# HALFTONE PHOTOGRAPHY

Library of Congress
Catalog Card Number: 75–18829
•
International Standard Book Number 0–911126–05–8

# THE HANDBOOK OF MODERN HALFTONE PHOTOGRAPHY

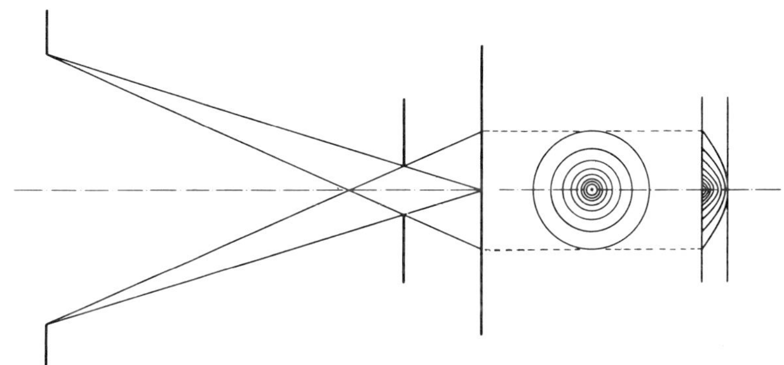

## WITH COMPLETE CONCEPTS & PRACTICES

By EWALD FRED NOEMER

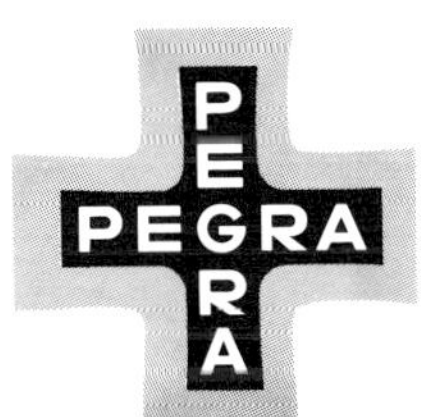


Publisher:

PERFECT-GRAPHIC-ARTS

SUPPLY COMPANY

P.O. Box 62 DEMAREST, N. J. 07627, U.S.A.

First Edition December 1965 Bb
Second Edition March 1967 Ab
Third Edition October 1968 Ab
Fourth Edition October 1969 Ac
Fifth Edition October 1972 A
Sixth Edition June 1975 Aa

PRINTED BY
MERICO PRINTING CORPORATION
117 CEDAR LANE
ENGLEWOOD, N.J. 07631, U.S.A.

ON WARREN LUSTRO OFFSET
ENAMEL DULL SUB. 100 BOOK PAPER

FROM S.W.I. PRL-SLN TYPE IV PLATES

# DEDICATION

The author of this book wishes to thank Agfa-Gevaert and gratefully acknowledges the permission granted by Messrs. Harald Guennel and Paul De Pelsmaker to reproduce material from their previously published Repro-Informations.

Also my sincerest thanks to Dr. Werner Rebner, for his great work as the spiritual originator of this complex matter.

I also extend my appreciation to the many craftsmen with whom I had the privilege of working with during my travels to research these specific applications in our trade.

A special thanks also to Mr. Albert Markarian, president of Kalmar Advertising and to Mr. Roy De Vries of De Vries Printing Company for their valuable help in preparing this book.

Lastly, but with deepest appreciation, I dedicate this book to my wife, Helga. Her patience and understanding, encouraged me to devote the necessary time and effort needed to document this portion of our great and consuming trade.

Ewald Fred Noemer

# PREFACE

This handbook is the single, most informative source for every required detail in modern halftone photography.

It is compiled into easy-to-read segments covering the most intimate variations and techniques for today's screening requirements, with quick reference index.

The total concepts behind screening and the solutions to every possible halftone problem are covered. More than 100 illustrations and charts aid the reader to visualize and easily apply every practice.

"Halftone Photography" has 11 chapters with 82 subtitles to help you immediately identify the particular screening question you want to resolve.

This new edition of "The Handbook of Modern Halftone Photography," is issued one year after the former printing. The previous thousands sold and the comments of complete satisfaction received from those who have been enlightened by its contents have convinced us that the efforts of compiling this authoritative document have indeed been justified.

While the science of film manufacturing has reached a high point of sophistication and graphic arts photographers have advanced their art to its finest achievements, the increased diversity of demands upon both can be most easily met only by a source for immediate and definitive answers to all the questions regarding halftone photography.

We believe this book is that source and hope you will find it a valuable companion and guide for time-saving and progressive photographic procedures.

Rene Aerts

President, Agfa-Gevaert, Inc.

# FOREWORD

## By Dr. Werner Rebner

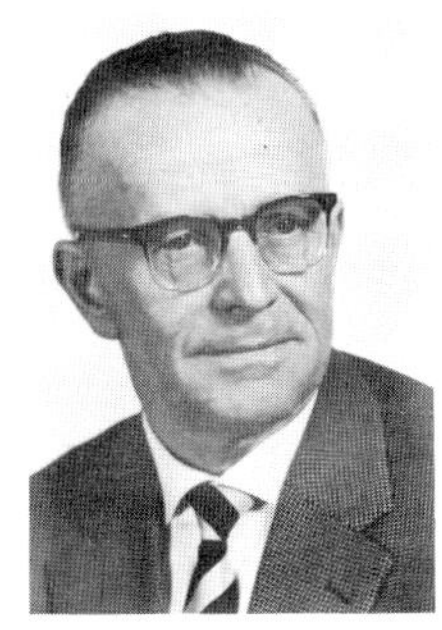

For many years the reasearch for halftone photography was a stepchild. Occasional attempts stagnated because of obscure and incorrect ideas regarding the actual facts and realties concerning the formation of halftone dots. This blockade was relieved only after the Lithfilms were created which provided for direct methods of obtaining final opaque and sharp halftone dots without additional manipulation with dot etching and intensifying. During the last decade, Agfa-Gevaert evaluated all these problems systematically based on previous investigations of Tritton & Wilson and Harrison. This unique comprehensive research program brought up new advanced recognitions which finally led to the creation and commercial manufacturing of new types of Negative Contact Screens and Positive Contact Screens. These new concepts and screens allow the making of perfect tone value corrected halftone negatives and halftone positives in one easy single step which is not possible with conventional contact screens. During the course of this year's long research program only some scattered information was published.

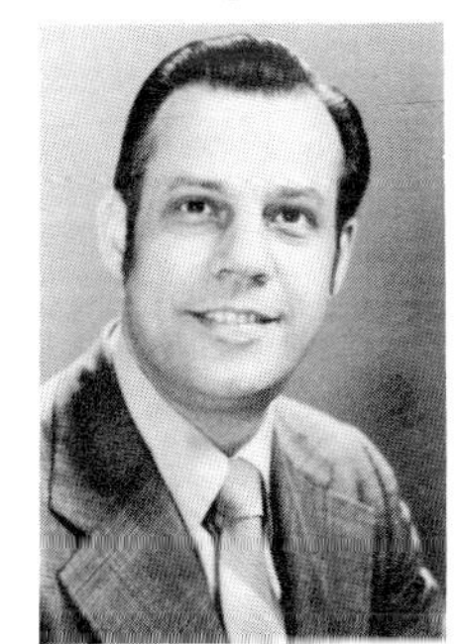

Mr. Ewald Fred Noemer, the author of this book, was my assistant in the vast Agfa-Gevaert research and quality control department for some time and also responsible for these new inventions. He is the first one to have combined all the old and new knowledge in a comprehensive way to make available to the trade these revolutionary achievements in an easy-to-understand way. His experience in this field is unique. He has spent more than twenty eight years in the camera department and other phases of the Graphic Arts Trade. Extensive business traveling took him to various European countries, India, Australia, New Zealand, Hong Kong, Thailand, Israel, and through the United States of America. He was Graphic Arts Technical Manager of Agfa-Gevaert Inc., Vice President for Klimsch-Repro, Inc., and now owns Merico Printing Corp. located at 231 Route 17, Rutherford, N. J. 07070. He is also an active licensed teacher in the New York School of Printing and member of many Graphic Arts organizations. He is also known for his trade magazine articles, some for which he was awarded "The Golden Keys Award".

It is highly recommended that this invaluable book gets trade-wide recognition. Besides being a textbook, it should serve every cameraman to acquire freedom in his daily work by solving his problems and at the same time especially enable him to keep up with the competitive requirements of our modern times.

# INDEX

# Chapter One

# THE CORRECT SCREEN EXPOSURE METHOD

## INTRODUCTION

Is it still worthwhile to discuss the glass screen and its complex application after the invention and the successful use of contact screens? The discussions among Graphic Arts craftsmen as to which of the two screens is most suitable never seem to end, and few people can genuinely make an objective decision.

This subject has been explored very carefully, and not one moment will be wasted in relating this information. The more time spent looking into the "mysteries" that glass screens seem to work, the more we will realize and understand the appreciation for the glass screen. The following information is intended to clear up a number of foggy ideas.

Besides other problems, the determination of the correct screen distance has undoubtedly remained a problem ever since 1852 when W. H. Fox Talbot's idea, to split up continuous tone pictures into dots, obtained the English patent No. 565. His screen, at that time simply consisted of dark textile fabric, but he was mainly concerned with photogravure. A few years later, in 1855 A. J. Berthold, in Paris, obtained a patent for an actual line screen. With this, however, it was necessary to turn the screen after 50% exposure had been given, to reverse the angle of the lines by 90°. A new branch of a profession had to be established, and only after many years of experience with halftone photography did it seem possible to enforce the degree of quality perfection possible to attain. Therefore, one would believe that after so many years of practical use, all possible experiences should have been gathered. Unfortunately, this is not so.

During the last generation, without noticeable opposition, definition of the theoretically correct screen distances were more or less accepted. These resulted from calculations based on definite multiples of the width of the screen window. In Germany, Dr. Schupp defended this theory and in England, W.B. Hislop did the same.

The factor by which the width of the screen window is to be multiplied in order to obtain the "correct" distance for all glass screens according to Hislop is as follows:

| | | | | | |
|---|---|---|---|---|---|
| with 40 or more lines/cm | or | 100 or more lines/inch | x 64 |
| with 30 — 35 lines/cm | or | 75 — 85 lines/inch | x 80 |
| with 20 — 25 lines/cm | or | 50 — 65 lines/inch | x 90 |

This fixed screen distance, calculated in this way for a screen with a definite number of lines, was considered to be characteristic for that screen, no matter what the scale of reproduction and the aperture with which the exposure was made.

## THE SCREEN KEY METHOD

This published method was compared in 1956, with the theories and the results of Agfa-Gevaert's experiences accumulated over many years.[1] In the meantime, a number of years have passed, and a great number of companies, mainly in Europe have become familiar with the Agfa-Gevaert Screen Key Method, and in turn have taken advantage of the security guaranteed by applying this proven system. An additional factor is that trade schools have included this method in their education programs.

*The expression "Screen Key" has become a technical term!*

It is unfortunate that there has been so little response outside of Europe to the Screen Key Method. Although details were published some time ago in the United States as well as in other countries and were made readily available, little acknowledgment has been given to the findings which were based on the Screen Key Method. There is, therefore, a regrettable absence of discussions regarding our statements concerning this method. The cameraman using the screen during regular working hours has seldom time to carry out systematic tests in order to satisfy himself with the usefulness of new facts. Investigations of this kind should be carried out by the institutes which occupy themselves with basic research for the Graphic Arts Trade. The assistance of these institutes in estimating the value of the Screen Key is especially desirable, because one must take into consideration the fact that an experienced man holds on to old established methods; only with hesitation will he depart from his basic experiences accumulated over a long period, even when these methods obviously should be regarded as obsolete.

## THE CORRECT SCREEN DISTANCE

When searching for the correct screen distance, this method is the key to all answers and it tells us what to do with a precision that exceeds the demands of practice. The Graphic Arts Trade should take an interest in bringing these facts to the attention of every camera operator. The fact that the investigations, which led to the Screen Key Charts, were made available by a film manufacturer,[2] should not at all be considered when estimating the value of these charts. The time spent with preparations, the installations and the material used have involved such efforts and expenses that if the method gets adopted, it promises prospects of reaching the goal!

This problem can be most effectively investigated by discussing the Screen Key Diagram itself. It will be seen in the course of this explanation that the performance of the ruled glass screens can be both tested and demonstrated with extreme facility. We shall refer to the following subjects:

1. Screen theory and the theory of diffraction.
2. The precautions necessary for a precise determination of the screen distance.
3. The density range which can be reproduced with the glass screen.
4. The definition of the screened image.
5. Deformation of the halftone dot under the influence of the diffraction of light.

*At this point the following facts must be stated:*

The values of the screen distances in the Screen Key Diagrams have not been calculated theoretically. More than anything else, they represent the conclusion of innumerable screen reproductions evaluated under variable testing conditions. Carefully examined, they represent nothing less than a systematic summary of experience gained in practice. Repetitions of these tests carried out by independent persons must, therefore, lead to the same results.

## THE SCREEN KEY DIAGRAM

It obligates the operator to work with precision. Before using the diagram one must know:

1. The number of lines per cm or inch in the screen,
2. The ratio between the transparent and opaque line,
3. The thickness of the cover glass of the screen,
4. The scale of the reproduction,
5. The lens aperture.

These five factors, set in the right combination, determine the correct screen distance. If only one of these settings is changed, another one also has to be readjusted in order to compensate.

*This proves:*

THERE IS ONLY ONE CORRECT SCREEN DISTANCE!

A straightline chart serves as a base for the Screen Key Diagram. It consists of three parallel, straight line columns.

The column on the left side of the chart indicates the scale for the reduction or enlargement.

The column on the right side indicates the lens aperture.

The center column indicates the screen distance in mm and /64 inches.

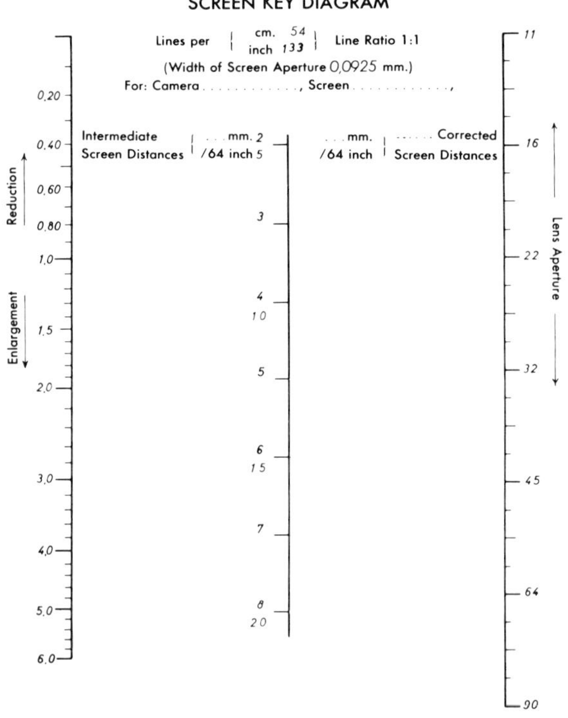


*Illustr. No. 1* **Screen Key Diagram for 54 lines/cm or 133 lines/inch.**

The values of the middle column are always strictly valid only for a definite width of the screen aperture. There are published Screen Key Diagrams, for the most commonly used screens on the pages 17 to 26 in this book:

lines per cm: 24, 28, 32, 40, 48, 54, 60, 70, 80 and 100

lines per inch: 60, 70, 80, 100, 120, 133, 150, 175, 200 and 250.

Illustrs. No. 1-4 show the Screen Key Diagrams for the following screens: 54/cm or 133/inch, 24/cm or 60/inch, 48/cm or 120/inch, and 100/cm or 250/inch. It is obvious that the only difference lies in the center column.

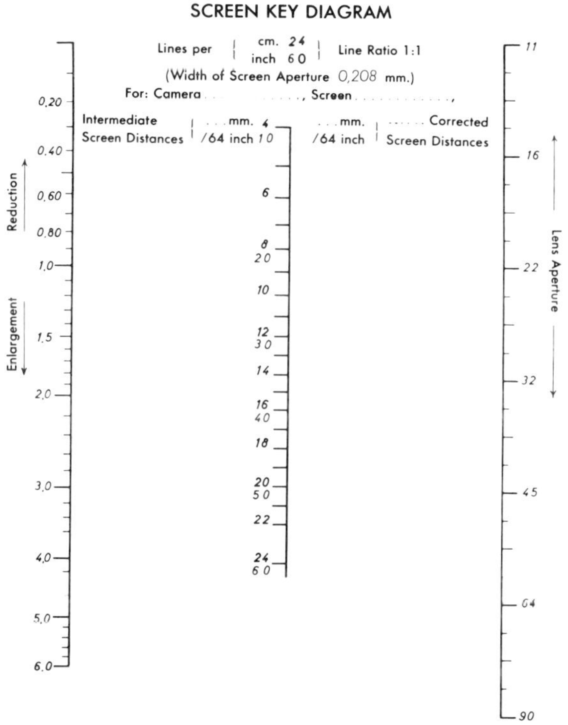

SCREEN KEY DIAGRAM

Lines per cm. 24 / inch 60 — Line Ratio 1:1

(Width of Screen Aperture 0,208 mm.)

For: Camera . . . . . . . . , Screen . . . . . . . . . ,

Intermediate Screen Distances . . . mm. / /64 inch — . . . mm. / /64 inch . . . . . Corrected Screen Distances

Reduction — Enlargement — Lens Aperture

*Illustr. No. 2* **Screen Key Diagram for 24 lines/cm or 60 lines/inch**

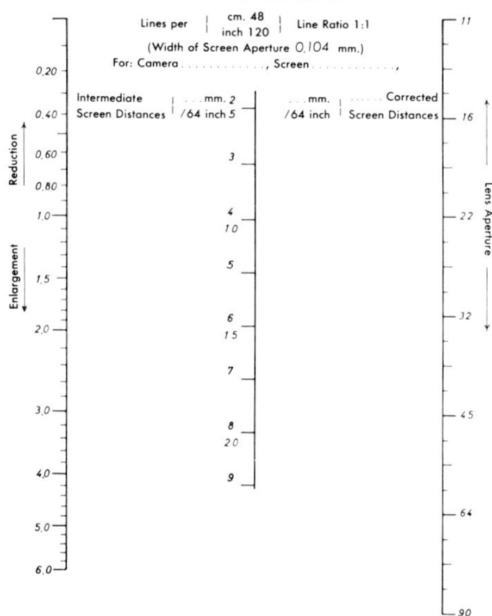


*Illustr. No. 3* **Screen Key Diagram for 48 lines/cm or 120 lines/inch**

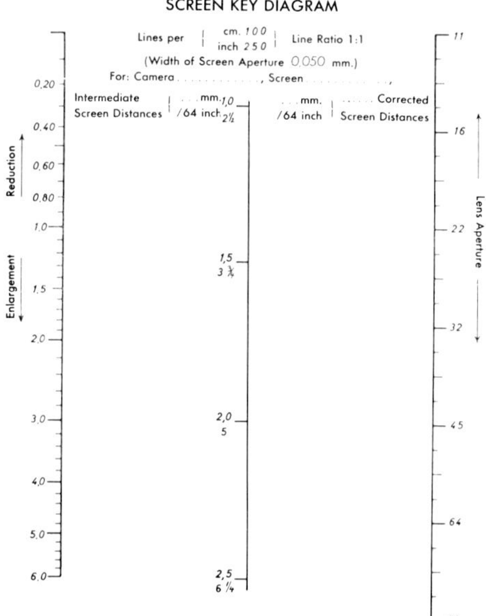


*Illustr. No. 4* **Screen Key Diagram for 100 lines/cm or 250 lines/inch.**

## PRACTICAL APPLICATION

To begin with, let us study the Screen Key Diagram without regarding its application to a screen with a certain number of lines.

In order to use the diagram, a ruler is put across it. Three points of intersection are obtained; these points are inter-related according to theoretical principles. Two of these intersection points can be chosen at random. The third intersection point associated with the two others is consequently fixed. If, for example, the screen distance has been chosen, then it is possible, according to the required reduction ratio, to read the diaphragm value for the prescribed screen from the centre column of the Screen Key Diagram. See illustr. No. 5.

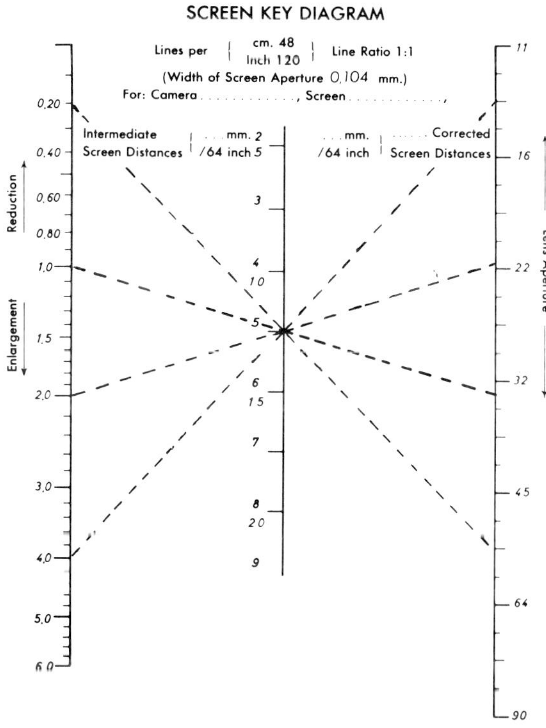


*Illustr. No. 5* **Screen Key Diagram**
**Explanation of the Diaphragm Column.**

If to begin with, the diaphragm has been chosen, one has to read the screen distance from the chart. See illustr. No. 6.

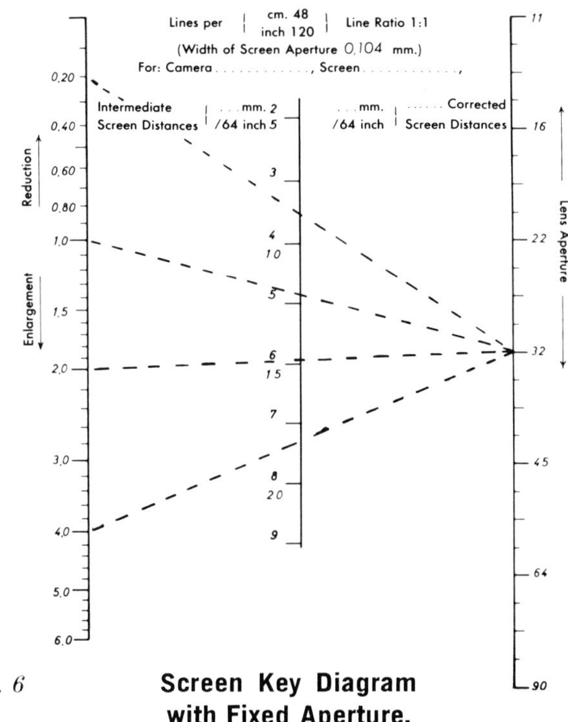


*Illustr. No. 6*

**Screen Key Diagram with Fixed Aperture.**

The detail on the Screen Key Diagram above the screen distance column refers to the width of the screen aperture. It is a common practice to define a screen by its number of lines per cm or inch. It is therefore clearly assumed that the screen in question has been ruled so that the ratio between transparent to opaque lines is 1 : 1 However, this assumption is relatively seldom fulfilled exactly.

Accuracy in the determination of the exact screen distance begins, as can be seen, with the screen itself. It is of course not simple to measure the existing screens on hand; however, if possible, it would be worth-while to do so.

The knowledge about the screen yields an immediate advantage, not only in the precise determination of the screen distance, but also in knowing what density range the screen can reproduce. In the future it may be expected that the manufacturers of glass screens will mention the ratio of the lines, in addition to the total thickness of the screen as well as of the cover glass. These factors will then be engraved on the cover glass in an effort to do away with unnecessary, and often inaccurate, guesswork.

## THE LAW OF LIGHT

According to scientific laws, light travels in straight lines. In this case the following equation is applicable:

$$\frac{\text{screen distance}}{\text{camera extension}} = \frac{\text{aperture of the screen}}{\text{diameter of lens aperture}}$$

We have calculated the screen distances with this equation and compared them with the distances found experimentally under corresponding conditions. This showed that practical results always lead to shorter values. For the scale of reproduction 1:1, the theoretically calculated distances were entered in the diagram illustr. No. 8 as dotted lines for three screens with 24, 48 and 100 line screen per cm. or 60, 120 and 250 lines per inch. On the abscissas of the coordinating system the lens apertures are marked. On the ordinates the screen distances are marked in millimeters and inches. The values for the experimentally found screen distances are connected with one another by a thick line. The shaded zones between these lines indicate that by decreasing the relative aperture (= an increase in the F:number of the aperture), the latitude for useful screen distances increases. The diffraction of light is responsible for this difference between calculated and practical values. From all light rays a certain portion of light is always diffracted. This proportion increases as the aperture size decreases. The aperture of the lens and the screen aperture could be very narrow openings indeed. The practical consequence of the partial diffraction of the light rays results in a shortening of the cone of light which would form behind the screen window if the light rays were to travel 100 per cent straight. It was very strange that capacities like Dr. Edor in Germany, P. Clerc in France and other authorities stated firmly that diffracted light did not play a part in the formation of the halftone image. However, Dollond and Tallent were one of the first ones to explain the penumbral theory, on which Deville's, from Canada, isophotes are based as shown in illustr. No. 7. The famous crossline screen manufacturer Max Levy and F. E. Ives also proved the effect of diffraction already in 1895.

*In summary it may be said that:*

The smaller the diameter of the lens aperture chosen and the narrower the aperture of the screen window, the greater is the defraction of light and the relatively shorter is the light cone.

*The length of the cone of light, which forms behind the screen window, is the correct screen distance!*

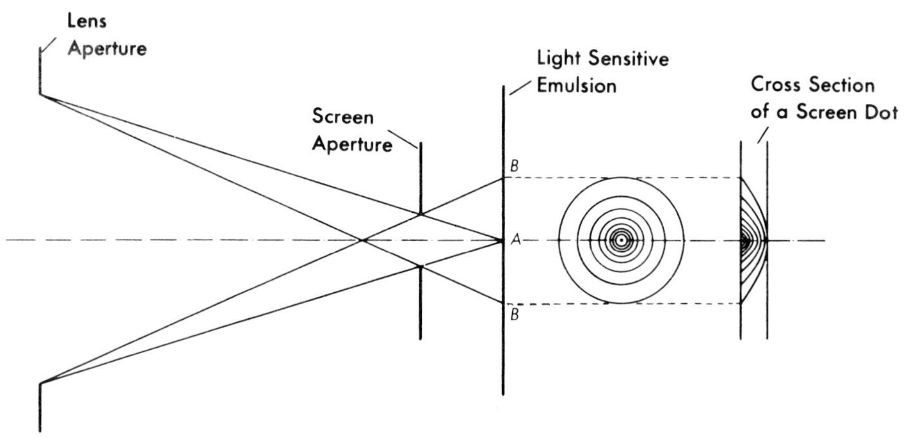


*Illustr. No. 7* **The Correct Screen Distance Penumbral Theory.**

The problem of the correct screen distances boils down to the question, by how much shorter—under the influence of the proportionate diffraction of light—does the screen distance become, compared with the one calculated according to the halftone theory. Calculations dedicated to this problem have often been published but without effort on practical applications. Only the Screen Key answers this question, and this, emphasized once again, has been done purely experimentally. The results achieved by it in regards to accuracy are amazing, and Dr. Werner Rebner deserves full credit and appreciation for his comprehensive explorations.

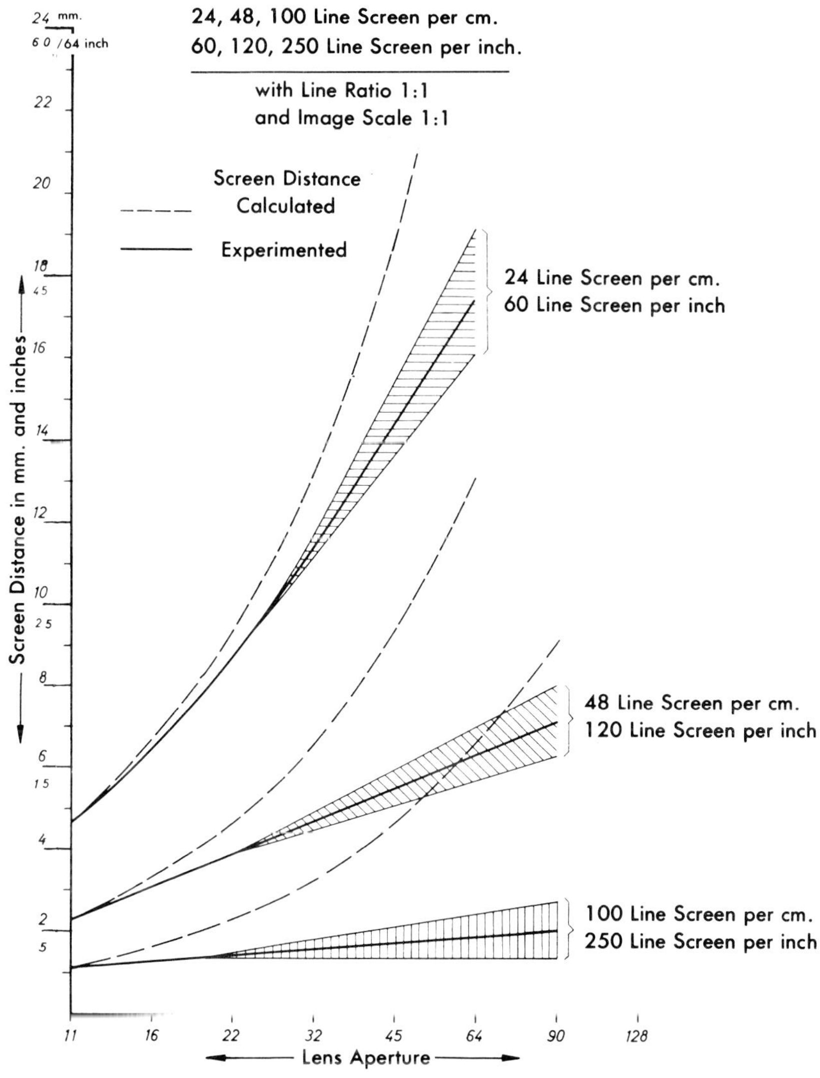


*Illustr. No. 8* **Calculated and Experimented Screen Distances**

Another fact should also be remembered. The light rays behind the screen aperture, apart from diffraction, are also subject to further influences. Examples of this principle are the differences in wave length and the diffusion of light within the emulsion layer. However, since these two factors are so minor, they need not be considered in practice.

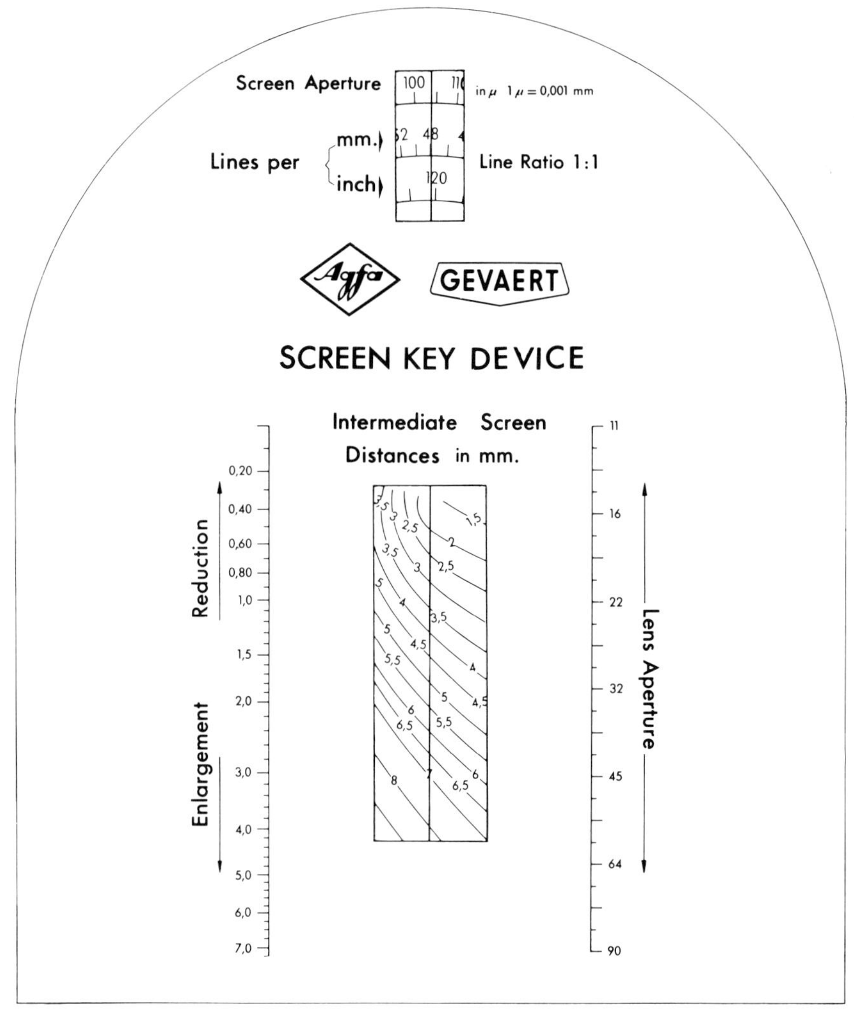


*Illustr. No. 9* **THE AGFA-GEVAERT SCREEN KEY DEVICE**

CONVERSION MILLIMETERS INTO INCHES

| mm | 1 | 1½ | 2 | 3 | 4 | 5 | 6 | 7 | 8 | 9 | 10 |
|---|---|---|---|---|---|---|---|---|---|---|---|
| /64 inch | 2½ | 3¾ | 5 | 7½ | 10 | 12½ | 15 | 17½ | 20 | 22½ | 25 |

Some time ago this universal Screen Key Device was introduced and provides information regarding the correct screen distance for all glass screens in use. This device has combined all test data into one single system. It contains a measuring disc, which is constructed similarly to the calculating circular discs used in the technique of reproduction and consists of a top plate with two window apertures and a central circular disc fitted underneath. This central circular disc can be rotated; the upper plate is inscribed. The center line in the device is arranged radially to the circular disc and is on a transparent window. In order to operate the device the applicable reproduction scale and the lens aperture chosen must be connected with a straight line. The points where the center line and the ruler cut through the set of curves, mark the desired screen distance for the screen indicated in the upper portion of the device.

The screen distances obtained from the Screen Key Device are "intermediate" values. This means that our data regarding the screen distances are not the experimentally obtained values themselves, but are the values after a conversion to a common basis. Without this conversion it is impossible to make a statement that is generally applicable. The reduced screen distance is valid for a camera in which there is no difference between the indication on the screen distance device on the camera and the actual measured distance between the screen ruling and the photographic emulsion. The "intermediate" screen distance would be correct for a screen without a cover glass only. For the conversion of the "intermediate" screen distance into the correct screen distance under specific working conditions, each Screen Key Chart bears the following correction-formula:

$$G = a + \frac{2}{3} b \quad \begin{matrix} \text{in mm} \\ \text{../64 inch} \end{matrix}$$

The value "a" indicates the actual distance required in millimeters or /64 inch (1 inch = 25.4 mm) between the surface of the cover glass of the screen and the emulsion compared with the theoretical distance read on the screen distance indicator on the camera. The correction value "b" indicates in millimeters or /64 inch how thick the cover glass of the screen is.

To calculate "a" let us assume that the screen distance indicator on the camera differs by +0.5 mm or 1¼/64 inch from the actual distance. To calculate "b", let us further assume that the screen has a total thickness of 6 mm or 15/64 inch. Should there be no indication on the screen regarding the thickness of the cover glass, we take half of 6 mm or 15/64 inch—3 mm or 7½/64 inch into the formula. Due to diffraction of light when passing through a more dense medium than air, only ⅔ of the actual thickness of the cover glass has to be taken into consideration. This will result in the following calculations:

G= 0.5 + ⅔ . 3.0 = 0.5 + 2 = 2.5 mm.
G=1¼/64+ ⅔ .7½/64 = 1¼/64+5/64= 6¼/64 inch.

By means of this equation it is now necessary to correct all given screen distance values on the center column of the Screen Key Chart by this deviation (illustr. 10). The new values obtained in this manner for the screen distances are valid for all reproductions with this particular combination: Camera + Screen only!

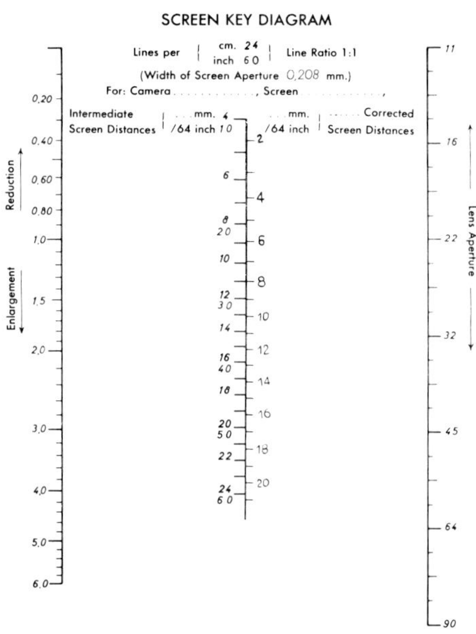


*Illustr. No. 10* **The Corrected Screen Distances**

As experienced from these considerations, the Screen Key Method enables the cameramen to work with a precision unknown until now. Let us repeat again the factors which we have to establish:

A. The aperture width of the screen.

B. The adjustment of the screen distance indicator on the camera.

C. The thickness of the cover glass of the screen.

## PRACTICAL EXPERIENCES

With the determination of the correct screen distance from the Screen Key Chart, our subject could actually be regarded as concluded. However, the significance of the Screen Key has made possible further exact studies of the performance of the glass screen because it gives complete assurance in determining the correct screen distance. Since this was lacking so far, further important characteristics of the ruled screens remained unknown until quite recently.

Let us once more ask the question: When is the screen distance correct?—*It is chosen correctly when the light cone, which is formed behind the screen window, just touches the emulsion of the photographic material with its point.* (Illustr. No. 11)

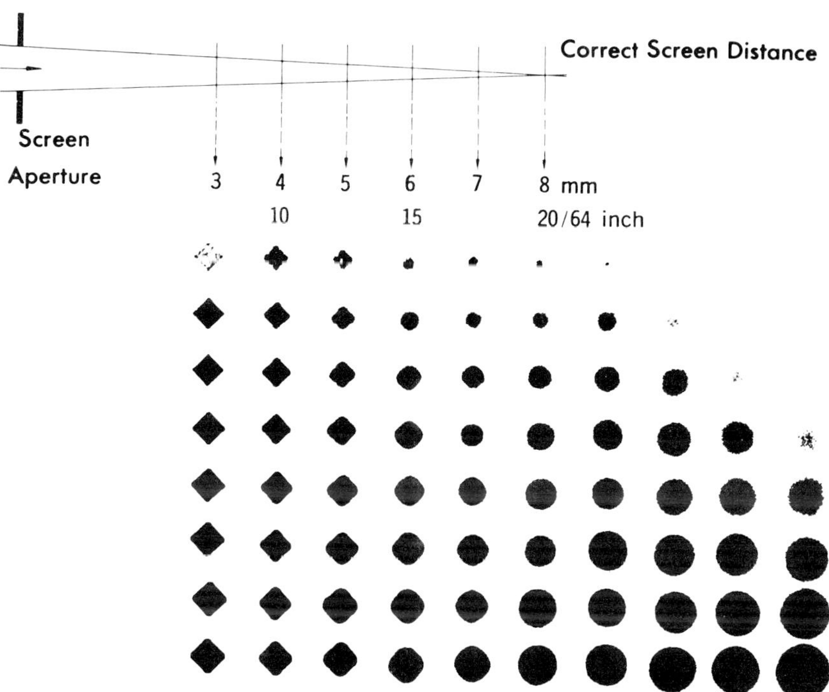


*Illustr. No. 11* **The Correct Screen Distance**

Only under these conditions is there a chance that the shadow details of an original will be reproduced without loss.

Illustration No. 11 makes this obvious. It shows single halftone dots, produced by a coarse screen where the screen distance was altered by 2 mm or 5/64 steps. Only within a very narrow zone of screen distances are halftone pinpoint dots created correctly with a big main exposure stop and no flash exposure. In the case of shorter distances, interference dots appear; and in the case of longer distances, the shadow dots are missing. Illustration No. 11 is very instructive. It explains visually the kind of damage done when the screen distance is incorrect. In the trade, almost without exception, the screen distances used are too great. This excessive screen distance prevents, as Illustration No. 11 shows, the formation of a pinpoint dot. In that case the light cone has its apex in front of the photographic emulsion layer. In the area where the shadow should be reproduced, the emulsion is only partly affected by diffused light. The greater the error in screen distance, the more extensive the loss of shadow dots and consequently in shadow detail.

In order to compensate for this loss, more and more flash exposure is given. Thereby only artificial halftone dots are created, but the actual shadow details can never be regained.

But this is not the only deficiency which occurs. As the last illustration also reveals, if the screen distance is too great the highlight end of the scale closes up very rapidly. For this reason the exposure must be cut down considerably in order not to clop these areas completely. This brings up even another drawback. As the exposure gets shorter, the details in the dark area of the picture become even more deficient, because they have already been neglected with imperfect screen distance. The shorter exposure does not allow the detail to receive enough light, reflected from the original, to influence the film to the point where it could bring out these details. The excess flash which would have to be given would not improve this situation either.

With too short a screen distance, proper graduation and contrast could not be built up. Rather than reproducing the image of the projected original, a contact of the screen would be made.

With proper screen distance the fine pin points are created from the dark areas of the original and contrast is increasing gradually, even so it is not perfectly in line with the original. This shortcoming can be compensated, however, with a no screen "bump" exposure, which will be discussed later. All this explains visibly the kind of damage done when the screen distance is not correct.

In all subsequent data we shall take for granted that the screen distance has been set "correctly".

# SCREEN KEY DIAGRAM

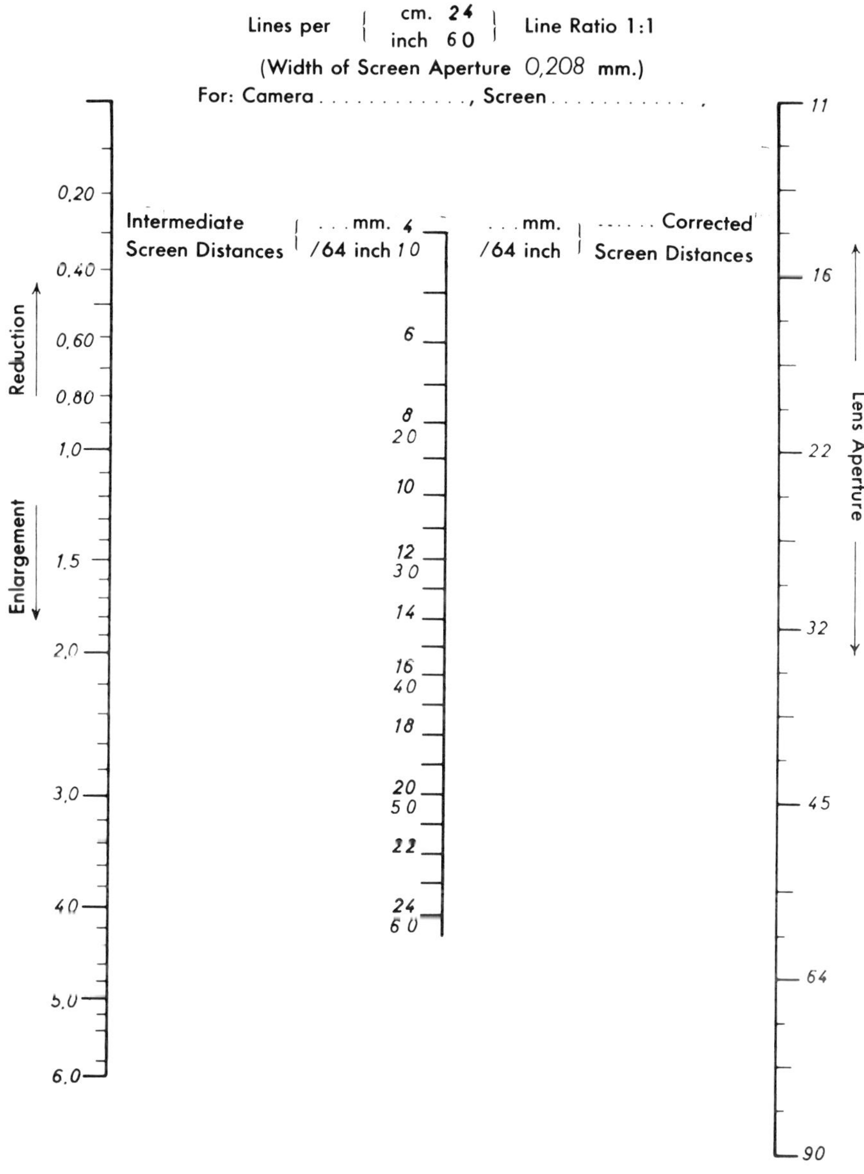

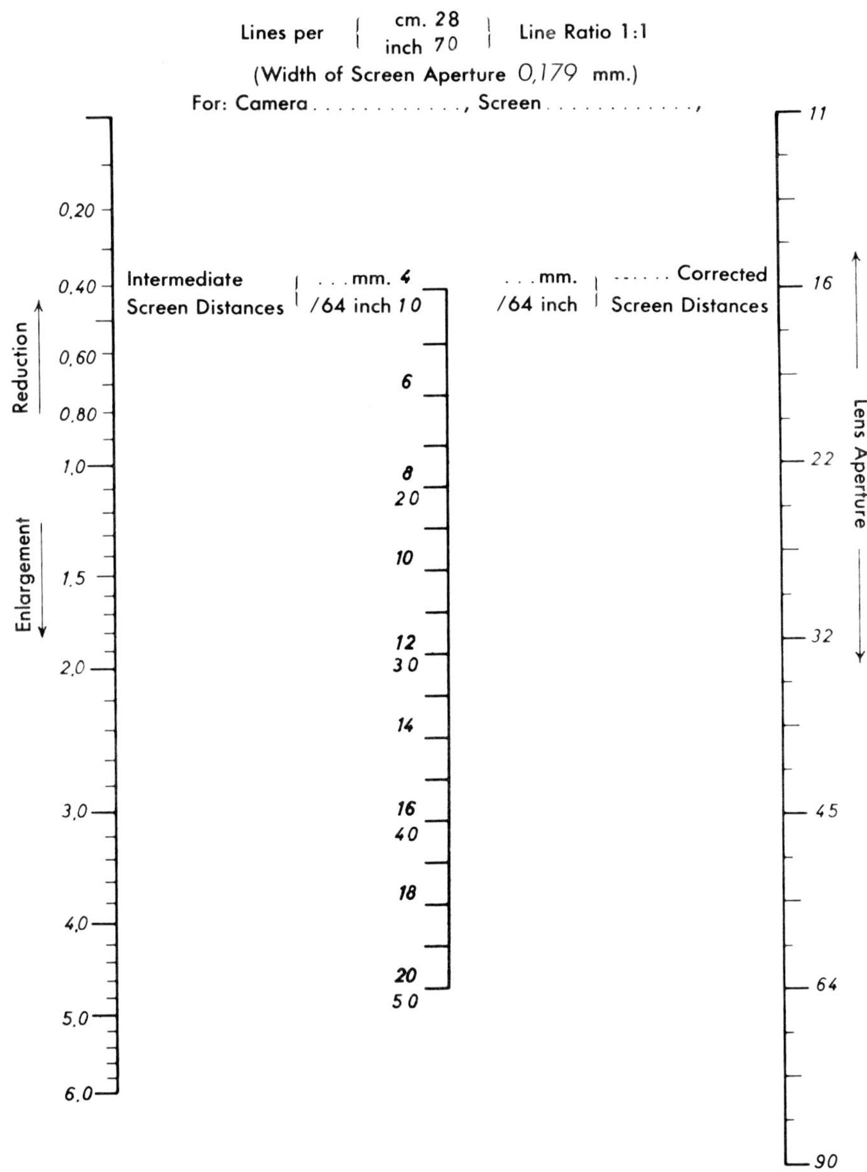
SCREEN KEY DIAGRAM
Lines per cm. 28 inch 70
Line Ratio 1:1
(Width of Screen Aperture 0,179 mm.)
For: Camera . . . . . . . . . . . . . , Screen . . . . . . . . . . . . . ,
0,20
0,40
0,60
0,80
1,0
1,5
2,0
3,0
4,0
5,0
6,0
Reduction
Enlargement
Intermediate Screen Distances
. . . mm. 4
/64 inch 10
6
8
20
10
12
30
14
16
40
18
20
50
. . . mm.
/64 inch
. . . . . . Corrected Screen Distances
11
16
22
32
45
64
90
Lens Aperture

## SCREEN KEY DIAGRAM

Lines per { cm. 32 / inch 80 } Line Ratio 1:1

(Width of Screen Aperture 0,156 mm.)

For: Camera . . . . . . . . . . . . ., Screen . . . . . . . . . . . . .,

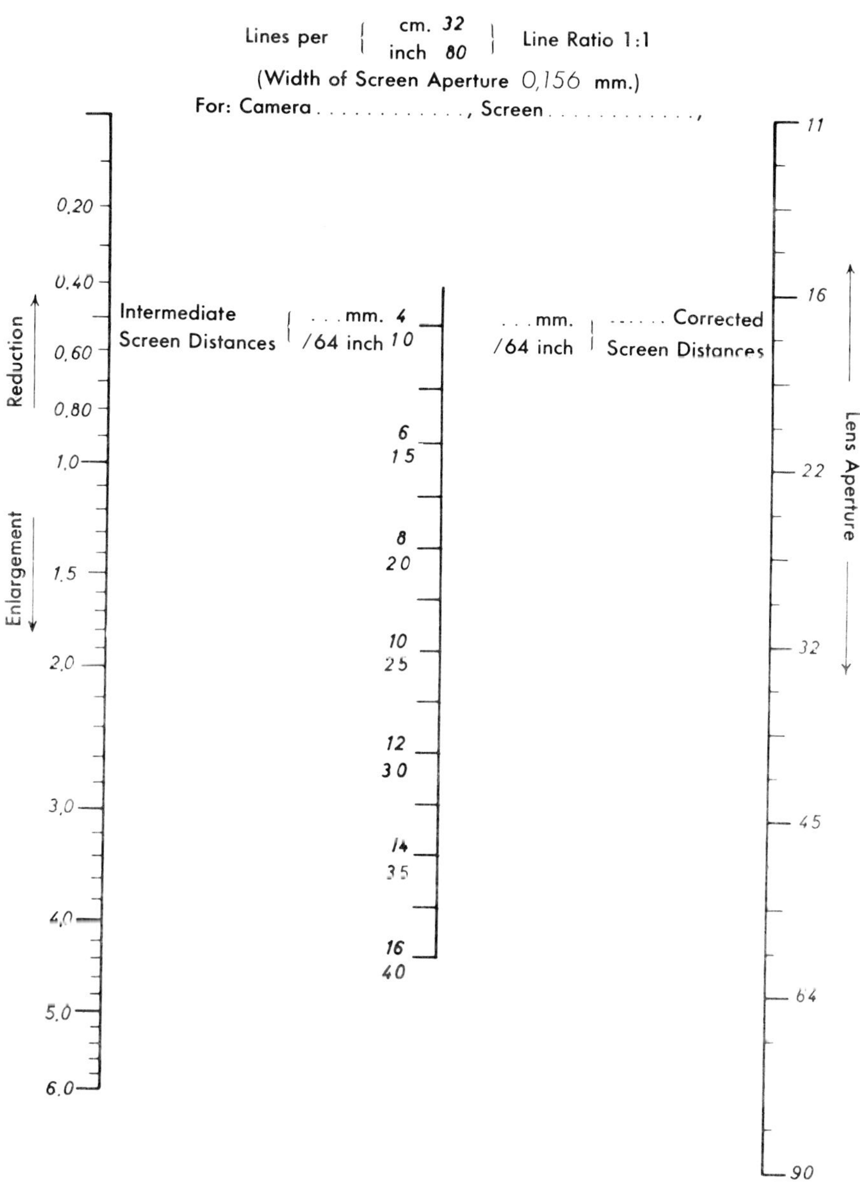

# SCREEN KEY DIAGRAM

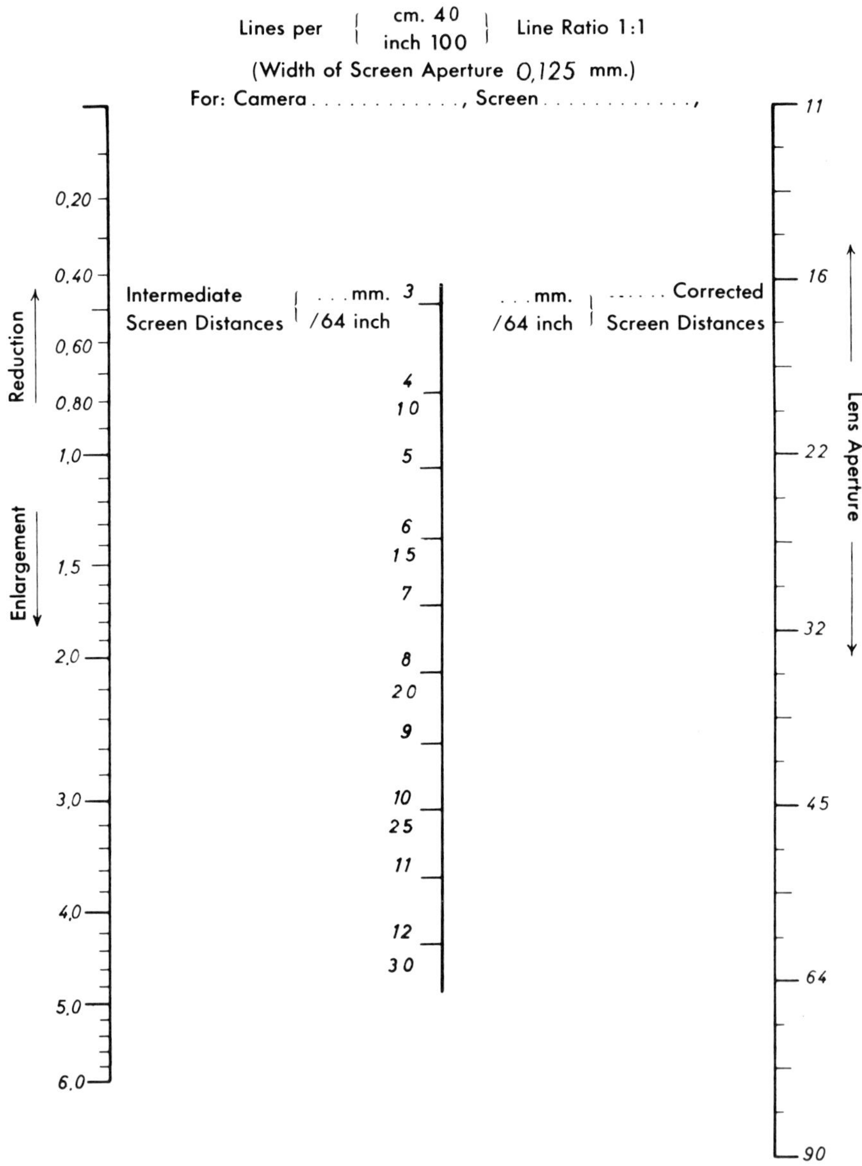

# SCREEN KEY DIAGRAM

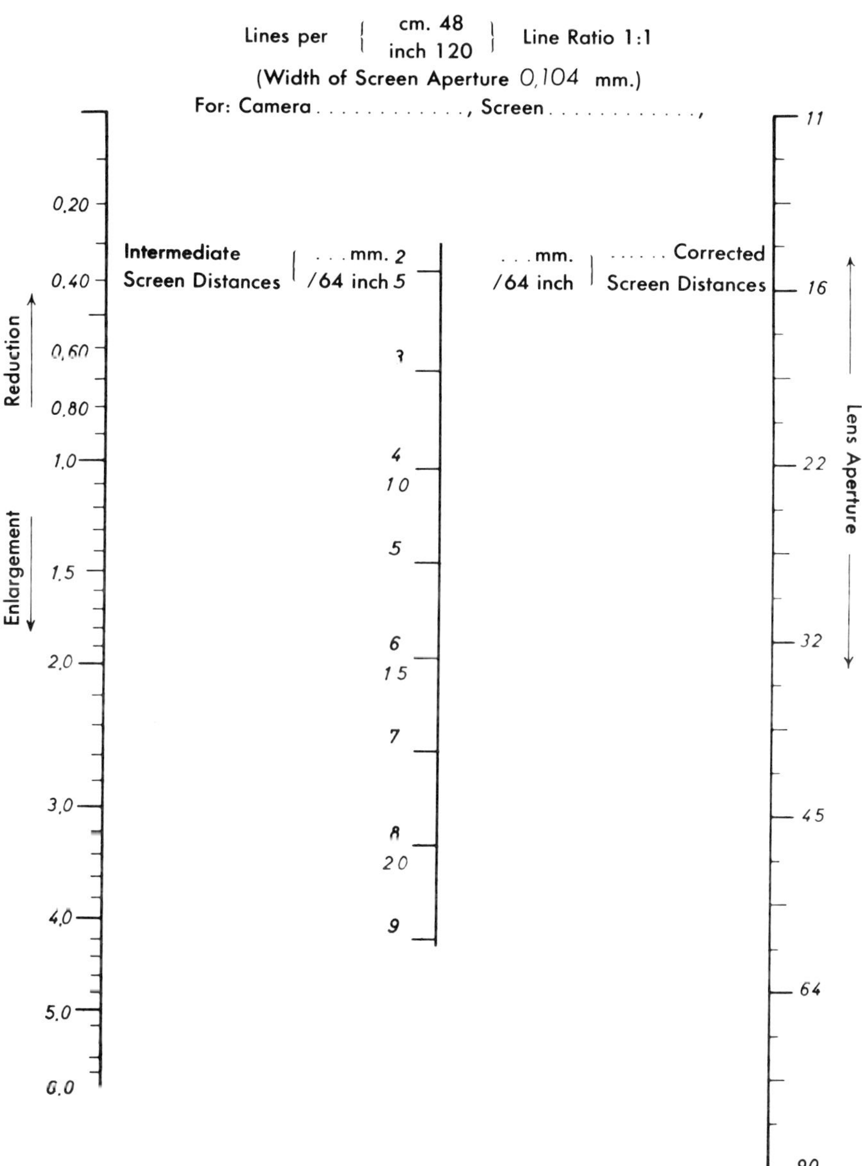

## SCREEN KEY DIAGRAM

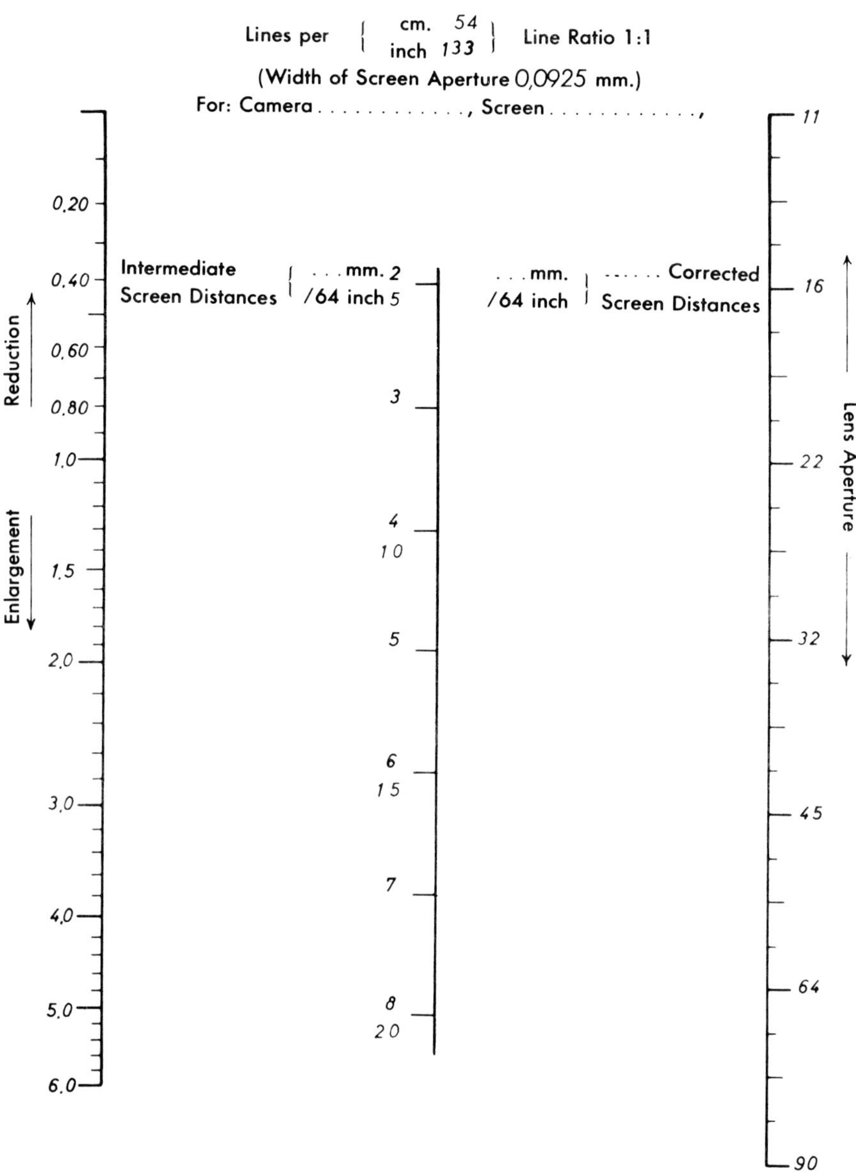

# SCREEN KEY DIAGRAM

Lines per cm. 6 0 / inch 150 — Line Ratio 1:1

(Width of Screen Aperture 0,0835 mm.)

For: Camera . . . . . . . . . . . . . , Screen . . . . . . . . . . . . . ,

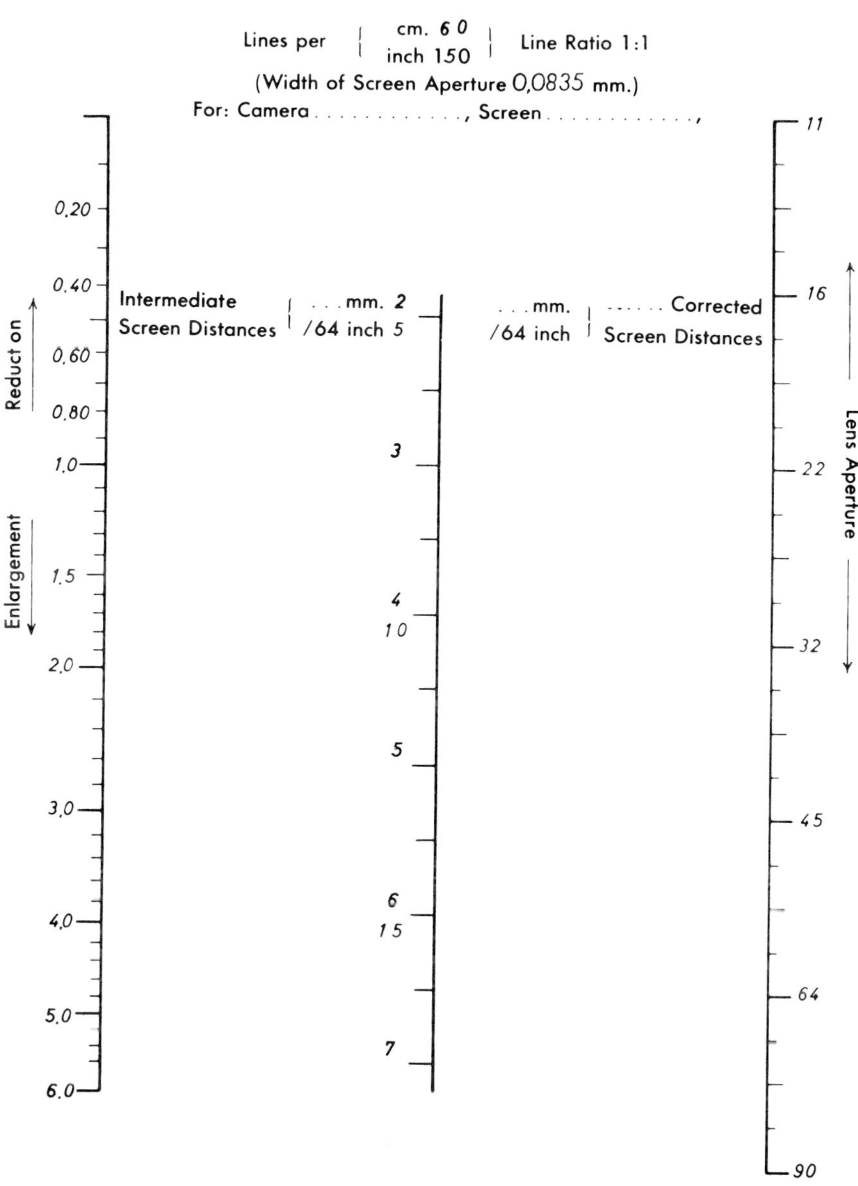

## SCREEN KEY DIAGRAM

Lines per { cm. 70 / inch 175 } Line Ratio 1:1

(Width of Screen Aperture 0,0715 mm.)

For: Camera . . . . . . . . . . . . ., Screen . . . . . . . . . . . . .,

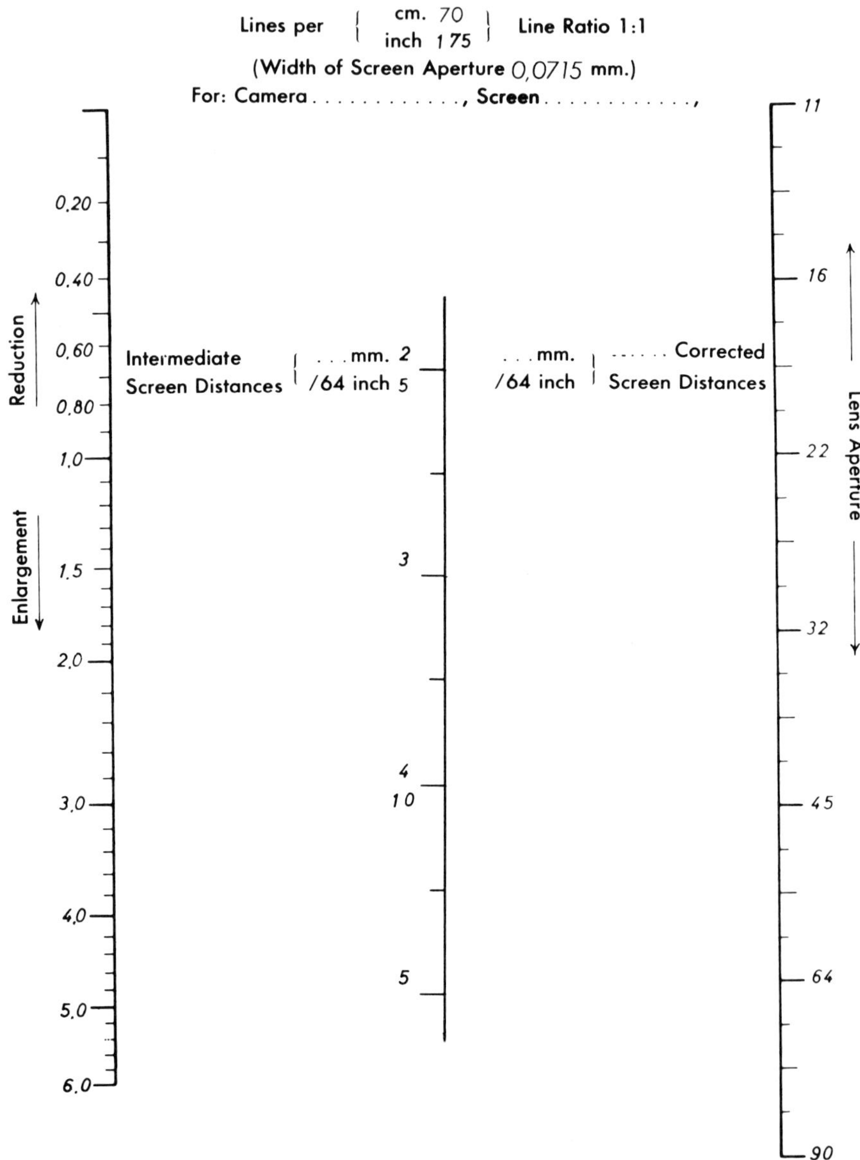

# SCREEN KEY DIAGRAM

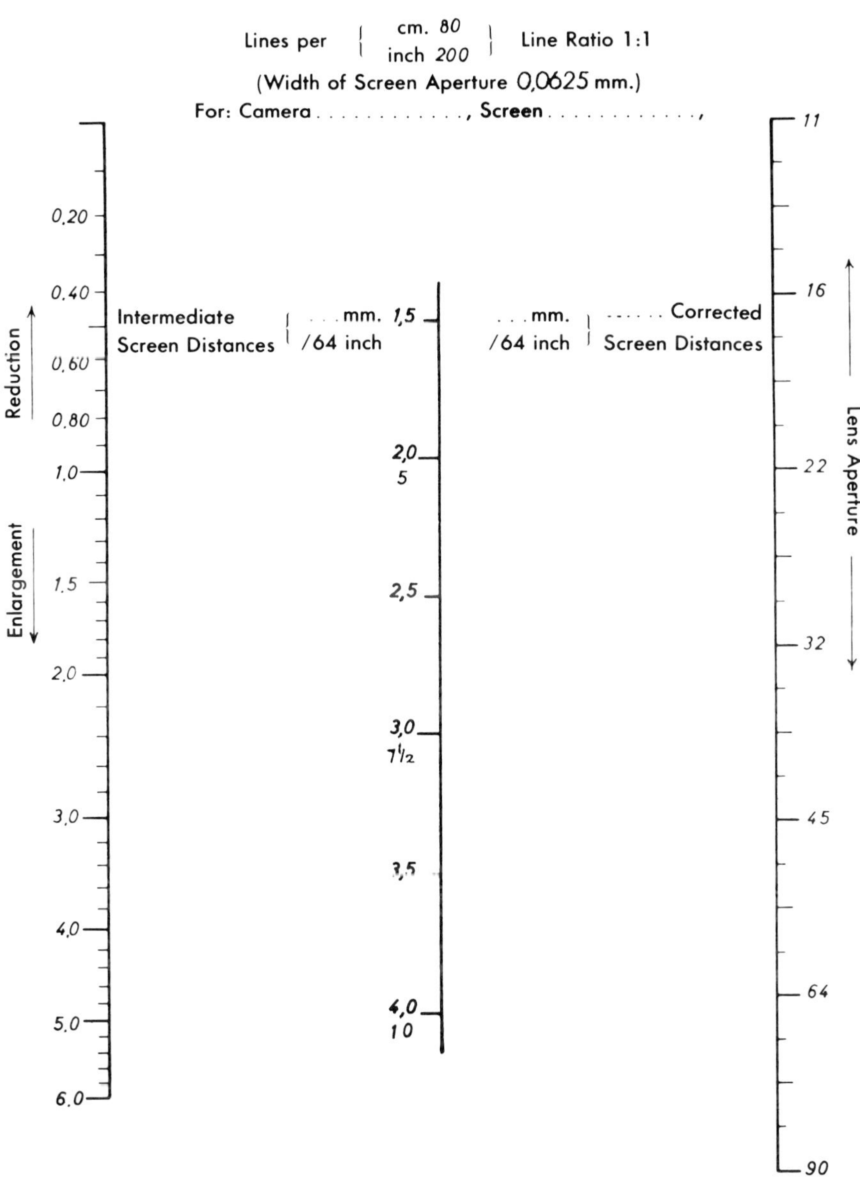

## SCREEN KEY DIAGRAM

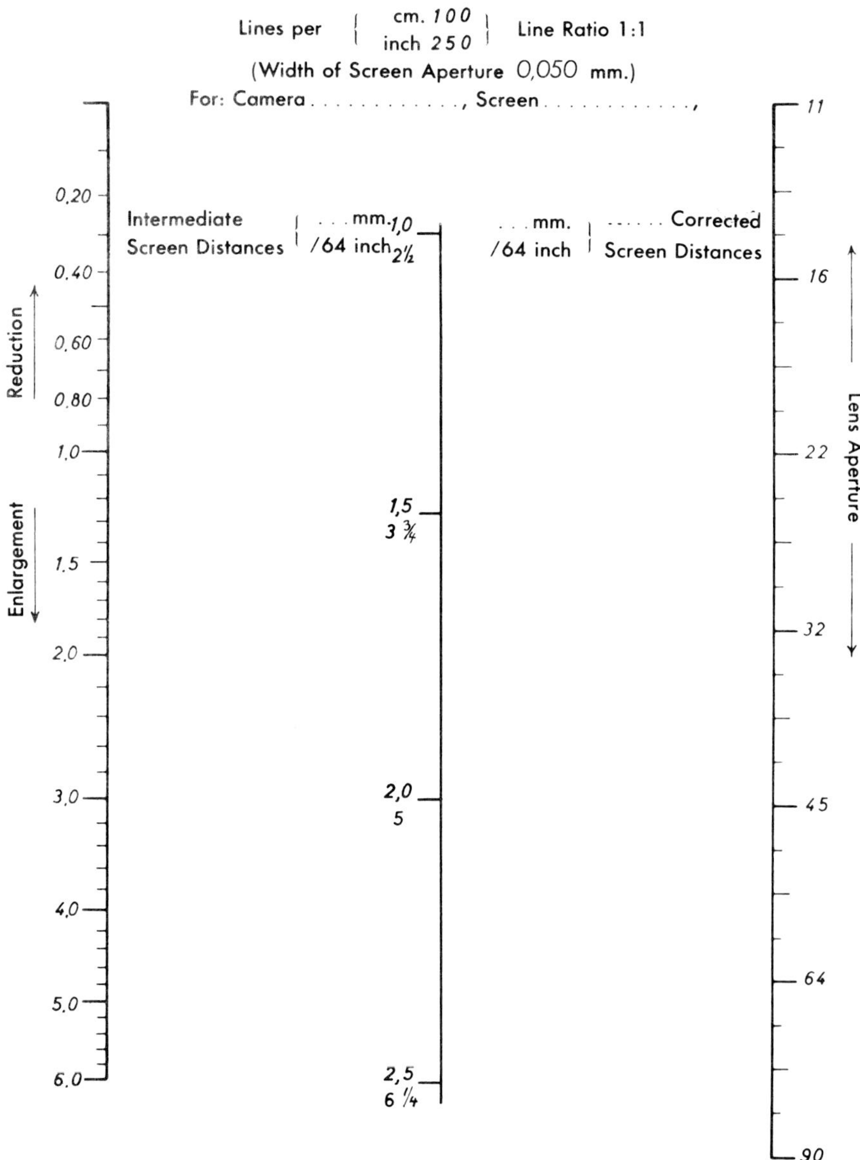

# Chapter Two

## THE REPRODUCIBLE DENSITY RANGE

To begin with let us ask the question: What genuine contrast range can really be reproduced by a screen? There was no literature concerning this matter, only the Screen Key has raised this question and made important measurements possible. These investigations have led to definite conclusions and revealed many interesting facts when screens of an equal number of lines, but with various line ratios were compared.[2]

In the diagrams shown in Illustrs. No. 12-15 we have reproduced the "gamma" curves of different screens obtained from a gray scale under identical working conditions. Glass screens with the following characteristics were used:

| Illustr. No. | Number of lines | | Line ratio | | |
|---|---|---|---|---|---|
| | per cm | inch | transp. | : | opaque |
| Illustr. No. 12 | 60 | 150 | 0.83 | : | 1.17 |
| Illustr. No. 13 | 60 | 150 | 1.02 | : | 0.98 |
| Illustr. No. 14 | 60 | 150 | 1.09 | : | 0.91 |
| Illustr. No. 15 | 60 | 150 | 1.23 | : | 0.77 |

We should not be satisfied with a visual comparison alone. The four diagrams show clearly that due to the line ratio of the screen its efficiency is considerably altered. This is comparatively easy to explain. Let us visualize narrow opaque lines between wide transparent lines. Excess light will fall through these large open areas and diffuse the narrow opaque lines rapidly. This is the same reaction as if too great a screen distance or too large a lens aperture had been chosen. Therefore, even with little exposure, the highlight areas in the negative close up too fast and do not allow for a long enough exposure, necessary to expose into the shadow end. This proves that screens with wider opaque than transparent lines give much better results. In practice they are usually referred to as "softer screens".

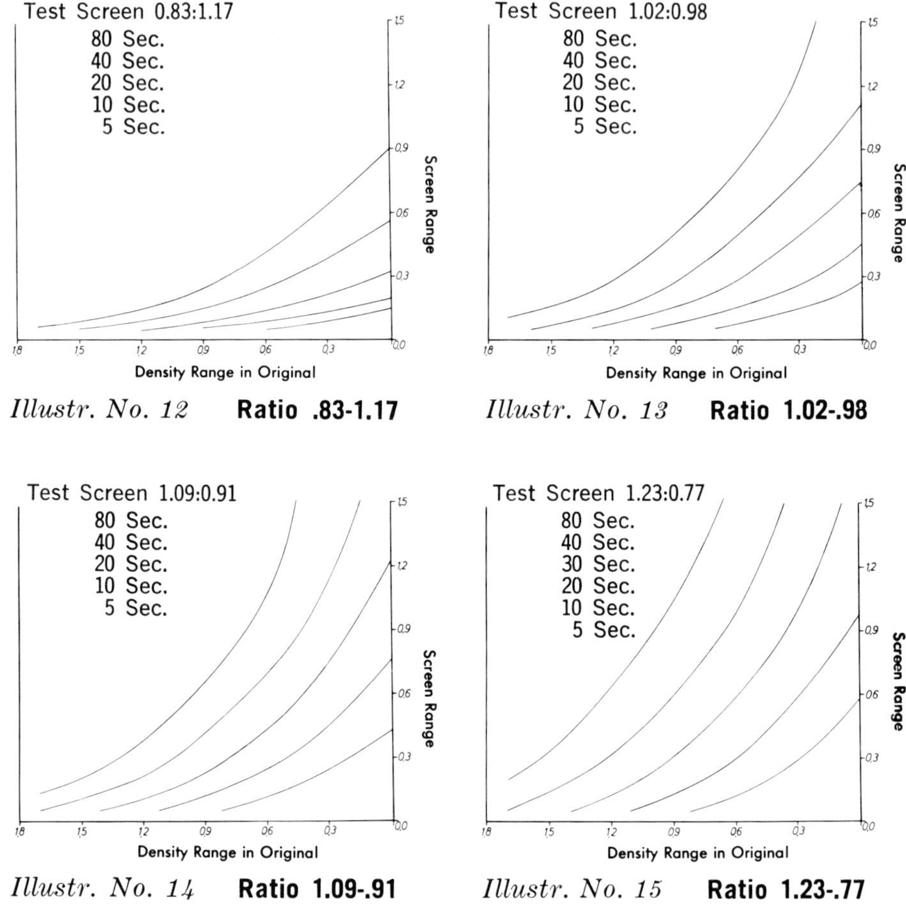


*Illustr. No. 12* **Ratio .83-1.17**

*Illustr. No. 13* **Ratio 1.02-.98**

*Illustr. No. 14* **Ratio 1.09-.91**

*Illustr. No. 15* **Ratio 1.23-.77**

**Glass Screens with Different Line Ratios**

The results of these statements are summarized in the following chart:

| Screen line ratio transp. : opaque | Reproducible density range | Reproducible brightness extent |
|---|---|---|
| 0.8 : 1.2 | 1.80 | 1 : 64 |
| 0.9 : 1.1 | 1.60 | 1 : 40 |
| 1.0 : 1.0 | 1.40 | 1 : 25 |
| 1.1 : 0.9 | 1.20 | 1 : 16 |
| 1.2 : 0.8 | 1.00 | 1 : 10 |

These results lead us to two fundamental conclusions:

1) The efficiency of a ruled screen fluctuates within wide limits according to the line ratio.
2) The contrast range, which can be reproduced by the 1:1 ruled screen, is relatively low. It corresponds only to an average original contrast, and is less than expected thus far.

It is necessary that these factual findings be explained. The majority of originals have a density range which, as can be seen from the records, is higher than the range a 1:1 ratio screen is able to cover.

The following question has been repeatedly raised with the manufacturers of screens: With what line ratio should a ruled screen in the future be provided? Our answer is as follows:

1) A good normal screen should be within the following tolerances:

| transparent | : | opaque |
|---|---|---|
| 0.9 ± 0.05 | : | 1.10 ± 0.05 |

2) For a special screen, we recommend the following line ratio:

| transparent | : | opaque |
|---|---|---|
| 0.85 ± 0.05 | : | 1.15 ± 0.05 |

Although we are dealing here with a new exploration, we already recommend that such screens be ordered.

## IMAGE SHARPNESS

A further important chapter on the effect of the glass screen is the image definition. In this case the Screen Key has again solved many problems.

To begin with, as is known from experience, the contact screens seem to give reproductions of finer definition than the reproductions with glass screens. Is this assumption true, and if so, what is the reason for this? The answer to the question is yes, it is valid, and it is due to the fact that behind the glass screen the light is partly diffracted, whereas behind the contact screen, diffraction is impossible.

Nevertheless, reproductions with sharp definition can also be obtained with the glass screen. Appreciable improvements are gained when care is taken so that the proportional amount of diffraction is reduced. This is achieved by exposing with larger lens apertures. With Illustr. No. 16 the proof of this claim is supplied.

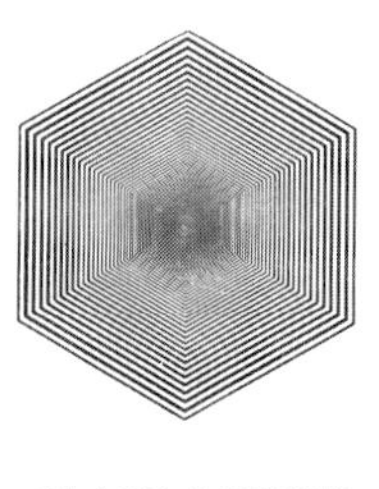

GLASS SCREEN

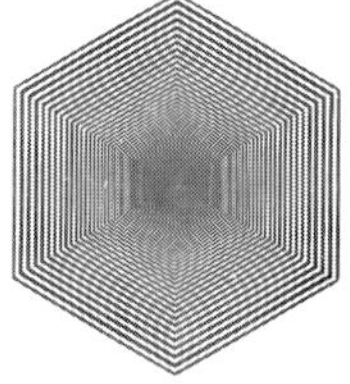

MAGENTA CONTACT SCREEN

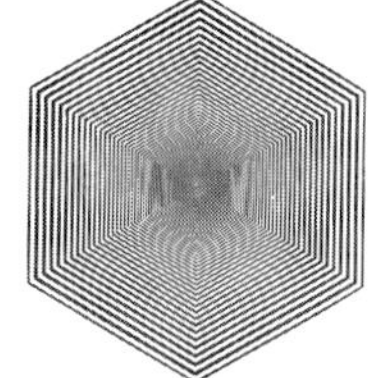

GRAY CONTACT SCREEN

*Illustr. No. 16* **Image Resolution**

A resolution chart was screened by using diaphragm 16 with a 48 lines per cm or 120 lines per inch glass screen. The same was repeated with two 48 lines per cm or 120 lines per inch contact screens of different brands. As can be seen, the glass screen reproduces at least equally as well as the contact screens.

However, diaphragm 16 which was used in these tests is unfortunately not very practical when applied to glass screens for the following reasons. The tolerances possible in the adjustments of the screen distance are very narrow in the case of diaphragm 16. In addition, this diaphragm requires working with such short screen distances that for obvious reasons it is usually impossible to come close enough to the film, especially when using fine screens.

Let us calculate in Illustrs. No. 17 and No. 18 the screen distance in the case of a screen with 54 lines per cm or 133 lines/inch.

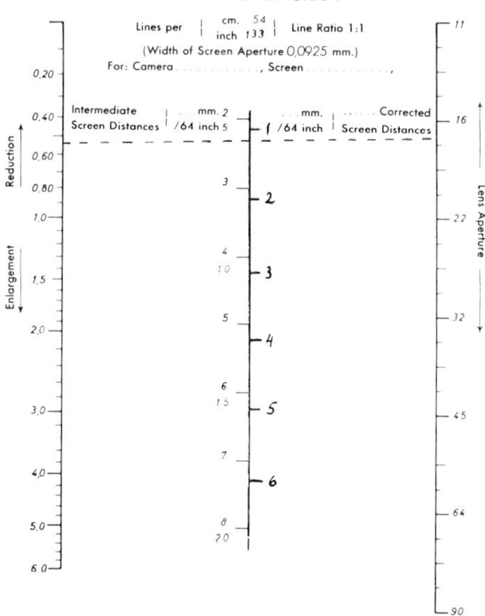


*Illustr. No. 17* **Screen Key Diagram Screen Distance Calculation.**

SCREEN KEY DIAGRAM

Lines per cm. 54 inch 133 Line Ratio 1:1

(Width of Screen Aperture 0,0925 mm.)

For: Camera ............, Screen ............

Intermediate Screen Distances ... mm. /64 inch — ... mm. /64 inch Corrected Screen Distances

Reduction — Enlargement — Lens Aperture

*Illustr. No. 18* **Screen Key Diagram Screen Distance Calculation.**

Let us assume the most favorable case for the adjustment of the camera: the correction value "a" equals zero. Let us further assume that the cover plate of the screen has a minimum thickness of 1.8 mm or 4½/64. Then the calculation will be as follows:

$$G = 0 + \tfrac{2}{3} \cdot 1.8 = 1.2 \text{ mm}$$
$$G = 0 + \tfrac{2}{3} \cdot 4\tfrac{1}{2}/64 = 3/64 \text{ inch}$$
(see Illustr. No. 17)

According to this calculation we have to correct the Screen Key Diagram for the 48 lines per cm or 120 lines per inch screen with the established correction of 1.2 mm or 3/64 inch. In this case with a minimum screen distance possible of 1 mm or 2½/64 inch and a diaphragm 16—we can carry out a reduction to one half of the original size only.

More reductions with diaphragm 16 would require screen distances which are less than 1 mm or 2½/64 inch. These cannot be adjusted any closer because for mechanical reasons the distance between the screen and the emulsion cannot be shortened to less than 1 mm or 2½/64 inch.

In practice, conditions are unfortunately always less favorable than those previously assumed. As a rule, the camera adjustment deviates by a minimum of ½ mm or 1¼/64 inch from the indicator, and the thickness of the screen cover glass amounts to 3 mm or 7½/64 inch and even more. In this instance our calculations would be somewhat like this:

$$G = 0.5 + \tfrac{2}{3} \cdot 3 = 2.5 \text{ mm}$$
$$G = 1\tfrac{1}{4}/64 + \tfrac{2}{3} \cdot 7\tfrac{1}{2}/64 = 6\tfrac{1}{4}/64 \text{ inch}$$
(see Illustr. 18)

If we have to correct for the 48 lines/cm or 120 lines/inch screens with the calculated correction value of 2½ mm or 6¼/64 inch then, with the screen distance of 1 mm or 2½/64 and with diaphragm 16, we are just able to expose an enlargement of 2/1 with the correct screen distance. No scale less than 2/1 can be reproduced with diaphragm 16 under the assumed conditions, because then the screen distance would have to be adjusted to less than 1 mm or 2½/64 inch.

These calculations can be carried on ad infinitum with the aid of the Screen Key Diagrams. It is surprising what terrific results can be achieved, and highly recommend the study of the Screen Key System.

The possibility of improving the definition with a ruled screen by increasing the aperture of the diaphragm and thereby diminishing the proportionate diffraction of light, relatively depends on the aperture of the screen or the number of lines in the screen per centimeter or inch. If the aperture of the screen is gradually reduced, then the required screen distances become shorter. The lower limit for the screen distance adjustment in the camera is 1 mm or 2¼/64 inch. By means of the calculated examples, as carried out by us just now, we have established that this lower limit for the diaphragm 16 is already reached with a medium-fine 48 lines/cm or 120 lines per inch screen.

In summary, we can prove that the glass screen offers—under ideal working conditions—the possibility of achieving the sharp definition of the contact screen. In practice, however, there might be limitations governed by the precision of the camera and depending on the thickness of the cover glass of the screen.

By using a relatively open lens aperture to improve the sharp definition with the ruled screen and by changing over from coarse to finer screens, we soon reach the limit for the shortest screen distance. Then we are forced to deviate exactly in the opposite direction; namely, to the side of the small lens aperture, in order to attain the correct screen distance.

Naturally, there would only be one solution; namely, to take a screen without a cover glass.

## THE SHAPE OF THE DOT

The light diffraction behind the screen window also produces another effect, which is of great significance. It deforms the shape of the individual halftone dot.

The shape of the halftone dot, when no diffraction at all is involved, is bound to represent the exact form of the diaphragm. If the latter is square, theoretically the halftone dots will be square also. For the sake of simplicity let us confine our attention to the round aperture. With a few experiments it is possible to prove that an increase in light diffraction causes increasing deformation of the halftone dots and makes their shape fuzzy. Illustr. No. 19 shows how the dot shapes change, when changing from a large to a small aperture, or from a coarse to a fine screen.

The dots in Illustr. No. 19 were photographed with a lith film. When developed in formaldehyde type developer, certain fine details which are of interest to us become suppressed.

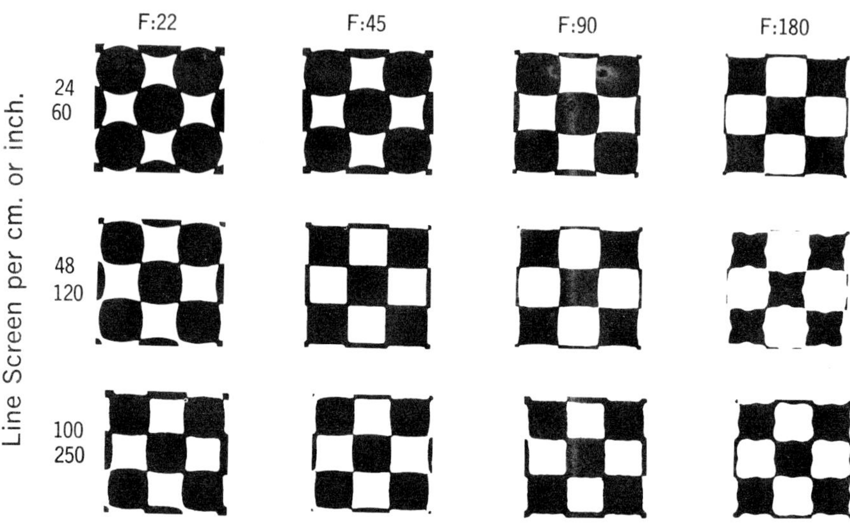


*Illustr. No. 19* **Dots Reproduced with a Lith Film and Lith Developer**

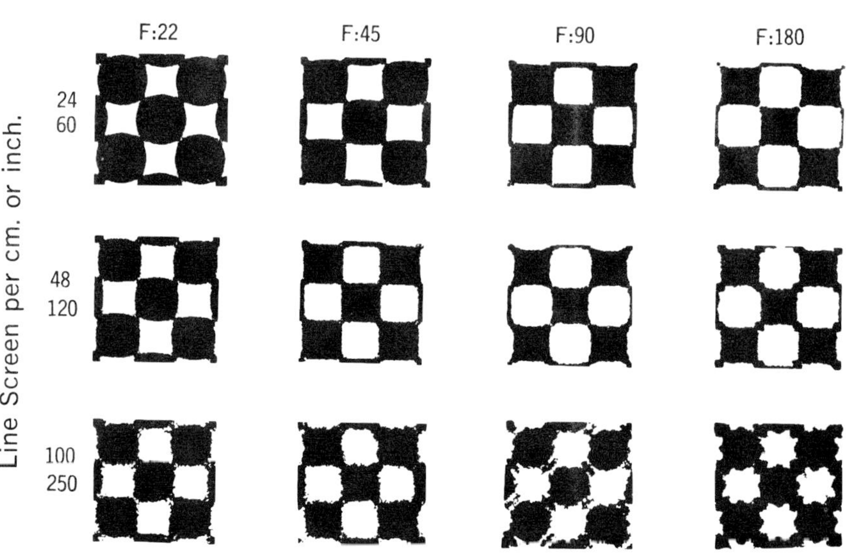


*Illustr. No. 20* **Dots Reproduced with a Softer Film.**

Illustr. No. 20 shows the same dots photographed with a softer film and developer combination. These results are therefore much more explanatory. One can clearly see in Illustr. No. 20 how the proportion of the diffracted light increases as we change to smaller lens apertures and to finer screens.

Both Illustrs. No. 19 and No. 20 explain and confirm a fact experienced in everyday practice. Halftone cameramen know that coarse to medium screens need a square diaphragm whenever perfect "checker board" dots are required, whereas in the case of fine screens, this shape can be achieved with a round diaphragm. Naturally, if a waterhouse stop is used to get a square dot, the stop must be perfectly positioned to be parallel with the ruling of the screen. Nevertheless, by shifting the waterhouse stop somewhat against the ruling of the screen, chaindots are obtained in the reproduction. This way it is possible to obtain the same elliptical dots with a conventional glass screen as it is otherwise possible only with an advanced contact screen.

As one can already see from these explanations, much valuable knowledge can be obtained by further studies of the glass screen based on the established research work which is offered by the principles of the Screen Key Method.

In conclusion, as a result of our findings the following question presents itself again: is it worth-while to make such a detailed study of the glass screen? Is not the contact screen on a fair way to push the glass screen out of the field? The characteristic properties of a contact screen depend entirely on the density and the definition of each individual halftone dot. This is determined by the conditions under which the contact screen is produced.

Many arguments support a growing appreciation for contact screens. Nevertheless this does not alter the fact that in producing the contact screen:

*The glass screen, as a master screen,*
*represents an indispensable preliminary step!*

# Chapter Three

## TONE VALUE CORRECTED REPRODUCTION

Our goal must always be to make halftone reproductions with perfect tone values in one direct step. Therefore the question arises: Is there a possibility to accomplish this strictly photo-mechanically? To be able to evaluate test series, it is important to find exact ways to read them systematically.[3] The only correct answer for this is:

## MODERN SENSITOMETRY

In this case it is necessary to measure halftone reproductions. This can be achieved on a reliable basis only if the screen dots are created with minimum halation and maximum density of at least 3.0 on an emulsion where the undeveloped areas remain perfectly clear. The only material to select for this purpose is a genuine lith film which must be developed in an ultra high contrast A + B formaldehyde type developer. However, only high quality lith films fulfill this to the required degree.

In order to obtain reliable readings, a photoelectric densitometer, such as is usually installed in the Graphic Arts Department, is used. The only importance is to take an aperture large enough to allow measurement of a series of dots together. 3 millimeters or 7½/64 inches is a safe diameter even for coarser screens. This kind of density reading is called an integral density reading, because the obtained values result from a mixture of opaque dots and transparent areas. On a screen pattern which is easy to follow a reading is explained very clearly. See illustr. No. 21.

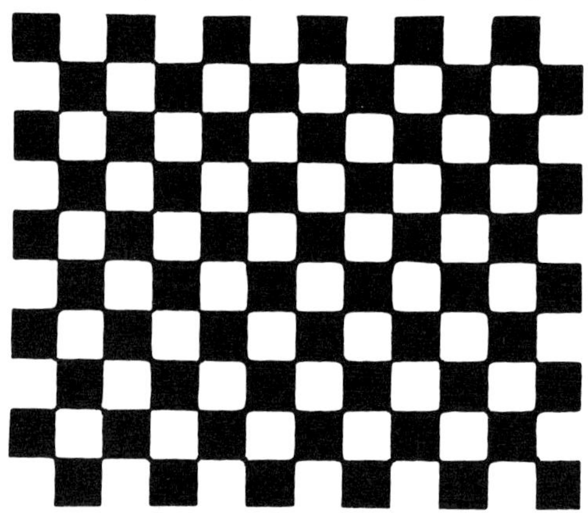

| | |
|---|---|
| density | : = 0.3 |
| transmission | : = ½ |
| opacity | : = 2 |
| log. 2 | : = 0.3 |

*Illustr. No. 21* **50% Dot Pattern**

This dot pattern represents a 50% halftone which is usually referred to as a "checkerboard." If such an area is measured on a densitometer, a density value of D 0.3 is obtained. The transmission of this area is ½ because 50% of the area is covered by opaque dots. This in turn represents an opacity of 2. As the density represents the logarithm of the opacity, our calculation results in: log 2 = D 0.3, which is the same as obtained on the densitometer.

As all test negatives have to be measured over the whole scale, an ideal original has to be used. A big continuous tone gray scale 18 x 24 centimeter or 8 x 10 inch is necessary. A transparent one would consist of 30 steps in increments of D 0.1 and therefore covering a density range of 3.0. A paper gray scale would consist of 20 steps also increasing by D 0.1, covering a density range 2.0*. Gray scales with these 0.1 subdivisions are known as $\sqrt[3]{2}$ scales and are at the same time positives as well as negatives.

With these important aids on hand one is able to begin the following investigations.

## THE CHARACTERISTICS OF GLASS SCREENS

It is a known fact that before an actual job can be printed, craftsmen are constantly asked to overcome problems. These include the printing itself, preparing of the printing plate and so forth. Unfortunately the influence from the camera end is the most serious one.

It is very informative to find out how a glass screen reproduces a $\sqrt[3]{2}$ gray scale. The foundation of this is to make "basically correct" screen exposures with the perfect screen distance as described under the Screen Key Method.

All tests have to be made with one single exposure only! Flash or highlight exposures would falsify the results. The lens aperture should not be smaller than F:22, in order to avoid excessive light defraction, which in turn destroys the true evaluation of the halftone reproduction. The following test is made. With a glass screen 48 lines/cm or 120 lines/inch and a line ratio of 1:1, a reproduction is made from the $\sqrt[3]{2}$ gray scale at same size and F:22. After the exposed lith film is developed in lith developer, a screened image is visible and shows various dot sizes starting from pin-

***Available through Perfect Graphic Arts Supply Company, P.O. Box 62, Demarest, N. J. 07627**

points and gradually increasing up to solid highlights. Each gray scale step in the reproduction is measured and the integral densitometer readings are transferred into the corresponding ordinate at the appropriate density in a coordinating system. See illustr. No. 22.

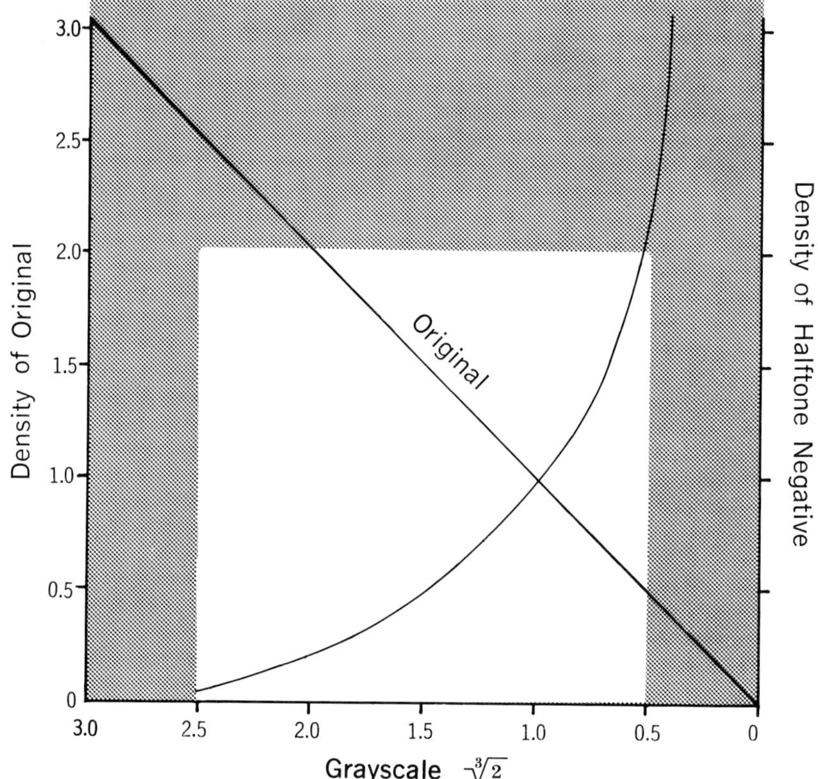


*Illustr. No. 22* **Characteristic Curve of Glass Screen Negative**

The judgment of the screen negative is based on completely different principles as known from continuous tone negatives. Certain areas in a continuous tone print appear uniformly gray to the eye. However, the same areas in a halftone print consist purely of mixtures of black and white dots and cannot be related with the naked eye. Besides that, of the twenty steps in the continuous tone gray scale, only about ten show usable screen dots. The rest of them are either without a dot or are already opaque. Tritton and Wilson[4] were the first ones who explored and described this mathematically as follows.

## THE IDEAL CURVE OF THE SCREEN NEGATIVE

Assuming a screen contact positive is made from an ideal halftone negative, then by no means has the negative and positive curve obtained the same shape as one is used to get when a continuous tone positive is made from a continuous tone negative under gamma 1. Nevertheless the opaque areas in the screen negative will be clear in the positive, and the clear ones in the negative will be opaque in the screen positive. This shows the clear areas in the screen negative and the clear areas in the screen positive add up to 1. In order to transfer these relations to the same basis applied with continuous tone, it is necessary to translate the transmission of the screen negative in density values. This is done in the following way.

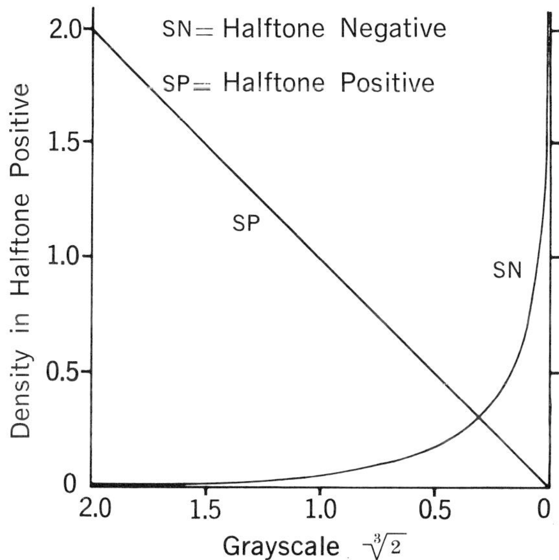


| Original | | Screen Negative | | Original | | Screen Negative | |
|---|---|---|---|---|---|---|---|
| Density d | Transmission $x = \frac{1}{\text{antilog. } d}$ | Transmission $1-x$ | Density $\frac{1}{1-x}$ | Density d | Transmission $x = \frac{1}{\text{antilog. } d}$ | Transmission $1-x$ | Density $\frac{1}{1-x}$ |
| 0 | 1.00 | 0 | ∞ | 0.6 | 0.251 | 0.749 | 0.125 |
| 0.01 | 0.977 | 0.023 | 1.64 | 0.7 | 0.200 | 0.800 | 0.097 |
| 0.02 | 0.955 | 0.045 | 1.35 | 0.8 | 0.158 | 0.842 | 0.075 |
| 0.05 | 0.891 | 0.109 | 0.96 | 1.0 | 0.100 | 0.900 | 0.046 |
| 0.1 | 0.795 | 0.205 | 0.69 | 1.2 | 0.063 | 0.937 | 0.028 |
| 0.2 | 0.631 | 0.369 | 0.43 | 1.4 | 0.040 | 0.960 | 0.018 |
| 0.3 | 0.500 | 0.500 | 0.30 | 1.6 | 0.025 | 0.975 | 0.011 |
| 0.4 | 0.398 | 0.602 | 0.22 | 1.8 | 0.016 | 0.984 | 0.007 |
| 0.5 | 0.316 | 0.684 | 0.16 | | | | |

*Illustr. No. 23* **The Ideal Halftone Reproduction**

The ideal screen positive in Illustr. No. 23 as per Tritton and Wilson is marked P. All densities in the dp curve are equivalent to the logarithm resulting from the opacity in the original.

$$dp = \log O$$

As opacity O represents the reciprocity of the transmission, t, it can also be described:

$$dp = \log \frac{i}{t} \quad (I)$$

The transmission in proportion to the incident light can only reach 1 as a maximum. If parts of an area are covered by screen dots, naturally the transmission must be less than 1. It would be 0 if no light was transmitted. Depending on the size of the halftone dots the transmission changes between 0 - 1.

If in (I) t is formulated t = x it results in:

$$dp = \log \frac{1}{x}$$

$$\text{or:} \quad x = 10^{-dp}$$

If x expresses the transmission of an ideal screen positive then in turn the transmission of the ideal screen negative must be 1 - x, because both transmissions add up to 1. The density in the screen negative dn is then:

$$dn = \log \frac{1}{1-x}$$

$$\text{or:} \quad dn = -\log \left(1-10^{-dp}\right)$$

If various densities from dp are derived in this way and plotted into Illustr. No. 23, the curve SN is obtained. It is obvious to the eye that the shape of the halftone negative curve must be completely different than that of the halftone positive. In the shadow areas of the negative little variation is noticeable but it changes almost suddenly into the extreme highlight areas. Therefore not even an expert is able to judge a halftone negative the way it is possible with a continuous negative. Tritton and Wilson were the first ones who recognized this and deserve full credit.

## HOW TO ACCOMPLISH THIS

In conclusion of these evalutions F. J. Tritton and E. T. Wilson stated:[4] "It has been shown that the normal screen negative is not capable of reproducing a scale of tones accurately as the dots are too large throughout practically the whole range, and in particular the reproduction of the highlights is unsatisfactory as it is not possible to get the dots to join up sufficiently rapidly with increase in exposure. — It is of interest to note that in the theoretical screen negative equal areas of black and clear represent a density 0.3 on the original; but the density range of 0.3 represents an exposure range of 2 to 1. Therefore doubling the exposure which produces a checkerboard pattern should cause the dots to close up to a solid black; no simple method for achieving this has been described —."

Sixteen years later Dr. V. G. W. Harrison[5] said the same. He had studied the relation between halftone negative to contact positive, between contact positive to deep etch offset plate and the print and checked the validity of the ideal halftone negative curve as described by Tritton and Wilson in all steps from negative to the printed sheet. It was commonly agreed that these new calculations and practical tests demanded an adjustment of Tritton and Wilson's theoretical curves. If the original has a density range of 1.45 it is necessary to obtain a screen negative curve as indicated with A; if the original has a density range of 1.8 then the screen negative curve has to be like curve B. Both curves lie between Tritton and Wilson's ideal and the screen negative curves usually obtained with a conventional screening method. See illustr. No. 24.

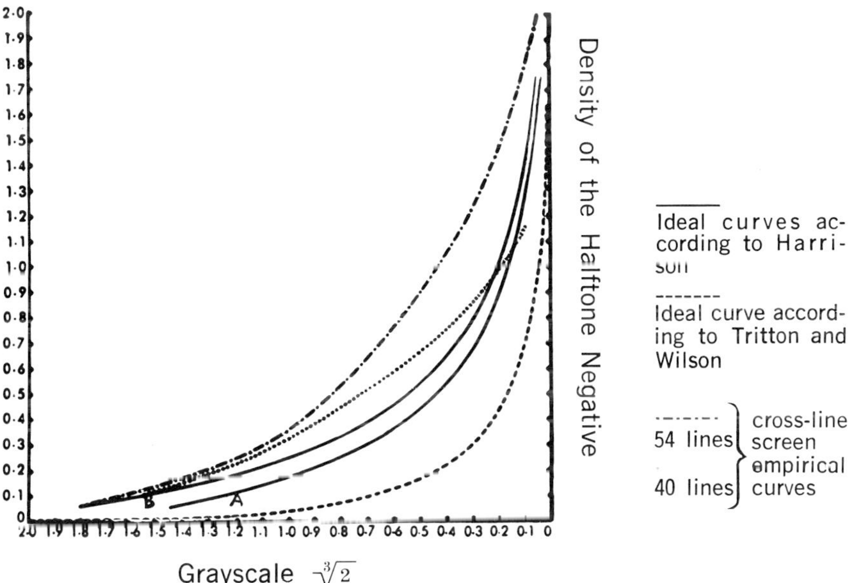


*Illustr. No. 24* **Screen Negative Comparisons**

Harrison stated further: At least in the shadow or highlight end should it be possible to come close to his ideal curves due to adjustments of the lens aperture, screen distance and exposure time. There is little hope of any improvement as long as ordinary glass screens continue to be used. — Theoretically, contact screens can be made to give any gradation desired and the preparation of a suitable contact screen would probably solve the problem of tone reproduction. Up to the present, however, this has not been done, but improvement of screens would undoubtedly bring about a substantial advance. However, so far no way was found to be able to reproduce a screen negative with perfect tone rendition throughout the whole scale. He also explains why Tritton's and Wilson's theoretical curves are not suitable for offset printing. It was found that areas in the negative reading less than 0.05 do not differentiate any more in the final print and appear solid. Therefore a great amount of shadow detail would be lost. We know that considerable changes occur during the various steps from negative up to the final print which up to that time was ignored. Still another point has to be considered. Yule and Nielsen found that due to light diffractions in the printed sheet the dot size appears bigger to the eye than its actual geometric area is.

| Original | Halftone Negative | Original | Halftone Negative |
|---|---|---|---|
| 0.03 | ∞ | 0.30 | 0.68 |
| 0.04 | 1.75 | 0.35 | 0.61 |
| 0.05 | 1.62 | 0.40 | 0.54 |
| 0.06 | 1.52 | 0.50 | 0.44 |
| 0.07 | 1.44 | 0.60 | 0.36 |
| 0.08 | 1.38 | 0.70 | 0.31 |
| 0.09 | 1.32 | 0.80 | 0.25 |
| 0.10 | 1.27 | 0.90 | $0.21_5$ |
| 0.11 | 1.23 | 1.00 | $0.17_5$ |
| 0.13 | 1.13 | 1.10 | $0.14_5$ |
| 0.15 | 1.04 | 1.20 | $0.12_5$ |
| 0.17 | 0.98 | 1.30 | 0.10 |
| 0.20 | 0.89 | 1.40 | $0.07_5$ |
| 0.25 | 0.77 | 1.45 | 0.06 |

*Illustr. No. 24a* **Densities of Screen Negative Required for Ideal Print.**

The ideal curves obviously have to be adjusted to suit printing conditions such as paper, ink, printing machine, etc. Since, however, our curves obtained in our final tests correspond well with the ones published by Gresham and by Clapper, an excellent result can be taken for granted.

The gradation of the ideal screen negative curve is contained in Illustration No. 24. However, as one might be interested to replot their own graph, all necessary values are given in table No. 24a.

## FINAL QUESTION

Are all of these previous findings still valid?

These theories explained by Tritton and Wilson and Harrison served as a valuable basis for the practical evaluations toward our goal. If we are able to accomplish in a direct way Harrison's suggested curve, then it is sufficient to check out the reproduction sensitometrically only. It eliminates our having to measure the following steps including the print.

Harrison's negative curve was applicable to offset only, as at that time there was no standard established for letterpress negatives in respect to their highlight dot size. Since the successful introduction of powderless etching, however, it is necessary to make equivalent offset and letterpress negatives with minimum highlight dots. As a matter of fact, this is a must to get the full benefit from this outstanding one-step etching method!

Our task was to create Harrison's curve under practical working conditions. The most important questions were:

1. What is the density range a glass screen can cover?
2. How is it possible to obtain perfect middletone and highlight rendition?

These questions are involved only in the making of halftone negatives. On the contrary, if it is necessary to make a perfect halftone positive, Harrison's curve is not applicable as the ideal curve for a screen positive has to be a straight line. It had to be assumed that a screen for the making of halftone positives has to have different characteristics than for negatives. Therefore, two more questions arose:

3. What kind of a glass screen is best suitable for making tone value corrected halftone positives?
4. Is it possible at all to make perfect halftone positives?

# Chapter Four

## THE MAKING OF THE SCREEN NEGATIVE

As pointed out before, the characteristic curves for halftone negatives versus halftone positives have to be completely different. Therefore, the evaluations have to go in two directions. In this chapter we will concentrate on the making of the screen negative only.[6]

## WHAT IS THE DENSITY RANGE A GLASS SCREEN CAN COVER

It is surprising that there is no literature which describes this important subject in detail. As a matter of fact we have to realize that each screen can cover only a certain density range. For instance, if one would try to reproduce a very high contrast original with one main exposure, then only the shadow detail would be obtained correctly. However, the middle tones would be too empty and the highlights would not have sufficient modulation. This is a result of the ratio between the opaque and transparent lines. Most screens have a line ratio of 1:1, nevertheless as it is not possible always to manufacture screens 100% exact, screens with different characteristics are known. An experienced cameraman talks about "good" and "bad" screens. He would determine a screen which is able to cover a high density range a good screen because with it he can give a longer main exposure to shoot more into the shadow detail without closing up in the highlights. If the line ratio of this screen would be measured with a microscope, we could clearly recognize the opaque lines being wider. The logical question arises:

## WHAT LINE RATIO IS MOST SUITABLE

The following evaluations are concerned only with glass screens for the making of halftone negatives. This brings up another important question: *What density range can be produced in the actual printing?* This, as we know, depends of course on a number of factors of which the most important ones are the quality of the paper and the ink used. Should these be very poor to start with, high quality could not be obtained as the density range would be suppressed. In this case it is suggested to retain as much highlight detail as possible, even though the shadow detail is bound to suffer. For reproductions of this kind a screen with a 1:1 ratio is alright. On the other hand, if it is important to make high quality reproductions, it is necessary to have a screen which can cover genuinely the complete range in a brilliant copy which averages about D1.7 or, in other words a brightness extent of 1:50. If halftone negatives have to be made from continuous tone positives, then it is advantageous to be able to adjust the range of the continuous tone positive to the suitable range required to fit the particular screen. If direct halftone negatives should be made from color transparencies with density ranges reaching up to 2.5, it would still be possible to make screens with the required line ratio. This, however, would not be a practical approach, especially as the indirect method via continuous tone color separations allow for color corrections with masks which at the same time lend themselves automatically to contrast reducing. Let us therefore evaluate the characteristics required in a glass screen best suitable for average originals of a 1.7 range. The experiments were made with a 60 lines per cm or 150 lines per inch screen. Naturally, all procedures were standardized as much as possible. This is of utmost importance as the developing in A + B formaldehyde developer can involve many variables, for instance, due to changes in temperature, age, usage, agitation, etc. To guarantee best uniformity in developing procedures, all tests were "brush developed." This means the developer is evenly distributed over the film to be developed by means of a soft camel hair brush of about 4 inches wide. It is also very important to use a tray with a perfectly flat bottom as any uneveness and for this reason especially ribs in the tray would show up in the halftone due to variations in the developer coverage. This would be even more fatal in still-developing.

It is also of utmost importance to prevent flare in the camera or intermediate surroundings. To minimize flare, the copyboard around the original has to be covered up with black paper, the walls and ceiling have to be painted in dark color, the lens system as well as the inside of the camera have to be clean. Unfortunately, it is not always realized to the full extent what damage is done by not obeying these laws. Deficiencies in screens, such as ragged lines, or imperfect contact between the two glass plates, might also influence the results. With screens 48 lines per cm or 120 lines per inch or finer, it would be ideal to work with screens without coverglass. Only then would it be possible to get the actual ruling of the screen close enough to the film plane, thereby allowing for big lens apertures which prevent diffraction of light, and in turn secures best image quality. Some of the tests were made with such special screens.

The tests were started to evaluate the characteristic curves obtainable with 60 lines per cm, or 150 lines per inch screens of the following nature:

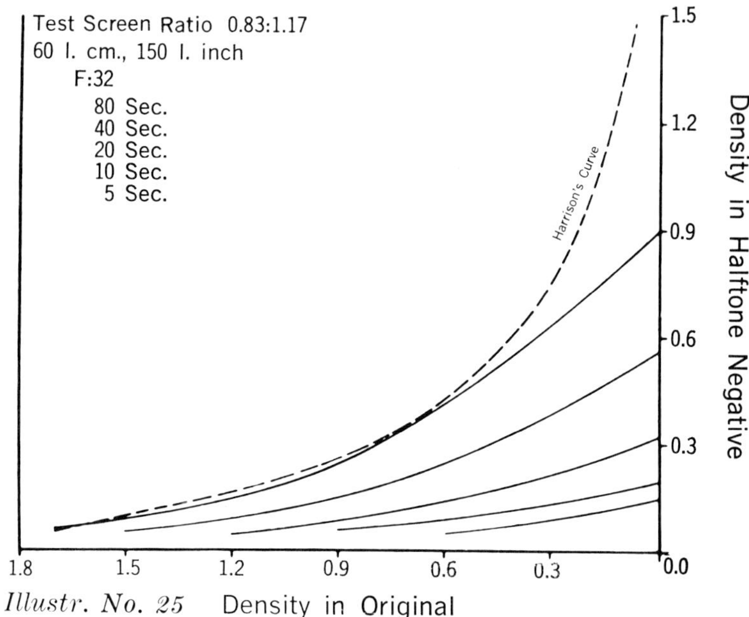


*Illustr. No. 25* Density in Original

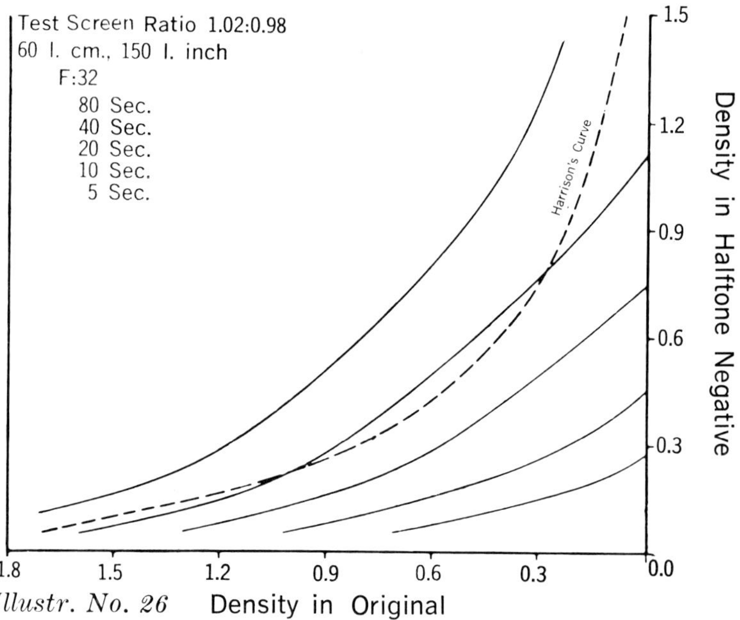


*Illustr. No. 26* Density in Original

**Screen Comparisons**

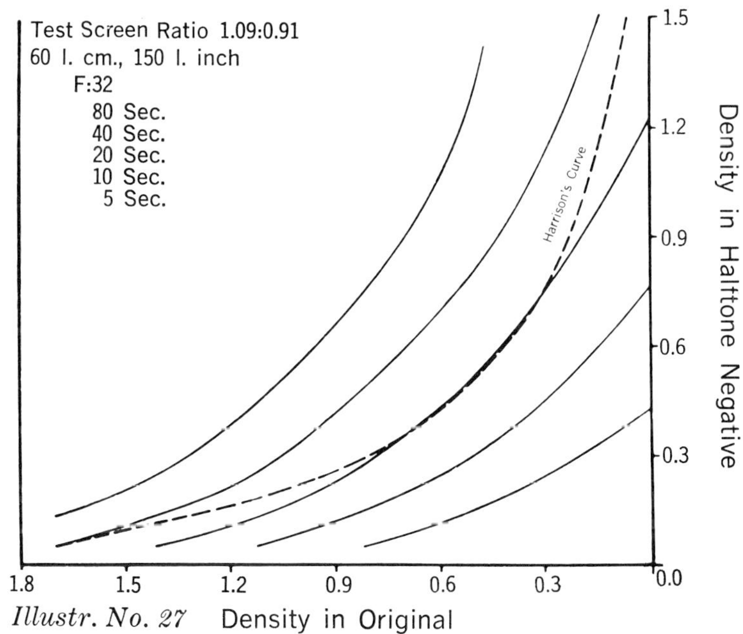


*Illustr. No. 27*

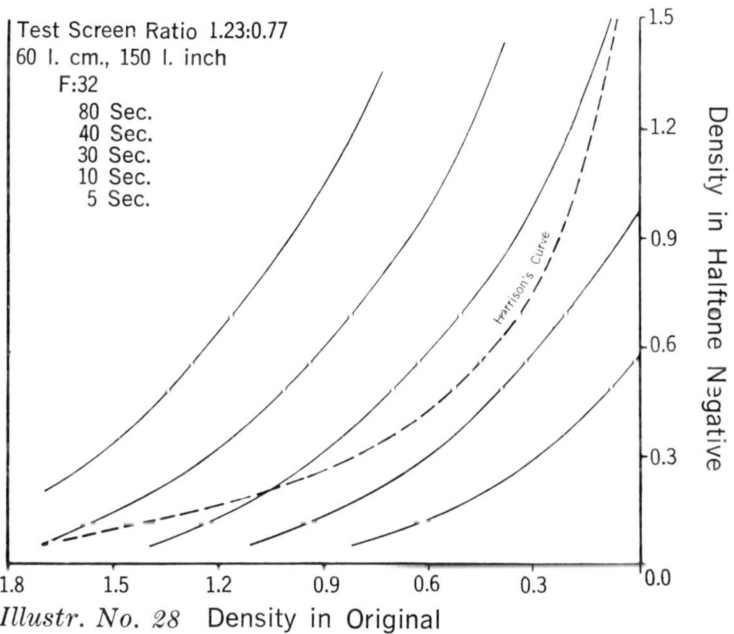


*Illustr. No. 28*

**Screen Comparisons**

The Illustrations No. 25-28 explain the density curves obtained with these different screens. The original used was an 18 x 24 cm or 8 x 10 inch wide step tablet $\sqrt[3]{2}$ 0.05 — 3.0. $\sqrt[3]{2} = 1.26$ in other words is the figure which can be multiplied 3 x with itself to make 2. The logarithm 1.26: log 1.26 = 0.1 represents an increase of the opacity of factor 1.26 and is equal to the density increase of 0.1 from step to step.) Single main exposures of 5, 10, 20, 40, 80 sec. were given at F:32 at same size. The screen distances of course were adjusted to be correct for the line ratios of the screens. To prevent variations in developing, all 5 exposures with the same screen were stepped up on 1 single film. All densitometer readings were reduced by 0.03 to compensate for the base of the film. The minimum densities start at 0.05 (.08 — .03) as densities below do not differentiate in the final print. Each diagram shows the ideal halftone negative curve as per Harrison in a dotted line in connection to a 1.7 original range.

In this test no attention was paid to the highlight details as we specifically wanted to find out the relation between the line ratios of the screens and the range possible to reproduce. Our goal is Harrison's ideal curve. To be able to obtain the best middletone details possible, it is necessary not to exceed any density which characterizes his suggested negative curve. The one test screen which fulfills this best is the one with the line ratio 0.83: 1.17 (see Illustr. 25). This illustration proves that the wider the opaque line in a screen the higher a density range it can cover! It is possible to find an exact relation between the line ratio of the screen and the density range it can cover by undertaking further studies, thereby learning how Harrison's curve can be duplicated under practical conditions.

## HOW TO OBTAIN THE CORRECT HIGHLIGHT DOT STRUCTURE

A dot exposed behind a glass screen grows proportionally to the light intensity given, however, only as long as the dots are not connected. Then, due to light diffractions, proceedings get more complicated as the joined dots do not gradually expand anymore, resulting in a considerable loss of highlight details. To compensate for this flattening effect it is necessary to give a supplementary highlight exposure. This recommendation was often a point of controversy. Even in trade literature it was repeatedly doubted that one is able to improve the highlights in this way. Innumerable suggestions were made to use especially shaped apertures and other procedures. It would only be a waste to spend time with all these manifold explanations, especially as there is one easier way to get better results by using the conventional round aperture but simply change to a larger opening for the highlight exposure. However, as explained later, this can only give limited improvements. Therefore, for best results, an actual "highlight bump" is necessary which was first described by J. O. Bow as follows:[7]

"A supplementary exposure given to the original with the screen removed or pushed foreward to the inoperative position showed that considerable increase in highlight contrast was possible. This technique is recommended by Kodak when using the Magenta contact screen and a study of the effect with the cross-line screen seemed worthwhile. Highlighting exposures made with the screen removed have been suggested and tried by many workers in the past, but the effectiveness is doubtful on emulsions other than "lith" type."

Illustrations No. 29 and No. 29a show the considerable improvements when giving supplementary exposures without a screen. *This was also experienced in our own, solely idependent tests made in 1956 and reveal the secret to a phenomenon unsolved till then.*

A 60 lines per cm, or 150 lines per inch glass screen with a 0.83:1.17 ratio was used. Main exposures of 100 sec. were given with F:32. After the screen was removed from the camera supplementary exposures from the original of 1½, 3, 6 sec. with the same stop were given. It was found to be absolutely necessary to remove the screen completely from the camera. If it were moved away only from the film, it would create excessive flare and destroy a considerable amount of detail. For the no-screen exposure it is a must to compensate for the thickness of the glass screen by means of a glass plate or by adjusting the cameraback.

Illustration No. 29 proves that, if the correct percentage of supplementary exposure is given, it is very well possible to meet Harrison's ideal curve very closely.

This practice can be successfully applied only since the availability of genuine lith emulsions. Developed in a good formaldehyde developer it accomplishes actual growing of the dots without creating any fog in the areas between them. It is surprising to what extent this can be carried on. For normal results the main exposure has to produce dots of a densitometer reading of 0.6 when making negatives for offset, or for letterpress when powderless etching is used. If conventional etching should be used, a densitom-

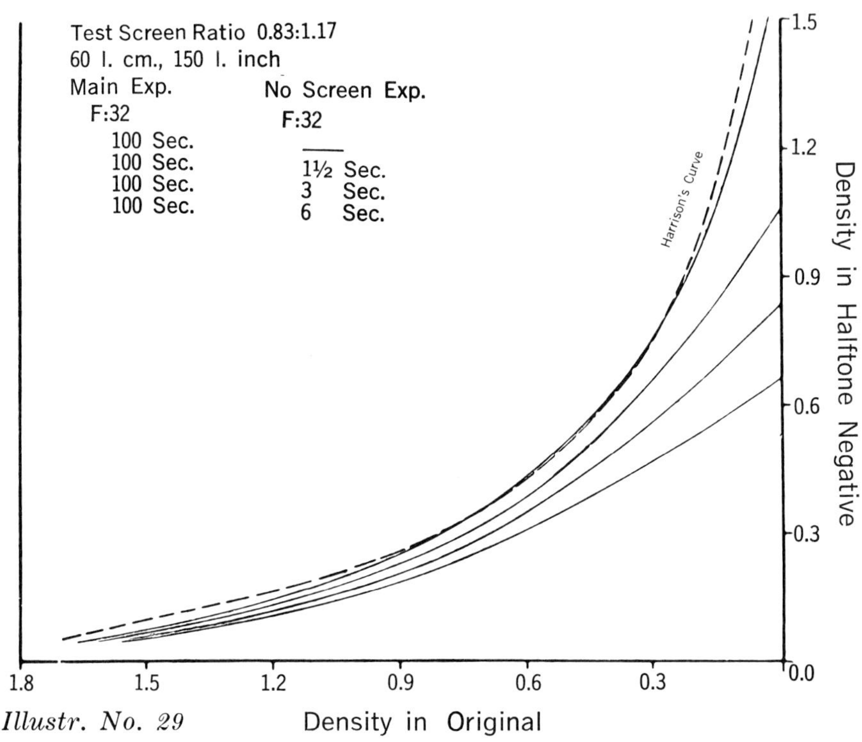


*Illustr. No. 29*

Basic exposure with screen only

| 5% | 10 | 15 | 20 | 25 | 30 | 35 | 40 | 45 | 50 | 55 | 60% |
|---|---|---|---|---|---|---|---|---|---|---|---|
| 5% | 10 | 15 | 20 | 25 | 30 | 35 | 40 | 50 | 65 | 85 | 95% |

Basic exposure with screen + 6% supplementary exposure without screen

*Illustr. No. 29a* **Effect of Supplementary Exposure without Screen**

eter reading of 0.3 should be obtained only, this is equivalent to a checkerboard and represents a 50% dot pattern. If the dots are smaller, in other words, disconnected, then it is difficult to obtain satisfactory highlight dots, as it goes beyond the limit of keeping perfectly clear areas between the extreme highlight dots. This is because the main exposure is not long enough to create sufficient effect below the inertia of the emulsion. An intermediate exposure of about ½% with an aperature 2 stops bigger than the main exposure stop can compensate for this. This recognition was the first necessary step before final controlled tests could be started, in order to evaluate all complexes involved. Some theories could be explained only after innumerable practical tests had proven this.

On the other hand if the main exposure exceeds a densitometer reading of 0.6 — 0.7, then as Illustr. No. 29 shows, it is not possible to get enough details in middle tones, as the supplementary exposure also affects these tones to an extent. The absolute maximum to stay in the limits of Harrison's curve is 0.7.

## THE RELATION OF THE LINE RATIO TO THE REPRODUCIBLE DENSITY RANGE

The line ratio between the transparent and the opaque lines governs the amount of main exposure which can be given to leave enough room for a supplementary exposure without a screen. If we examine once more the Illustrs. No. 25 - 28, we can see the effects of different screens:

| Illustr. No. | Line Ratio transp. : opaque | Reproducible Density Range | Reproducible Brightness Extent |
|---|---|---|---|
| Illustr. 25 | 0.83 : 1.17 | 1.60 | 1:40 |
| Illustr. 26 | 1.02 : 0.98 | 1.25 | 1:18 |
| Illustr. 27 | 1.09 : 0.91 | 1.05 | 1:11 |
| Illustr. 28 | 1.23 : 0.77 | 0.95 | 1: 9 |

These measurements are correct within ± 0.05 and show obviously these interrelations. Further comparisons were made with 18 other screens. Illustr. No. 30 shows the ratios between transparent and opaque lines and the useable density range possible to obtain.

As can be seen in this Illustration, No. 30 the ranges obtainable are very similar even with screens of different lines per cm or inch, as long as the line ratio is similar. However, comparing very coarse against very fine screens it is indicated that with very coarse screens the ranges will extend slightly faster if the screen window gets smaller than with very fine screens.

We can take for granted that the basic range obtainable can be extended by at least 0.2 with a minimum flash exposure. (This is explained later on under "The Flash Exposure".) Therefore, it can be expected that average screens have the following characteristics as shown in Illustr. 31.

It is very well possible to manufacture screens with these specifications within minor tolerances. However, if the line ratio is between 0.80 : 1.20 or 0.90 : 1.10, then a satisfactory density range is obtainable.

| Lines: cm. | inch | Line Ratio transp. : opaque | Reproducible Density Range |
|---|---|---|---|
| 24 | 60 | 0.82 – 1.18 | 1.9 |
| 24 | 60 | 1.0 – 1.0 | 1.3 |
| 24 | 60 | 1.02 – 0.98 | 1.3 |
| 48 | 120 | 1.0 – 1.0 | 1.2 |
| 48 | 120 | 0.98 – 1.02 | 1.3 |
| 54 | 133 | 1.02 – 0.98 | 1.2 |
| 54 | 133 | 1.0 – 1.0 | 1.3 |
| 54 | 133 | 0.94 – 1.06 | 1.3 |
| 54 | 133 | 0.95 – 1.05 | 1.3 |
| 54 | 133 | 0.85 – 1.15 | 1.5 |
| 54 | 133 | 1.1 – 0.9 | 1.0 |
| 54 | 133 | 1.2 – 0.8 | 0.9 |
| 60 | 150 | 1.02 – 0.98 | 1.25 |
| 60 | 150 | 1.0 – 1.0 | 1.25 |
| 60 | 150 | 0.83 – 1.17 | 1.6 |
| 60 | 150 | 1.09 – 0.91 | 1.05 |
| 60 | 150 | 1.23 – 0.77 | 0.95 |
| 100 | 250 | 1.06 – 0.94 | 0.9 |

*Illustr. No. 30* **Line Ratio and Reproducible Density Range**

| Line Ratio transp. : opaque | Reproducible Density Range | Reproducible Brightness Extent |
|---|---|---|
| 0.8 : 1.2 | 1.80 | 1:64 |
| 0.9 : 1.1 | 1.60 | 1:40 |
| 1.0 : 1.0 | 1.40 | 1:25 |
| 1.1 : 0.9 | 1.20 | 1:16 |
| 1.2 : 0.8 | 1.00 | 1:10 |

*Illustr. No. 31* **Screen Characteristics**

All screens should be provided with exact information concerning the characteristics of the line ratio, thickness of the cover glass as well as of the total screen. This would enable the camerman to determine in advance what the particular screen can do for him. If these data are not given, extensive tests are necessary to familiarize the camerman with the new screen which might often become a surprise. To perform this test it is best to reproduce a gray scale and establish the density difference between the steps producing 0.6 – 0.7 and a good printable shadow dot. The advantage hereby is that the test is valid for the actual working conditions.

It is important to point out again that all our tests were made in lith developer with brush development in a tray with a flat bottom. A 4 inch wide camelhair brush was slowly moved over the films for smooth developing. The kind of development used has a big influence over the results obtained and is shown in Illustr. No. 32.

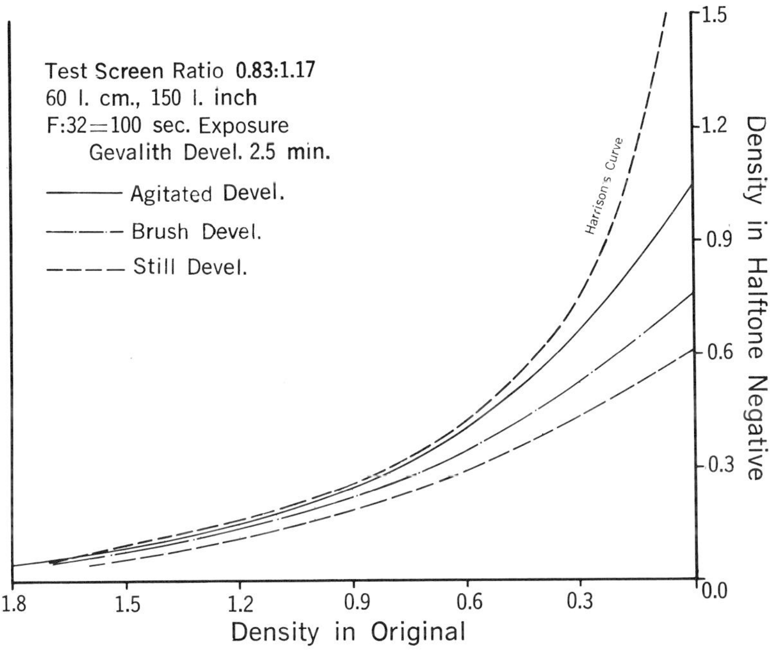


*Illustr. No. 32* **Developing Characteristics**

These results were obtained after a 18 x 24 cm or 8″ x 10″ inch step tablet $\sqrt[3]{2}$ was exposed with a 60 lines per cm. or 150 lines per inch screen, with a line ratio of 0.83 :1.17. The film was cut into three parts and then developed separately with agitation, brush and still developing. Tests with screens of different lines per cm or inch rulings gave equivalent results. If the curves obtained in Illustr. No. 32 are lined up cover the same density range of 1.6, then the results are as shown in Illustr. No. 33 and explain even better the actual differences.

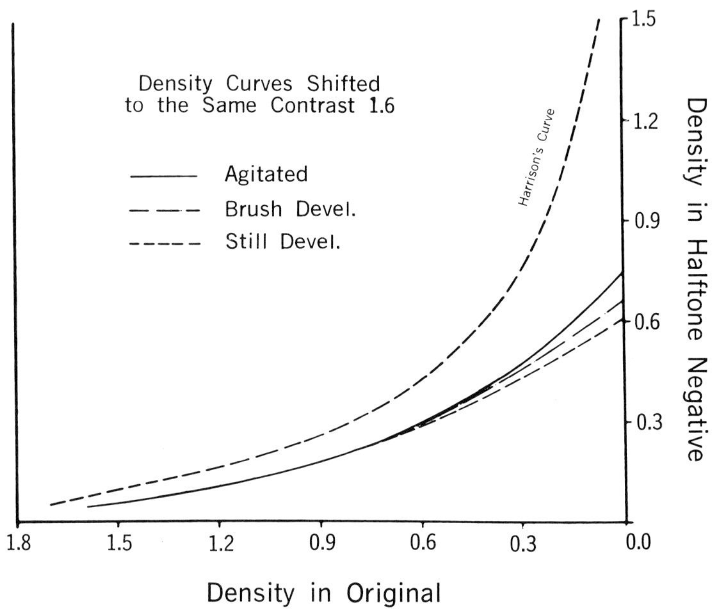


*Illustr. No. 33* **Developing Characteristics**

## PERFECT DOTS THROUGH LITH GRADATION

A perfect dot has to have a density minimum of at least D 3.0 and should not show any halation at all. This ideal cannot be fulfilled; however, with genuine lith materials it is possible to come very close. This was true even at times when "wet emulsions" were in use. These of course had to be specially etched and intensified. These steps are eliminated with modern lith films when processed in good formaldehyde type developers. Comparisons of various brands of these film and developer combinations makes one realize the considerable variations which show up much more due to the different developing characteristics in lith developing. Therefore it is interesting to analyze these points.[8]

A. What is a lith gradation, and why is it necessary?

B. What happens in lith developing?

C. What demands have to be met in lith processing?

## THE LITH GRADATION

The first question will be, is it correct to speak about gradation when determining the sharpness of a dot? The answer is a definite yes. *The steeper the gradation of a film the sharper the dots reproduced with it.*

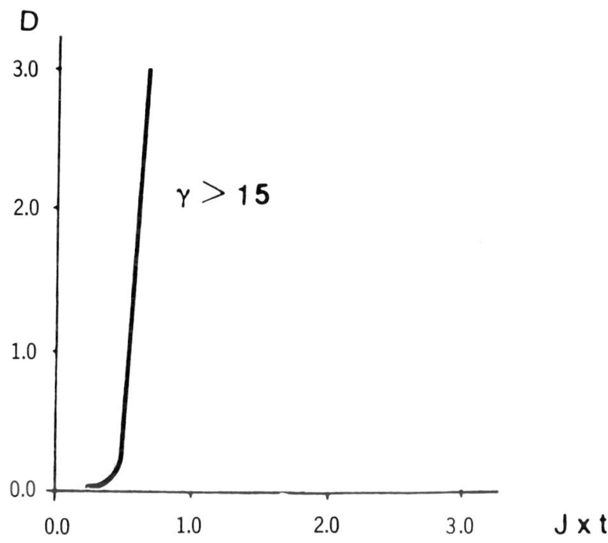


*Illustr. No. 34* **The Lith Gradation**

There is no doubt, that the contrast of a lithfilm and the dotsharpness obtained with it is at least relative! Naturally experience has shown that there can be discrepancies caused by the way the film is being developed which has quite an influence on how the exposed areas and the silversalt is converted into metallic silver which again has quite some influence on the resulting dot sharpness. Processing machines with a slower throughput or less developer turbulence indicate a lower gradient on a "continuous tone" processing control strip as compared to one which has been developed with a much more active processor. Nevertheless, when comparing the actual dot sharpness, there is not necessarily as much difference. Unless something else had influenced the final result, I have not seen a deficiency in dotsharpness when a very high gradient was evident over one where the gradient was much lower. As a matter of fact many tests have indicated that when using the same film and developer combination in a tray, the gradient obtained in an automatic processing machine, where the developer turbulence was quite vigorous, was about 3 lower and in a processor with little agitation about 5 lower. The dots however were not so decisively different in respect to sharpness but always at least somewhat better with a higher gradient.

If a gradient in a machine falls way below 7, a sharp dot is just not obtainable anymore, while I have never experienced an unsharp dot when exceptionally high gradients of 15 (which might be equivalent to a gamma of 20) were obtained in a tray. This is why I feel quite confident when making the statement that the gradient and the dotsharpness is relative.

In continuous tone photography, gradation means gradual differentiation from shadows to highlights. Depending on how many steps show in between, we speak of a soft or a hard gradation. In scientific photography it is common to determine this with the number of the tangent which represents the angle of the gradation curve. Films with relatively low gammas are not suitable for first generation screening as they would create dots with considerable halation or possibly not even enough density maximum resulting in no core in the dot.

For halftone reproductions it is necessary to have films with gammas of at least 15.0 The higher the gamma the sharper the dots obtainable. This extreme contrast can be reached with lith film and lith developer only. The highest contrast is just good enough.

It would be wrong to believe that this would directly affect the details in the reproduction. As a matter of fact:

*The contrast of the film material used, basically has no influence over the tone rendition obtained in the screen reproduction.*

The following evaluations explain why this statement must be correct. Behind each screen window of a glass screen in a camera a light cone is formed. A lith film strictly reacts to the light intensity of this cone. With minimum light intensity pin dots are created, as the dots jump over the inertia of the emulsion. With more intensity these dots grow bigger, join in a checkerboard pattern and as an absolute maximum close up to a solid area.

With contact screens the same principle is in effect. The only difference is that the cones of the light are formed by distinct densities in the contact screen dots. Basically the lith film serves only as a medium to register different light intensities, reflected or transmitted by an original, resulting in small or larger dots. Any attempt to influence the tone values in the reproduction has to be made through changes in the exposure technique such as supplementary exposures, etc. In every case, however, the lith film will guarantee perfect dot construction in respect to density and sharpness.

## THE FORMALDEHYDE-DEVELOPER

The main differences between lith developers compared to regular developers is the presence of only a single developing agent—hydroquinone—and the limited amount of sodium sulfite in action during the developing process. The bulk of the sulfite present is linked together with formaldehyde and therefore not able to react. If, during the developing process free sodium sulfite is used up, then in turn the formaldehyde compound releases a definite amount of sodium sulfite. This chemical mechanism is called "buffer" and assures a satisfactory sulfite level in order to achieve the "lith" effect. This is of utmost importance as there should be just enough free sodium-sulfite present in the developer to prevent the rapid oxidation of the solution. However, there must be little sulfite present to inhibit the oxidation occurring during the developing reaction itself. This assures the loss of energy of hydroquinone in areas of maximum development and prevents development in adjacent areas which have received only slight exposure through diffraction or halation. The "infectious developing time" must be short enough so that the less exposed areas are not developed. This is because the maximum sharpness would then be lost again and the contrast of the film would fall below gamma 15.0, resulting in halated dots or lines. This of course would be most unfavorable as the control for the next step, such as platemaking, would be completely lost.

In other words, the developing must be stopped or rather suddenly interrupted by immersing the film in an acetic acid stop bath. Another purpose of the stop bath is that it reduces the active developer transferred into the hypo bath where the fixation of the undeveloped silver salt takes place.

## FUNCTION OF A STOPBATH

When using tray processing, development must be stopped, or rather suddenly interrupted, by immersing the film in an acetic acid stop bath. A 3% solution is prepared by adding 30 cc. or 3 oz. of acetic acid (glacial) into 1000 cc. or 100 oz. of water. If acetic acid of a concentration of 28% is used, 100 cc. or 10 oz. of the latter has to be used for 1000 cc. or 100 oz. of water.

The acidity of the stopbath opposes the alkalinity of the developer and puts the developing agents into an inert stage thereby instantaneously stopping the development action.

The stop bath not only interrupts the developing action immediately, but also prolongs the life of the fixer considerably. In addition, it prevents stain and streaks which can lead to "dichroic fog." This is a chemical fog which can occur when too much developer is carried over into the fixer, which will then be contaminated. If a film is not put into a stop bath, or if it is not properly rinsed and is therefore covered by a still active layer of developer when it gets into the fixer (especially when the latter is not fresh or sour enough), a chemical reaction occurs and deposits a dichroic fog on the surface of the film.

It can easily be recognized by its rainbow color appearance, which becomes especially obvious when inspecting the film — not with transmitted but with reflected light at a 45° angle. Fortunately, dichroic fog is easily removed with a very weak solution of Farmer's Reducer. It should be so diluted that the actual image is not in any way affected. Needless to say, such an extra procedure should not be required and can be prevented by the proper handling of the film in the first place and by keeping the chemicals in good condition.

The stop bath fulfills its task only if it stays sufficiently sour. It can be checked with blue litmus paper which must readily change to red; otherwise the stop bath must be renewed. If a stop bath is not used, the film should be rinsed in clean water. This, however, does not stop development but only slows it down.

As is realized, when mechanized processing is utilized, a stop bath is not used because there is simply no provision for it in a machine. For this reason it is most important to make sure that the acid fixer used is kept in perfect condition. This can only be assured by constant replenishing and a good circulation in the fixer tank. If this is not done, the developer carried over from the previous tank can accumulate on the upper level of the fixer tank and build a pocket, which again can lead to dichroic fog and many other difficulties.

## FIXER AND ITS PROPER USE

It is often asked how long a film should be fixed. A safe rule is to leave it in at least twice as long as it needs to clear out. The fixer must be mixed to comply with the manufacturer's recommendation. It is often thought it would be a good idea to use a much stronger hypo concentration to assure better and faster fixing. Quite the contrary is true, however!

Tests were made with a high quality fixer and a good quality lith-film to find the relation between its fixing time and concentration. The manufacturer's recommendation called for a dilution of the liquid fixer concentrate with three parts of water and the addition of the normal amount of hardener. Nevertheless, varying dilutions from too high to too low were used at 70° F and the results shown in the table were experienced.

| DILUTION | CLEARING TIME |
|---|---|
| 1 + 1 | 20 sec |
| 1 + 2 | 17 sec |
| 1 + 3 | 14 sec |
| 1 + 4 | 16 sec |
| 1 + 5 | 19 sec |
| 1 + 6 | 23 sec |

As can be seen, contrary to popular belief, too concentrated hypo slows down the fixing time rather than speeds it up. The suggested dilution of 1/3 gives the best result.

The same could be experienced when an overly amount of hardener is used. This seems to harden the emulsion, slowing down the fixing time by retarding the penetration of the hypo into the emulsion.

An excess quantity of hardener is usually used if transport or drying problems are experienced in automatic processing machines. Even though this will sometimes help momentarily, it is definitely not a good practice. Too much hardener can cause the hardening chemical to precipitate and deposit in the fixer replenisher storage tank, on the hoses which lead to the fixer tank and also on the rollers in the fixer tank where it can create deposits on the film. This is generally referred to as sludging which, however, can also have other causes.

Even if the proper dilution is used, the previously described trouble can occur if the solutions are not perfectly mixed. Fixer concentrate and hardener must never be put together, but the hypo must always be diluted first before the hardener is added. It should be remembered that these chemicals are very heavy and do not mix easily unless an extra effort is used. When heavy hypo sits on the bottom of a fixer tank (even if water has already been added) the hardener, which is quite heavy too, also sinks down to the bottom and can create precipitation. Casual stirring can hardly mix the solutions, for which reason a plunger should be used in a regular up-down motion. If these rules are neglected all sorts of difficulties can occur in the processor, such as poor drying, slow clearing, etc., which one would not associate with the original mixing problem.

Insufficient fixer replenishment or improper circulation, besides difficulties already mentioned, can also give elastic-like deposits on rollers and fixer tank walls. This could be calcium-aluminum-gelatine composites which are usually more prevalent in hard water areas. Most of the trouble found with improper drying or film transport must be attributed to improper fixing. There is no doubt that there is much more to the "fixing" of a film than just simply clearing it!

Although a good fixing bath has considerably longer life and capacity than a developer, it is still subject to deterioration. To be able to find out instantly the condition of the fixing solution, Agfa-Gevaert has made available a uniquely devised method called "Agfa-Gevaert Fixing Aid". This kit consists of two small rubber balls—one white and one black—each of a selected specific gravity. When placed in the fixer tray, the white ball will sink to the bottom and the black ball will float to the surface if the fixer solution is at the proper dilution. The position of either ball will act as a guide for replenishment through use or evaporation. If the fixer is too strong, both balls will float; if the fixer is too weak, both balls will sink.

Indicator paper strips are also supplied with the kit to check the acidity balance and silver content of the mixture. Instructions are also included.

## THE MAKING OF THE SCREEN NEGATIVE UNDER PRACTICAL CONDITIONS

All these evaluations are bound to be theories only, unless they can be applied practically under shop conditions in photoengraving as well as in offset. Since it cannot be expected that present screens on hand will be eliminated in order to buy new ones with these recommended characteristics, the question arises how useful the conventional screen is. The answer is very encouraging provided certain rules are being observed.

First of all it is important to have a camera where the screen can easily be removed during the exposure and compensated with a glass compensator or cameraback adjustment for a supplementary exposure. Furthermore, it is necessary that the cameraman has perfect control over the lith processing. It is important to know that in lith developing a definite maximum of sharpness is obtained only during a comparatively short interval. Only genuine lith films reach this stage and the latitude depends strictly on the quality of the film and developer combination. After this stage the gradation gets softer again and the growing dots start to build up a noticeable halo due to the "infectious" developing which acts like a chain reaction as it partly converts unexposed silver haloids into metallic silver. This is contrary to metol hydroquinone processing where the developing levels or shoulders off in the final stage. In lith developing the density does not increase gradually. It needs close to one minute to show an image. Then in the following minute the density increases rapidly and jumps suddenly up to its final maximum. This is the time to interrupt the developing process. To be able to control this critical stage it is best to use a transparent tray in a temperature controlled sink which can be illuminated with red or yellow light from the bottom. Only in this way it is possible to provide for smooth, even developing, especially still developing, as the film does not get touched or streaked due to handling. If this should not be available right away, it is suggested to use a bright red darkroom safelight at a distance as close as 25 cm or 10 inches to the tray. Illuminated from a 45° angle it allows at least some inspection with a magnifier. As the emulsion desensitizes considerably after the first 2 minutes of developing, this light is then not harmful to the film anymore.

We know that the first step in preparing for a screen exposure is to determine the combination: Screen used, aperture chosen, reduction or enlargement ratio, to find out the correct screen distance.

The "Screen Key" serves hereby as a unique tool.

The second step is to accomplish the Harrison curve. For this it is necessary to use two to three exposures such as: main exposure, supplementary exposure and necessarily a flash exposure.

## THE FLASH EXPOSURE

The following illustrations No. 35 and No. 36 show the effect of flash exposures with two 60 lines per cm or 150 lines per inch screens with different line ratios.

As can be seen from the illustrations it is possible to gain about a 0.2 higher range with a minimum flash exposure. This flash exposure alone without any main exposure would not be intensive enough to create a shadow dot all by itself. It only allows the dots insufficiently exposed during the main exposures to jump over the inertia of the emulsion. This minimum flash helps genuinely to cover more density range without destroying shadow detail. If the flash exposure is increased beyond this stage, then the shadow details flatten out more and more as they get covered up with foreign dots not naturally created by the original. The illustrations show clearly the deteriorating effect of excessive flash exposure and should therefore be kept to a minimum. A safe rule is to use only half the exposure as would be required to create a shadow dot with a flash exposure alone.

## THE MAIN EXPOSURE

As this was extensively explained before, let's explain in summary the most important facts: The main exposure has to guarantee the creation of maximum middletone and shadow details. How far the scale can be extended depends on the line ratio of the screen. It is of utmost importance to have the correct screen distance for this main step. If it is chosen correctly, it is possible to create a fine pinpoint even from extremely dark originals with densities as high as 2.0. This is because at least 3% of light is always reflected from any medium. If enough exposure time is given, the light will accumulate to sufficient intensity and create a perfectely dense pin dot.

The duration of the main exposure is determined by the reduction ratio, aperture used and density of the original. If the screen does not cover to high a density range of an original without exceeding an integral density of 0.6-0.7, then it is necessary to limit the exposure to that point only and substitute for the shadows with a

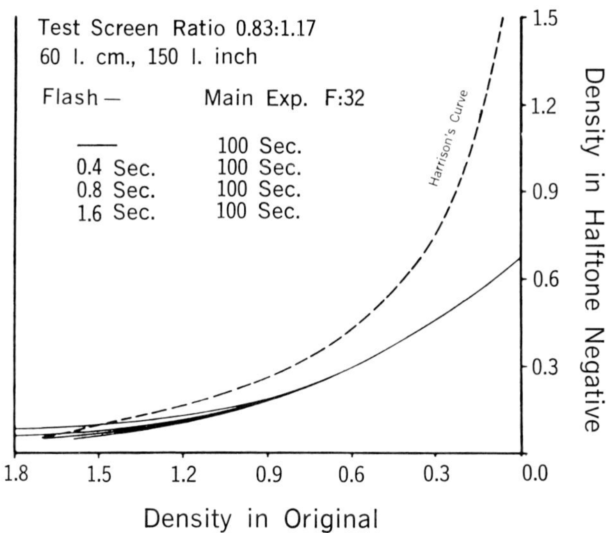


*Illustr. No. 35*

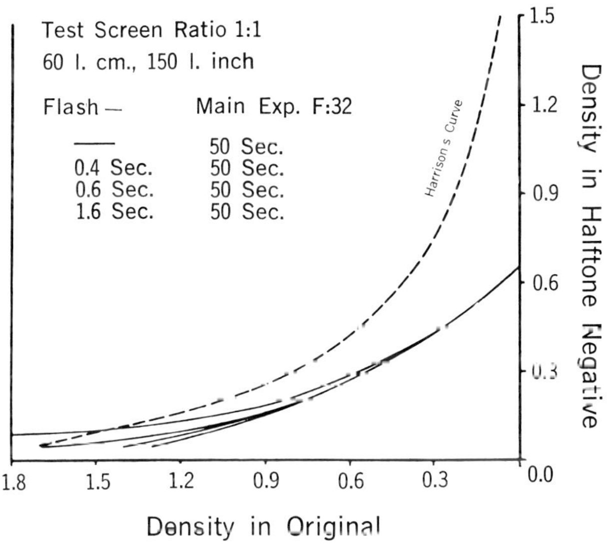


*Illustr. No. 36* **Effect of Flash Exposures**

flash exposure. A screen with a 1:1 ruling covers about a 1.25 useable range as shown in illustration No. 30. In other words, this limited range of 1.25 is characteristic for this particular screen under the specific working conditions. If a suitable aperture is used, for instance F: 22, it results in the following relation:

Exposure = A x B
(A=Factor for exposure and size ratio
(B=Factor for exposure for film material and exposure technique.)

Factor A can be obtained from Illustration No. 37.

Factor B has to be obtained with a test exposure.

There will be no change in B as long as there is no change in the photographic material nor in the light intensity or color-temperature of the light source.

| | Size Ratio | 0.45 | 0.60 | 0.75 | 0.90 | 1.05 | 1.20 | 1.35 | 1.50 | 1.65 | F:22 Ratio |
|---|---|---|---|---|---|---|---|---|---|---|---|
| | | ← Density in Original → | | | | | | | | | |
| Reduction ↑ | 0.2 | 3.2 | 4.5 | 6.5 | 9.1 | 13.0 | 17 | 26 | 36 | 52 | 36.7 |
| | 0.3 | 3.8 | 5.3 | 7.6 | 10.3 | 15.1 | 21 | 30 | 42 | 61 | 33.8 |
| | 0.4 | 4.4 | 6.2 | 8.8 | 12.3 | 17.7 | 24 | 35 | 49 | 71 | 31.5 |
| | 0.5 | 5.0 | 7.1 | 10.1 | 14.1 | 20.2 | 28 | 40 | 56 | 81 | 29.4 |
| | 0.6 | 5.8 | 8.2 | 11.7 | 16.4 | 23.4 | 32 | 47 | 65 | 93 | 27.5 |
| | 0.7 | 6.4 | 9.1 | 12.8 | 18.2 | 26.0 | 36 | 52 | 72 | 104 | 25.9 |
| | 0.8 | 7.2 | 10.2 | 14.6 | 20.4 | 29.2 | 40 | 58 | 81 | 117 | 24.5 |
| | 0.9 | 8.2 | 11.5 | 16.4 | 23.0 | 32.8 | 45 | 66 | 91 | 131 | 23.2 |
| | 1.0 | 9 | 12.6 | 18 | 25.2 | 36 | 50 | 72 | 108 | 144 | 22.0 |
| Enlargement ↓ | 1.2 | 11 | 15.8 | 21.8 | 32.0 | 43.6 | 61 | 87 | 121 | 175 | 20.0 |
| | 1.4 | 13 | 18.1 | 26.0 | 36.2 | 52.0 | 72 | 104 | 144 | 208 | 18.4 |
| | 1.6 | 15.2 | 21.3 | 30.4 | 42.6 | 61.0 | 84 | 122 | 169 | 243 | 17.0 |
| | 1.8 | 17.6 | 24.7 | 35.3 | 49.3 | 71.0 | 98 | 141 | 196 | 282 | 15.7 |
| | 2.0 | 20.2 | 28.4 | 40.5 | 56.7 | 81.0 | 113 | 162 | 225 | 325 | 14.7 |
| | 2.5 | 27.5 | 38.5 | 55.0 | 72.0 | 110.0 | 153 | 220 | 306 | 440 | 12.6 |
| | 3.0 | 36.0 | 50.4 | 72.0 | 100.0 | 144.0 | 200 | 288 | 400 | 576 | 11.0 |
| | 3.5 | 45.5 | 63.6 | 91.0 | 127.0 | 182.0 | 252 | 363 | 505 | 727 | 9.8 |
| | 4.0 | 55.4 | 79.0 | 113.0 | 155.0 | 226.0 | 313 | 450 | 625 | 887 | 8.8 |
| | 4.5 | 68.0 | 95.0 | 136.0 | 191.0 | 272.0 | 378 | 545 | 756 | 1090 | 8.0 |
| | 5.0 | 81.0 | 114.0 | 162.0 | 237.0 | 325.0 | 450 | 648 | 900 | 1300 | 7.3 |

*Illustr. No. 37* **Factor for Size- Exposure- and F:22 Ratio**

## THE SUPPLEMENTARY EXPOSURE

The conventional way for the additional highlight exposure is to change to the next or second next stop. The results obtained in this way, with a 60 lines per cm or 150 lines per inch screen, with a line ratio of 0.83:1.17 are shown in the illustrations No. 38, 39, 40 and 41.

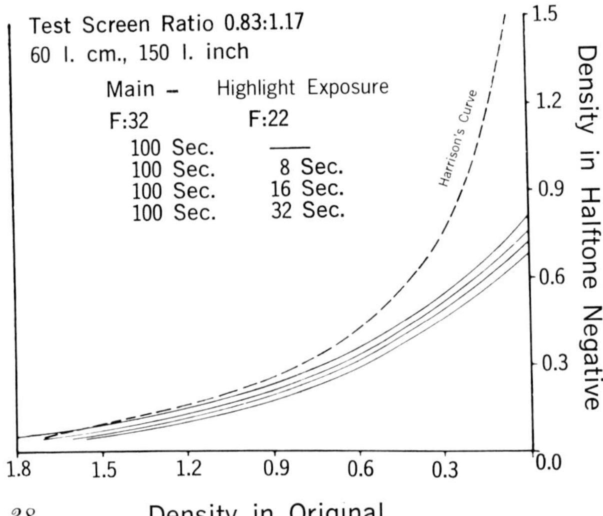


*Illustr. No. 38*

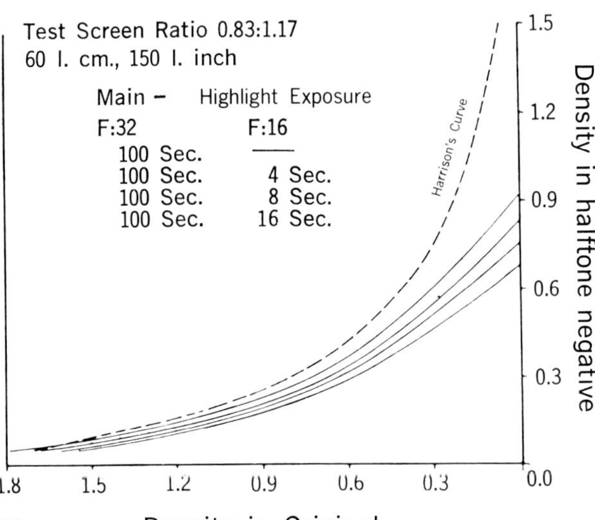


*Illustr. No. 39*

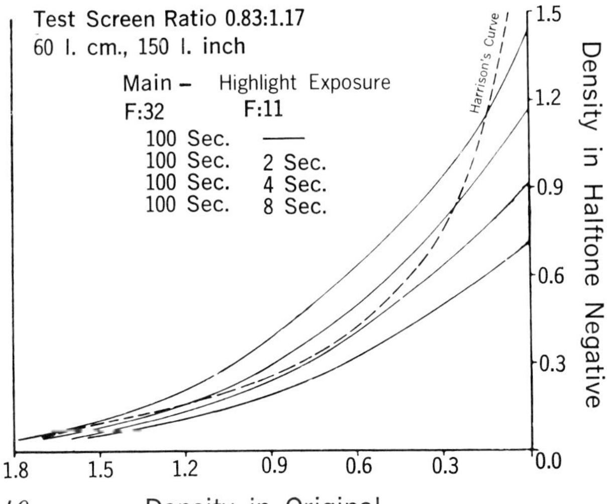


*Illustr. No. 40*

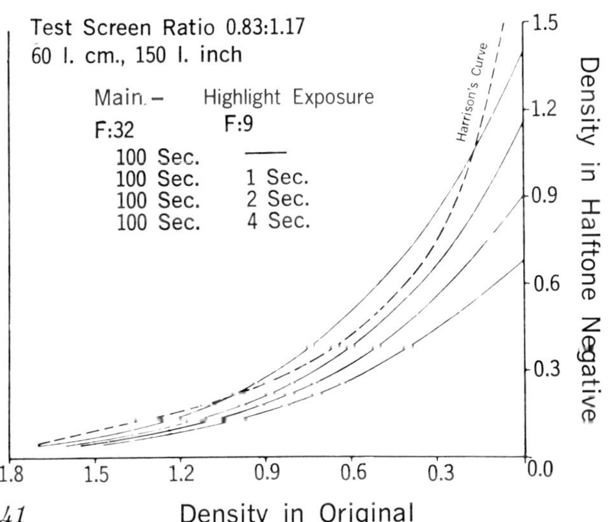


*Illustr. No. 41*

**Effects of Supplementary Exposures with Different Apertures**

To open only one stop has practically no effect as seen in Illustration No. 38. The curve shapes maintained are similiar to the one obtained with the main exposure and could be almost duplicated by simply giving a longer main exposure.

To open two stops shows slight improvements and more saturation in the highlight areas as shown in Illustration No. 39. However, as the shadow areas also advance, there is still not enough exaggeration remaining.

To jump three stops really steps up the highlight areas, as evident in Illustration No. 40. Unfortunately, by the time the highlight dots close up to the correct size, the dots in the middletone area are far too large and the negative curve obtained considerably exceeds Harrison's ideal curve.

If four stops are opened, the closest gradation is obtained as seen in Illustr. No. 41. Nevertheless, it is still not possible to meet the ideal curve. Another disadvantage would be the excessive amount of flare created by interferences of the light with this "wrong" screen distance, resulting in a very noticeable loss of details.

These evaluations prove sufficiently that there is no possibility to obtain the correct negative characteristics with any one of the conventional ways. Comparing these results to the one obtained with a supplementary exposure without screen and shown in Illustr. No. 29 proves clearly the superiority of the no screen exposure.

*As a matter of fact, only this method guarantees perfect construction of the completely correct negative curve without loss in either shadow, middletone and highlight areas.*

If the supplementary exposure is made with the screen removed, it is equivalent to an additional lineshot from the original and gives therefore unsurpassed sharpness of all highlight details.

It is suggested to standardize all procedures as much as possible. The only changes necessary are the compensation for the reduction or enlargement and for the different reflexion densities of the originals. These adjustments are given in Illustration No. 37 and enable instantly the correction for the applicable exposure. If the camera is equipped with a lens ratio indicator, then the corrections should rather be made in that way as it automatically takes care of the exposure time, reciprocity failure and the correct screen distance which is of utmost importance. An average supplementary exposure amounts usually to approximately 7% of the main exposure or proportionately less or more depending on specific conditions. To be able to better control this short exposure without screen, which is made with the main exposure stop, it is recommended to use a neutral density filter to gain more exposure latitude.

Screen negatives in this described way are not only the ultimate for offset but just as well for photoengraving, especially for powderless etching. The best degree of highlight exposure depends finally on the way of etching but can be adjusted to any requirement as can be seen in illustration No. 29.

## DARK-FIELD ILLUMINATION

It is recognized that the inspection of dots with bright field illumination does not easily disclose halation. An experienced craftsman, therefore, evaluates dots by 'winging' them from a bright light into a shadow area when inspecting the film with a magnifying glass. The change in dot size shows the amount of halation. There is a much more sophisticated method in doing this. A light box* with an open area for inspection can be easily made in the way outlined in the following illustration No. 41a. A moveable diffusing glass is mounted between the light source and the inspection area. For bright light illumination the dot is inspected with the diffusing glass in place, for dark field illumination the diffuser is removed and the dots appear as shown in the illustration, clearly revealing the amount of halation.

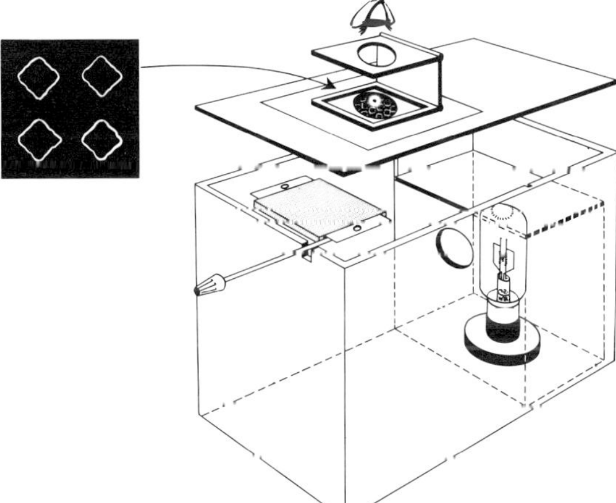

*Illustr. No. 41a*

***Available through Perfect Graphic Arts Supply Company, P.O. Box 62, Demarest, N. J. 07627**

## THE KLIMSCH ALLTON GRADAR HALFTONE SCREEN

This new special glass screen with clear transparent magenta crosslines is designed for use as negative screen in process cameras and consequently serves for screening from positive black and white orignals. The following features of the Klimsch Allton Gradar Halftone Screen are of particular interest. It assures excellent tone rendition, since the intense reflections of the highlights of the original are readily transmitted through the magenta lines of the screen. The effect of a highlight exposure is achieved in the camera, and favorable gradation curves are obtained without any subsequent operational steps. A separate highlight exposure is no longer required. The exposure time with this screen is shorter than with any other screen. Clear unveiled highlight areas are produced in the negative due to the darker intersections of the crosslines on the new Allton Gradar screen. Negatives produced with the Klimsch Allton Gradar Halftone Screen Type ANK show a slight chain formation in the middle-tones which warrants a perfectly smooth blending of the tones. The dot formation in the highlights and shadows is normal. The Klimsch Allton Gradar Halftone Screen incorporates all advantages of a glass screen: remarkable long life without any decrease in quality, simple handling, almost no risk of damage, no failures due to dust, no contact trouble.

The use of the Klimsch Allton Gradar Halftone Screen in practice corresponds in all respects to the method adopted for standard black and white glass screens. Normal originals are reproduced without filters. Due to the excellent rendition of details this new screen makes it possible to obtain with a coarser ruling the fidelity of a finer conventional glass screen which offers considerable advantages for the press-run. Negatives on lith-film produced with the Allton Gradar Halftone Screen are particularly suitable for Offset-Litho printing as well as for Photoengraving in conjunction with powderless etching processes. Thus, the Klimsch Allton Gradar Halftone Screen is a remarkable contribution in the technology of glass screens.

A complete assortment of these exceptional glass magenta screens are now available:

Type ANK — Negative screen with chain dots for screening from positive black and white reflection and transparent copy.

Type 3000 — Negative screen with chain dots for exposures with halogen lamps (3000° K)

Type RO Negative screen with extended density range and reduced saturation in the middletones. This screen was especially designed for web offset.

Type APK Positive screen with chain dots for screening from continuous tone negative separations.

# Chapter Five

## THE MAKING OF THE SCREEN POSITIVE

In this chapter, the requirements for making correct halftone positives are evaluated.[9]

First of all we should realize that, in order to make a halftone positive, it is necessary to have a continuous tone negative. In the preparation of this it is of great advantage to be able to adjust the density range of the negative to the range which the available screen can cover.

In a screen positive, contrary to a screen negative, the highlights are represented with fine dots. Tests have shown that it is easier to obtain good highlight rendition in a positive with a main exposure which creates small dots, than with a supplementary exposure without screen for a negative which creates large, up to 95% dots in the negative. Here again of course, the basis is the perfect screen distance as previously described. In the making of a screen positive this is even more important than in the negative. This is because to the eyes, highlights are much more obvious than shadows. A flash exposure in compensation for an incorrect screen distance would eventually produce some pinpoints in a positive but would undoubtedly destroy highlight details.

The ideal curve for a screen positive is a perfectly straight line. Slight deviations toward Person's curve might be necessary to differentiate the highlights and shadows better in case of unfavorable printing conditions.

## THE IDEAL CURVE OF THE SCREEN POSITIVE

It is important to know what results can be obtained with a regular glass screen by simply giving a main exposure only. As an average continuous tone negative we took a transparent gray scale $\sqrt[3]{2}$ with 30 steps reading from 0.0-3.0. The screens used were the same ones as used before to make the screen negatives, with 60 lines per cm or 150 lines per inch and the following ratios:

| transparent | : | opaque |
|---|---|---|
| 0.83 | : | 1.17 |
| 1.02 | : | 0.98 |
| 1.23 | : | 0.77 |

Illustration No. 42 shows how these screens perform. The exposure time was adjusted to get respective density readings of 0.05 in the screen positive from the 1.8 density in the continuous tone negative.

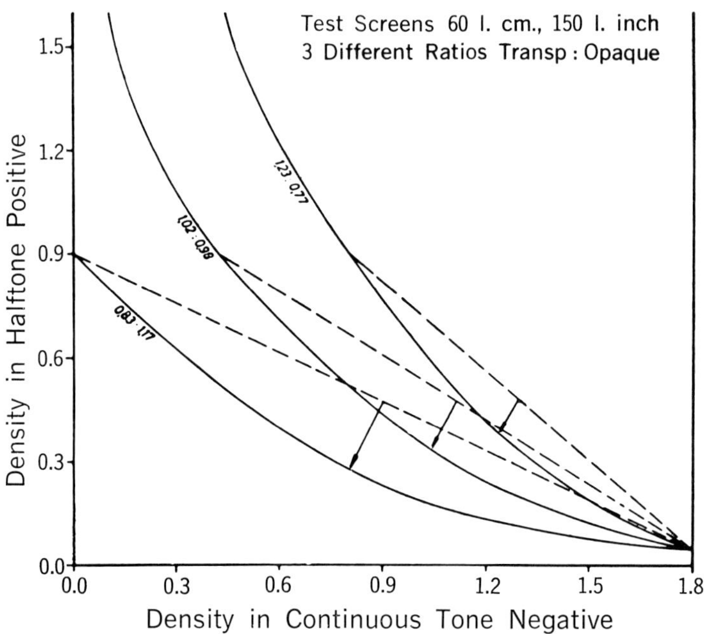


*Illustr. No. 42* **Characteristic Curves of Glass Screens**

These results are not surprising. As learned from the making of the screen negatives, the density range the glass screen is able to cover depends on the ratio between the transparent to opaque lines. Exactly the same characteristic is true here. The curves obtained as shown in Illustr. No. 42 are far away from the required ideals. The highlights are very flat, the middletones are empty and the shadows are harsh. The dotted lines, however, show that the wider the transparent line of the screen the lesser the bow in the curve shape. This means that for making of screen positives, screens with wider transparent lines are more suitable than for making screen negatives. Nevertheless screens like this still don't come close to a straight line and would limit the reproducible density range to a minimum. To solve this problem we have to refer again to Tritton and Wilson:[4] The continuous tone negative from which a screen positive has to be made must meet different requirements. It has to have a shape which guarantees a straight line when made with the screen available. As each of the three screens in Illustr. 42 can be adapted, it is preferred to use screens as already available. All following tests were therefore made with screens of a 1:1 ratio and therefore represent equivalent results.

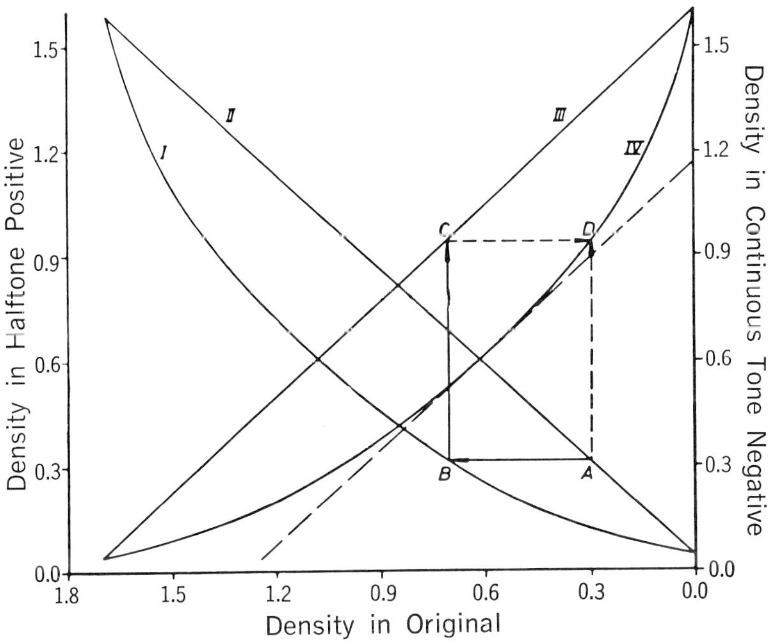


*Illustr. No. 43* **Relation of Continuous Tone Negative to Screen Positive**

This illustration explains the relation between continuous tone negatives to screen positives. Any spot on curve II for instance A, has a related point on curve I such as B. The density B in the screen positive is a result of the density of the ordinary continous tone negative and represented in point C of curve III. If AB and BC are connected with straight lines and C to A are joined with parallel lines then they will meet in point D. This point D is representative for the density of the ideal continuous tone negative which in turn leads to the density A in curve II. If this procedure is repeated for curve II, then if these dots are connected it results in curve IV which represents the adjusted continuous tone negative. The dotted line parallel to curve III and next to curve IV points out the discrepancy between an ordinary continuous tone negative and one especially adjusted and suitable for making an ideal screen positive. The major differences are in the exaggerated highlights and in a long toe.

These results cannot be obtained with a regular continuous tone negative unless an additional highlight mask is applied or better, a double emulsion film is used which gives an automatic highlight masking result. For the following tests the Agfa-Gevaert CO23 highlight masking film was used. The screen positives obtained from these improved continuous tone negatives were indeed very close to a straight line, except in the extreme shadow areas. This final correction is possible with a supplementary exposure with an aperture of at least three times larger than the one used for the main exposure, or with no screen. The basis for this lies mainly in the comprehensive knowledge and control of the particular highlight masking film used. As the CO23 Film lends itself in an outstanding way to this intermediate step it is necessary to explain this material in more detail.

## CHARACTERISTICS OF THE CO23 HIGHLIGHT MASKING FILM

This special highlight masking film consists of two emulsions. The continuous tone emulsion which is blue sensitive, is coated directly on the base and the highlight mask emulsion which is orthochromatic is coated on top of it. Due to this arrangement it is possible to reduce the highlight densities with Farmer's Reducer with hardly any effect to the shadow end. The speed difference between the two emulsions equals about five stops when carbon arclight is used. (In other words, one-stop corresponds to factor two and is equivalent to 0.3.) If an average original is exposed to get a shadow density of .3, then the mask gets effective in highlight areas where the original exceeds a range of 5 x 0.3=D 1.5. An original with a range of 1.8 would be masked in the three last steps. If the exposure time is increased, then of course the highlights get noticeably more density. The shadow end will change only slightly. This is because of the different gammas of the two emulsions. The soft continuous tone emulsion has a gamma of approximately 0.9 against the steep highlight emulsion with a gamma of about 2.5. The latter has therefore much less exposure latitude and corresponds much more to exposure variations. This is an advantage in balancing different range copies to same range negatives. For instance, if twice the exposure is given then the mask covers 0.3 more range and thereby extends into densities of D 1.5-0.3=1.2. Only a short test exposure is necessary to get familiar with the characteristics of this film.

The speed between the two emulsions can also be governed with the application of blue or yellow color compensating filters.

The continuous tone emulsion is distinguished by means of a very straight gradation. This characteristic is maintained, even if developing time is varied or developer concentration is changed. This lends itself in an outstanding way to developing adjustments in a wide range to control the density between the continuous tone emulsion and the highlight mask. This is shown in the Illustrations No. 44-47.

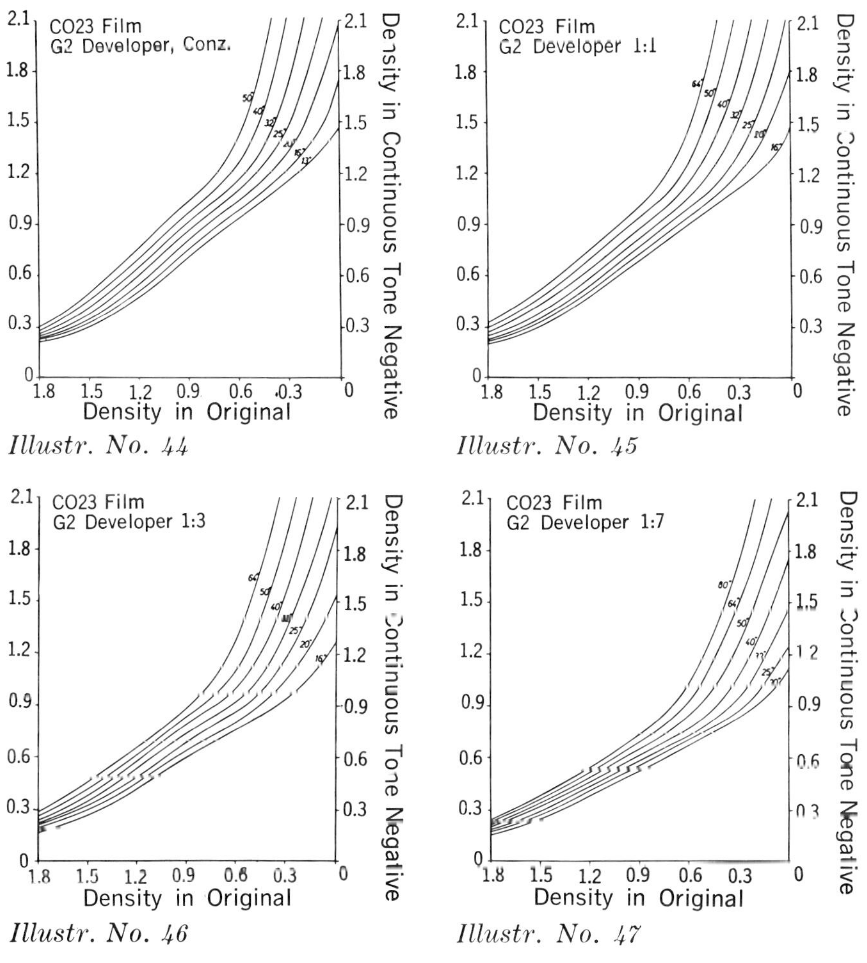


*Illustr. No. 44*

*Illustr. No. 45*

*Illustr. No. 46*

*Illustr. No. 47*

**Variation in Developer Concentration**

The previous illustrations explain the results on CO23 Film obtained with different exposures and different developer concentrations.

Illustration No. 44=Agfa-Gevaert G2 developer concentrated

Illustration No. 45=Agfa-Gevaert G2 developer 1 : 1 diluted

Illustration No. 46=Agfa-Gevaert G2 developer 1 : 3 diluted

Illustration No. 47=Agfa-Gevaert G2 developer 1 : 7 diluted

The changes in the curves are obviously the results of the developer strength. The more dilution the softer the continuous tone gradation, however with little change in the highlight mask. All tests in Illustr. No. 44-47 were developed for 5 minutes. Instead of changing the developer strength it is equally possible to vary the developing times, as can be seen in Illustration No. 48.

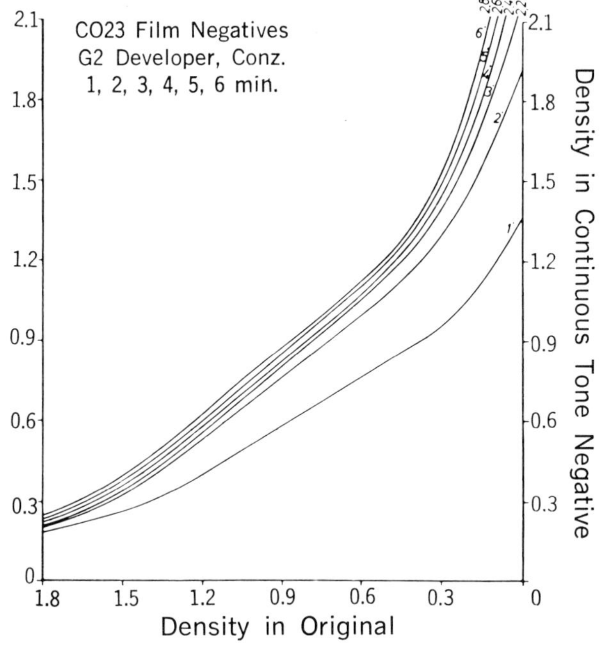


*Illustr. No. 48* **Variation in Developing Time**

In these tests in illustr. No. 48 the same exposure was given but G2 was used for 1-6 min. processing. It can easily be recognized that the two emulsions do not build up proportionally when developing time is increased, and it is therefore necessary to bring the developing process under perfect control. Should it be noticed during developing that the exposure was on the long side, then it is still necessary to complete the standard processing time, because it is possible to manually reduce the highlight mask with Farmer's Reducer, with hardly any effect on the shadow areas, as illustr. No. 49 proves.

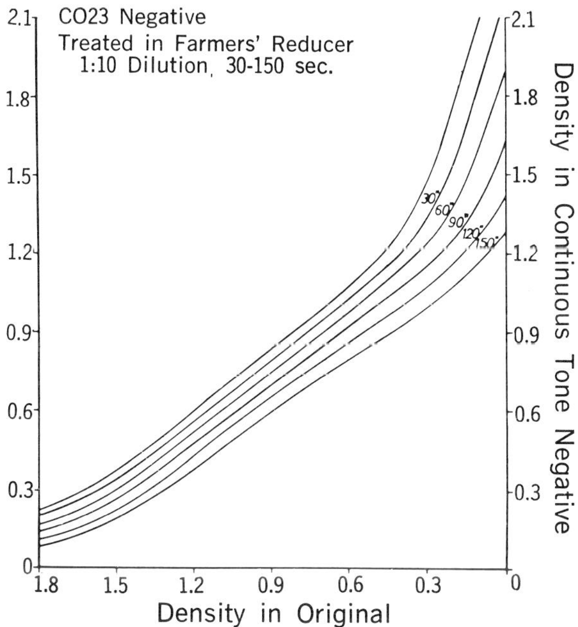


*Illustr. No. 49* **Highlight Correction**

The results in Illustr. No. 49 were obtained with concentrated developer and then etched with Farmer's Reducer 1:10 dilution, step by step with 30 seconds intervals.

## THE MAKING OF THE SCREEN POSITIVE FROM THE ADJUSTED CONTINUOUS TONE NEGATIVE

First of all it is important to find out what characteristics are necessary in the continuous tone negative to be able to obtain a straight line halftone positive. For this reason several test exposures were made from steptablets originally made on highlight masking film with the 60 lines per cm or 150 lines per inch screen of a 1:1 line ratio. All screen positives which produced a density of 0.05 from the last highlight step of the continuous tone steptablet were plotted.

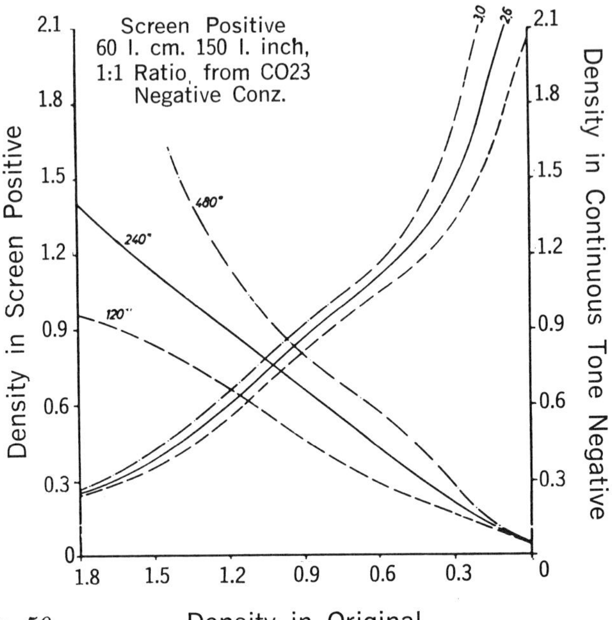


*Illustr. No. 50*

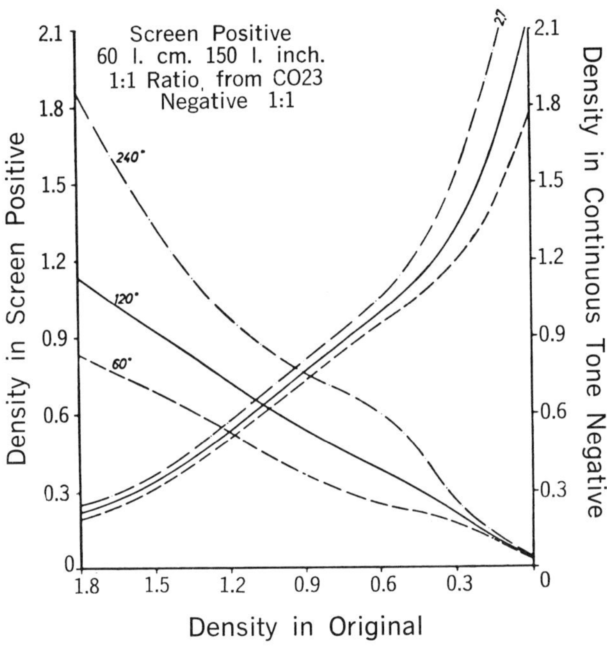


*Illustr. No. 51* **Screen Positives Obtained From CO23 Negatives**

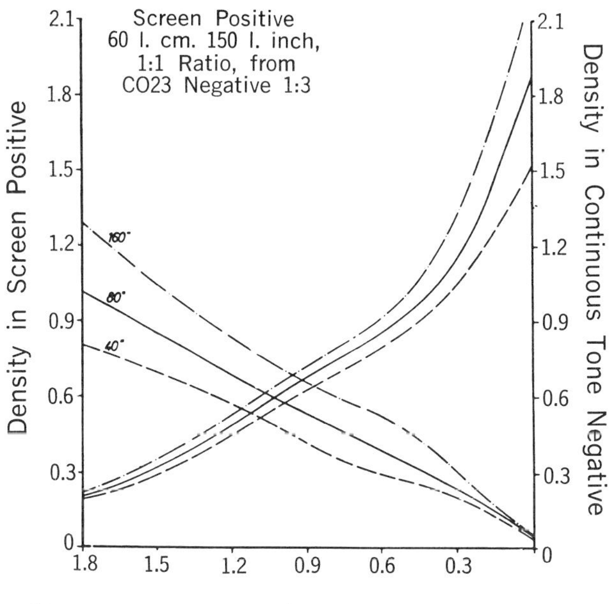


*Illustr. No. 52*

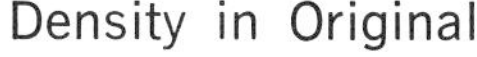


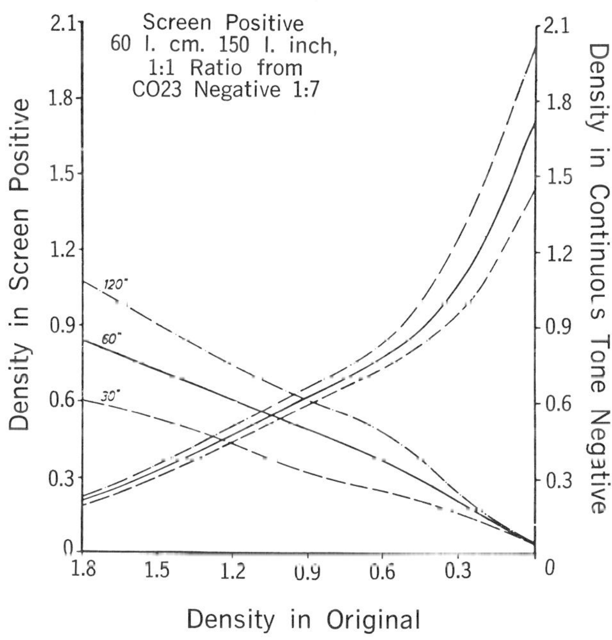


*Illustr. No. 53* **Screen Positives Obtained From CO23 Negatives**

The continuous tone negatives in each illustration were made with three different exposure times. The screen positives obtained from the particular negatives are shown with the equivalent dotted line. It is amazing how uniformly the screen positives in Illustrs. No. 50-53 compare. In each case they prove the dependence between the proportion of the mask to the positive curve obtained, such as:

A. Not enough middletone density.

B. Fairly straight line.

C. Too much middletone density.

From this we learn that the mask has to be 50-60% of the total range of the continuous tone negative in order to produce a straight line screen positive. The developer dilution does not seem to affect the shape of the curve too much as long as the mask is exposed up to 50-60% of the total range. A normal CO23 negative suitable for gravure has to have a highlight mask of only about 20%. The developer dilution has thus more influence. As it has not much effect on the intermediate negative for screening, it is advantageous to choose the higher dilution to obtain a negative with lower densities, which in turn allows for shorter exposures in the final screening. Illustr. 52 and 53 also show what end densities, respectively what ranges are obtained with the different dilutions. One can select the most appropriate dilution for their particular requirement. A 1:5 dilution is recommended as a good basis. The contrast of the continuous tone negative should be such that with just the main exposure a fine highlight dot is created in the screen positive and about a 75-80% shadow dot with a densitometer reading of about 0.60-0.70. This is necessary to still be able to give a supplementary exposure without screen or a jump to three apertures larger to increase the shadow contrast and the shadow detail.

## THE SUPPLEMENTARY EXPOSURE FOR THE SCREEN POSITIVE

If we refer to Illustr. No. 29 as well as No. 38-41, we can again recognize the changes due to the increase of the supplementary exposures. In this case it is not necessary to create a bow shape but only intensify and lift up the shadow end of the curve in the screen positive. To obtain this with the least complication, a jump to three stops bigger is sufficient. However to get maximum sharpness in these shadow details, the supplementary exposure without screen is superior. Illustrations No. 54-57 demonstrate both ways. They are the results of CO23 negatives developed in G2 Metol-hydroquinone developer diluted 1:3 and 1:7.

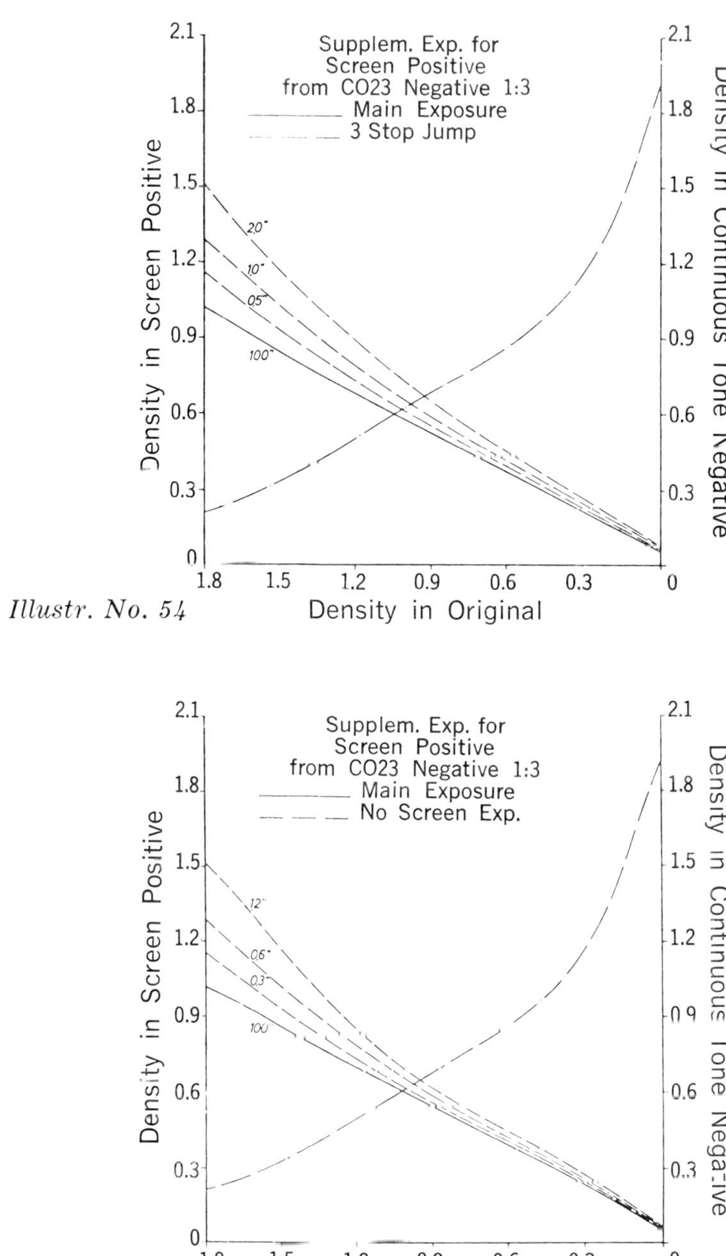


*Illustr. No. 54*

*Illustr. No. 55*

**Supplementary Exposures for Screen Positives**

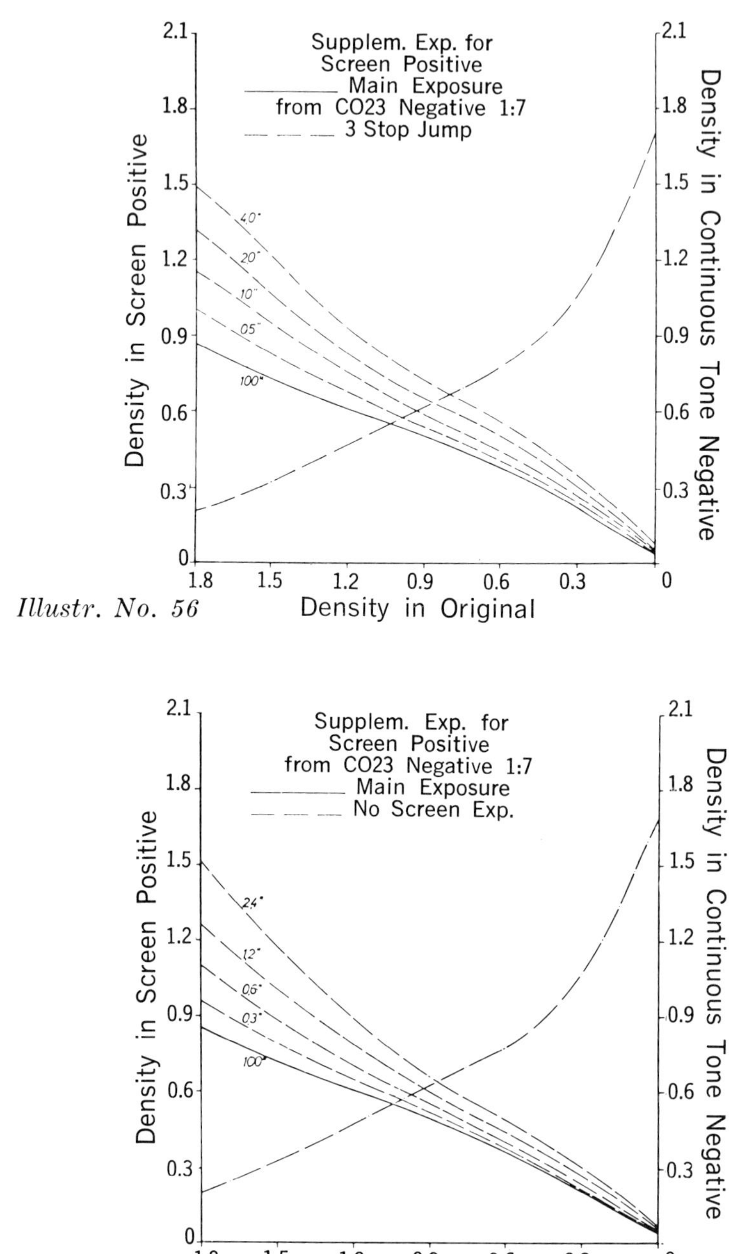


*Illustr. No. 56*

*Illustr. No. 57*

**Supplementary Exposures for Screen Positives**

Experience has shown that in offset printing dot areas of more than 97% and an integral reading of 1.50 usually print solid. The tests we made were therefore limited to the maximum density of 1.50.

## THE MAKING OF THE SCREEN POSITIVE UNDER PRACTICAL CONDITIONS

In conclusion, let's repeat in a comprehensive way how a perfectly tone value corrected screen positive can be made photomechanically. The continuous tone negative from which the final halftone positive has to be made, must be highlight corrected with a mask of about 50-60% proportion, to get a fairly straight line positive. The tests have shown that the developer dilution is not directly significant for the actual shape of the continuous tone curve, as long as the mask is exposed up to 50-60% of the total range. However a 1:5 dilution should be a good basis to provide for an ideal intermediate for making the halftone positive with a reasonable short exposure time.

To establish exact information the tests were made with CO23 Film. Nevertheless two separate films would perform in a similar way.

Complete standardization of all factors involved must be guaranteed to get repeatedly dependable results.

It is most important to balance the continuous tone negative to the range which the screen available can cover with the main exposure only, as flash exposure is very harmful. However allowance should be made for a supplementary exposure to lift up the shadow details in the positive. The basis for all this is of course the perfect screen distance, which was explained in Chapter One.
All steps explained in these extensive evaluations were practiced by the author already in 1956 and actual proofs were demonstrated early in 1957 during the "Graphic Exhibition" in Lausanne, Switzerland.

## COMPARISON BETWEEN REGULAR AND IDEAL CURVE SHAPE

The results so far accomplished are really considerable. From the previous graphs we can see what a screen should do and what it is in reality able to produce. Let us finally compare these curves to learn what adjustments should be made.

Suppose a step tablet $\sqrt[3]{2}$ representing a continuous tone negative is used to make a halftone positive with a glass screen then instead of an ideal straight line positive, one with a bow shape is obtained which is characteristic for a glass screen. See illustration No. 58.

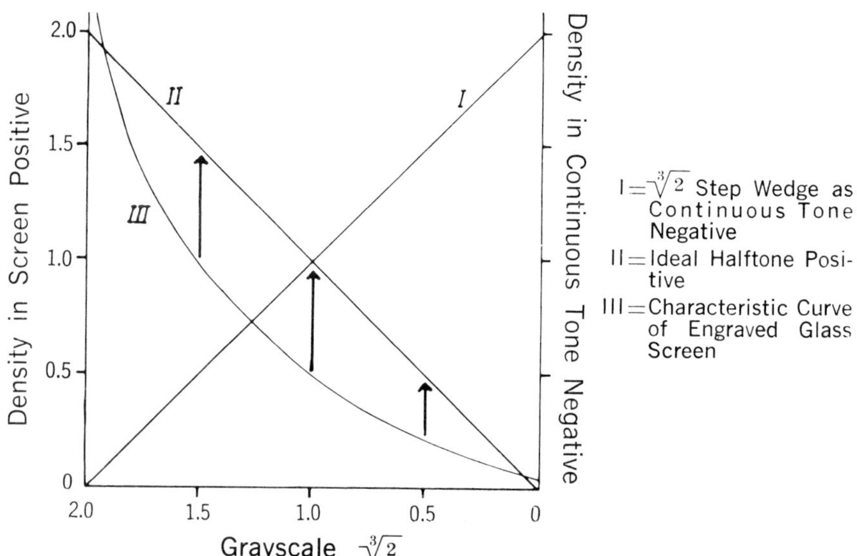


*Illustr. No. 58* **Characteristic Curve of a Glass Screen**

As illustr. No. 58 shows, there is a considerable lack in the middle tones resulting in the usual flat and empty reproductions like curve III. To correct this it would be necessary to change the glass screen in this way that it lifts up the middle tones and finally produces an ideal straight line positive like curve II. On the other hand if a reflection copy is used to make a halftone negative with a glass screen, the ideal curve shape II as per Harrison should be obtained. See illustration No. 59.

This in fact is exactly the contrary as required for making a positive. We are therefore confronted with two exactly opposite requirements. If it were possible to alter the glass screen it would be necessary to design a positive as well as a negative screen. However these demands cannot be satisfied. The only change possible is to alter the ratio between the transparent and opaque line. Nevertheless only the reproducible range could be effected, still leaving other faults to be corrected.

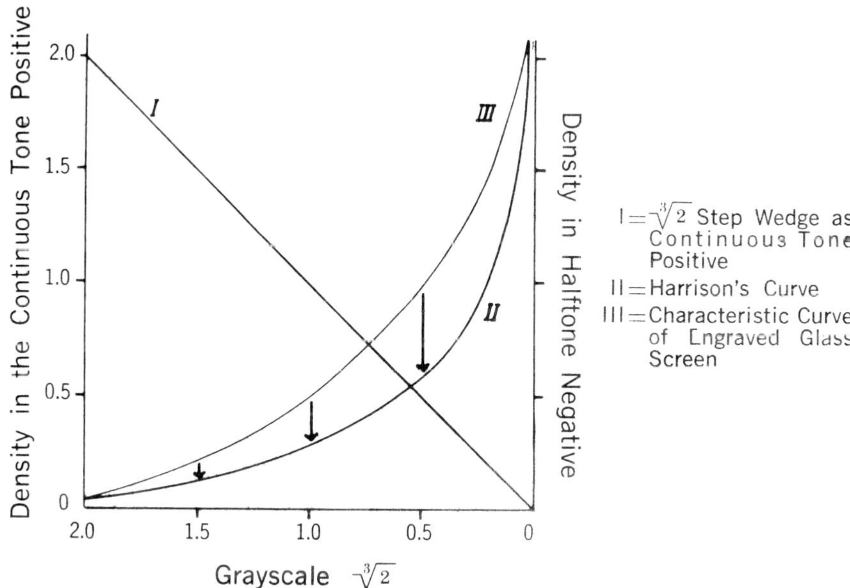


*Illustr. No. 59* **Characteristic Curve of a Glass Screen**

In the absence of a double emulsion film a separate, continuous tone film and a highlight mask accomplishes the same results.

# Chapter Six

## CONTACT SCREENS

Let us see if there is another chance to get correct halftone negatives and positives in one single step.

What could not be accomplished with the glass screen should be possible with a contact screen!

Only now, after all these extensive evaluations and tests are we prepared and ready to begin our studies about contact screens. These explorations start with the same question as previously investigated with the glass screen:

## WHAT IS THE CHARACTERISTIC CURVE OF A CONTACT SCREEN

Here again a continuous tone gray scale $\sqrt[3]{2}$ is the basis for all following tests. Fortunately these are much less complicated than in the case of the glass screen, because no screen distance, light diffraction, size of aperture etc. are involved. From this point of view no error is expected. However it is still a must to give one single main exposure only! Any supplementary exposure such as flash or highlight exposure would falsify the true evaluation of the screen itself.

For the practical tests an available contact screen with 48 lines per cm, or 120 lines per inch is used. The gray scale is now reproduced same size on a lith film through the contact screen after it is put with its emulsion to the emulsion side of the film to be exposed. Good vacuum is recommended to assure perfect contact. The exposed lith film has to be developed in a genuine lith developer with the developing time recommended by the manufacturer. This usually amounts to 2½-3 minutes at 20°C or 68°F. The reproduction, if properly exposed, shows a certain number of gray scale steps starting in the extreme shadow area with a fine pinpoint and on the other extreme, such as the highlight area, with fine open dots which gradually close up to solid.

Again, we measure all the gray scale steps and mark these integral readings in a coordinating system corresponding to the gray scale used. After these dots are lined up we have obtained the characteristic curve of the contact screen used. The bow shape obtained will very closely match with the characteristic curve of the glass screen. This is no surprise as we know that the contact screens are made photographically from the glass screen, from which we know is obviously the master screen. Therefore all failures were automatically reproduced and captured in the contact screens as well!

Exact analyses have shown that different brand contact screens, as long as they were made in a conventional way from glass screens, show the same faults in respect to the unsatisfactory curve shape obtainable. The only variations might be in the contrast ranges which they are able to cover. However the characteristic curves obtained with all the conventional contact screens corresponded very closely to the ones of the glass screens with hardly any exception. This is not too surprising as an experienced Cameraman has constant trouble in getting the perfect tone values in the reproductions, regardless whether he is using a glass or a contact screen.
Again, it is of great value to have carefully studied the peculiarities of the glass screens. We had to realize that the requirements are twofold, depending whether a halftone negative or positive has to be made. With a glass screen it is possible only with extra manipulations to obtain acceptable negatives or positives. The screen itself is not flexible at all. There is no chance to alter the glass screen. On the other hand with the contact screen it is very well possible to vary the dot structure simultaneously in each individual dot according to specific requirements. In reality the key to tone value corrected screen negatives as well as positives lays alone in the particular structure of the contact screen dot.

Before we continue in our studies it is important to know how the density of a tiny contact screen dot can be evaluated. We can measure a dot from its lowest density to its peak density with a microdensitometer as indicated from A to B in illustration No. 60.

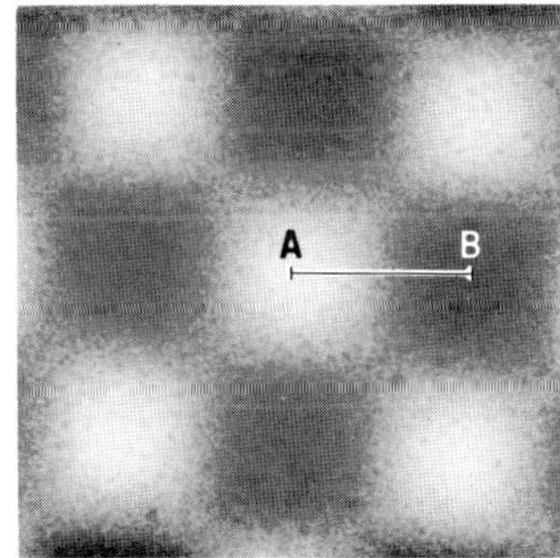


Negative Contact Screen Dots

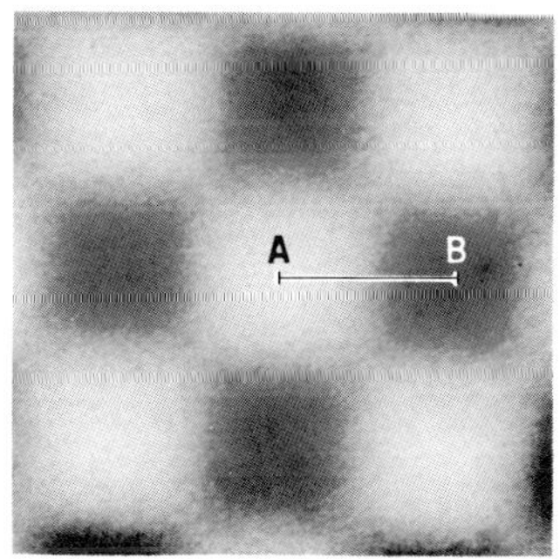


Positive Contact Screen Dots

*Illustr. No. 60*

**Micro-Photographs**

When these readings are plotted into a coordinating system then a characteristic curve is obtained as shown in illustr. No. 61. These readings of course might be completely different from another contact screen as the dot structure might vary considerably from one screen to another.

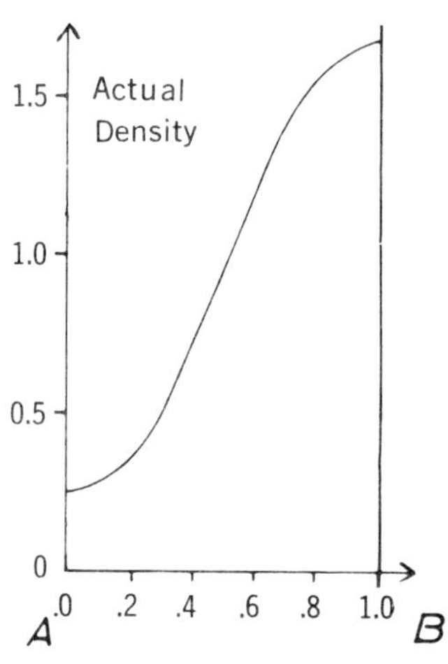


**Actual Density Reading**

*Illustr. No. 61*

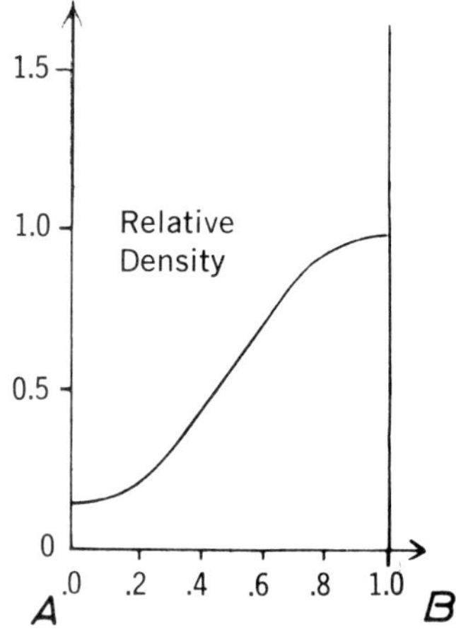


**Relative Density**

*Illustr. No. 62*

The calculation for these readings require a basis for comparison as follows.

$$\frac{\text{Density Reading}}{\text{Maximum Density}} = \text{Relative Density}$$

In the illustrations to come screen dot shapes are shown in which the different density ranges are equalized through a calculation into relative density as shown in illustr. No. 62. Nevertheless the density range of an actual screen dot determines the contrast range the screen is able to cover. This particular characteristic however is of no importance in the evaluation of the actual shape of the dot.

## WHAT DOT STRUCTURES ARE NECESSARY IN CONTACT SCREENS

Let us evaluate this question. Only after years of extensive research the following conclusions could be drawn:

It is absolutely necessary to have two types of screens.

*A "Positive Screen and a Negative Screen."*

The dot structures necessary for the positive or negative contact screen are shown in illustrations No. 63 and No. 64.

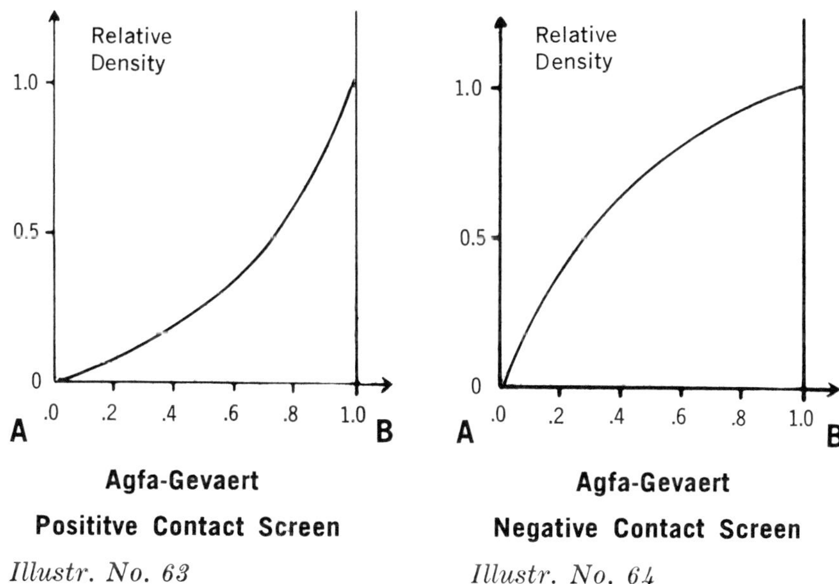


**Agfa-Gevaert**
**Posititve Contact Screen**

*Illustr. No. 63*

**Agfa-Gevaert**
**Negative Contact Screen**

*Illustr. No. 64*

Illustration No. 63 shows the dot structure of a good positive contact screen. As can be seen, its density starts very slowly. From A to B the density increases rather uniform and finally reaches its maximum density in B. The curve obtained has a slight distinct bow shape and is responsible for the perfect curve shape of the halftone positive.

Illustration No. 64 shows the dot structure of a good negative contact screen. Contrary to the positive contact screen its density increases rather rapidly. Towards B the density starts to fall off more and more and reaches finally its minimum increase. The curve obtained has a very distinct shape like a dome and is responsible for the perfect curve shape of the halftone negative.

Illustration No. 65 compares the performance of

A—Conventional contact screen,
B—Perfect positive contact screen,
C—Perfect negative contact screen.

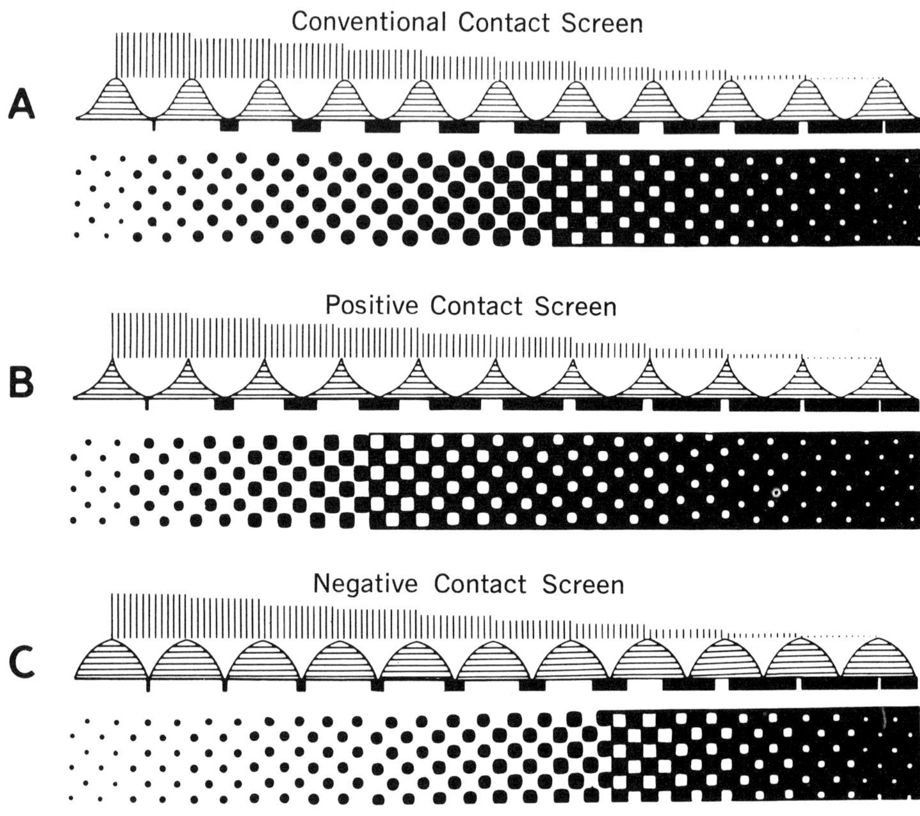


*Illustr. No. 65* **Different Contact Screens**

In each case as indicated, the same amount of light was given. when exposing through a gray scale and the different type screens. The gray scale is indicated with a step wedge. The contact screen dots are indicated with horizontal lines. The solids on the bottom of each illustration indicate the dot size obtained with the particular screen.

It is obvious that the growth of the dots on the lith film is determined and governed by the amount of light transmitted through the particular shape of the contact screen dot. This proves that:

*It is possible to influence the tone value in the reproduction according to the dot shape provided in the contact screen.*

This flexibility of the contact screen dot makes the contact screen superior to the glass screen! Only now after all these comprehensive studies are we able to fully recognize the potentialities and exact performance of contact screens.

## FUTURE OUTLOOK

Time does not stand still and sometimes it is surprising how fast generally established technical knowledge and habits must be replaced with improved techniques.

Since the invention of glass screens many theories were recognized. In most cases, however, these were only partial explanations which could not be practically applied because of imperfections and many other limitations and shortcomings.

On the contrary the evaluations in this book are strictly based on practical studies, confirmed by mathematical calculations. *For this reason and with these fundamental proofs on hand, it can be claimed that the complete complex of "screening" is herewith accessible and for all practical purposes basically established.*

This is the reason why Agfa-Gevaert in Leverkusen, Germany, had started to manufacture Positive and Negative Contact Screens, which are available as gray and magenta screens. The positive screens produce a tone value corrected straight line halftone positive from a straight line continuous tone negative. The negative screens produce a tone value corrected bow shaped halftone negative from continuous tone positives either reflection or transparent copies.

When screening black and white reflection copies or intermediate continuous-tone separations, the possibility of contrast variation is an advantage. That is why Agfa Gevaert provides special magenta contact screens in connection to their "Gevarex" system. This, electronically selects the appropriate blue/yellow split filter exposure to adapt to any contrast provided in the continuous-tone image thereby extending or compressing the range the screen can cover. The range obtainable in the halftone reproduction is naturally limited by the range the printer can reach. This of course depends very much on the grade of paper and ink used. In newspaper printing the contrast range producible is relatively short but when printing on coated stock it can be extended to about 1.6. Usually lower quality paper requires a coarser screen for printing. On the other hand finer screens can be used as the paper quality improves. The average range for a screen print can be expected as follows:

24 lines per cm or 60 lines per inch = 1.2

48 lines per cm or 120 lines per inch = 1.4

80 lines per cm or 200 lines per inch = 1.6

The Agfa-Gevaert Contact Screens meet these requirements in very close tolerances and are again characterized through their specific dot structure. Therefore under normal conditions only one exposure is necessary, eliminating any supplementary exposure without screen, as the "bump" effect is built into both screens. In the negative screening this improves the middletone and highlight details, and in positive screening it improves the shadows. The advantages in respect to time savings and quality improvement are amazing. This is of utmost importance not only for offset but also for letterpress when using powderless etching machines and relief image photopolymer printing plates.

It is necessary to point out again that only the dot structure of the contact screen dots is responsible for the tone rendition obtained in the reproduction. It is inconsiderate and unjustified to claim that the same single contact screen could be used either for the making of perfect screen negatives as well as for screen positives. The lens aperture is also of no consequence as unfortunately, so often mistaken. The aperture, when using a contact screen, is responsible only for the amount of light passing through. The density range of the contact screen dots also have no influence on the curve shape obtained in the reproduction. It solely determines the contrast range the contact screen can cover. The entire function of the contact screen depends exclusively on the particular shape of the screen dots. It is therefore required to build in the needed screen characteristic right into the screen dot itself.

Illustrations No. 66 and No. 67 show the conventional contact screen characteristics against the ones theoretically calculated, and finally compared to the actual Agfa-Gevaert Contact Screens.[10] The double lines represent a conventional screen. The arrows point up and down and indicate the changes necessary for making an ideal negative or positive screen.

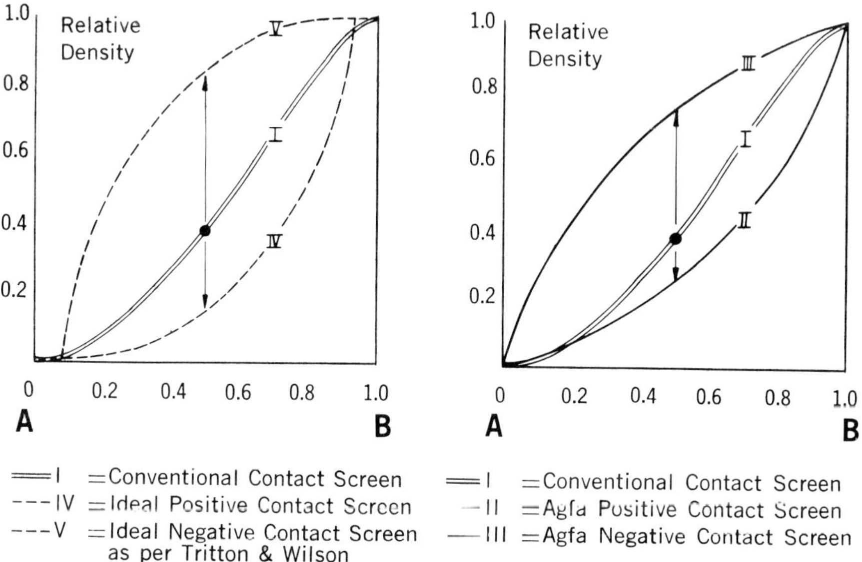


*Illustr. No. 66* *Illustr. No. 67*

**Relative Density of Contact Screen Dots from Density Minimum A to Density Maximum B.**

The more picturesque illustrations 67a-67d show very clearly the considerable improvements between the results obtained with an Agfa-Gevaert Contact Screen.

When studying the two different halftone negatives it becomes very obvious that it is almost impossible to make a true judgment on the quality of a halftone negative. Due to the considerable bow shape, the shadow areas in a good halftone negative appear to empty all the way up to the middle tones. Therefore almost everyone would be inclined to instantaneously choose the incorrect negative made with the conventional contact screen as it seems to show more details in the shadow areas. As a matter of fact, the shadows and especially the middletone areas in the conventional halftone negative are so heavy and dense, that these important tones print far to light in the positive.

This is clearly revealed only in the contact positive or in the print which proves that precautions must be made for not making too hasty judgments in the negative stage but make a true evaluation only of the final print.

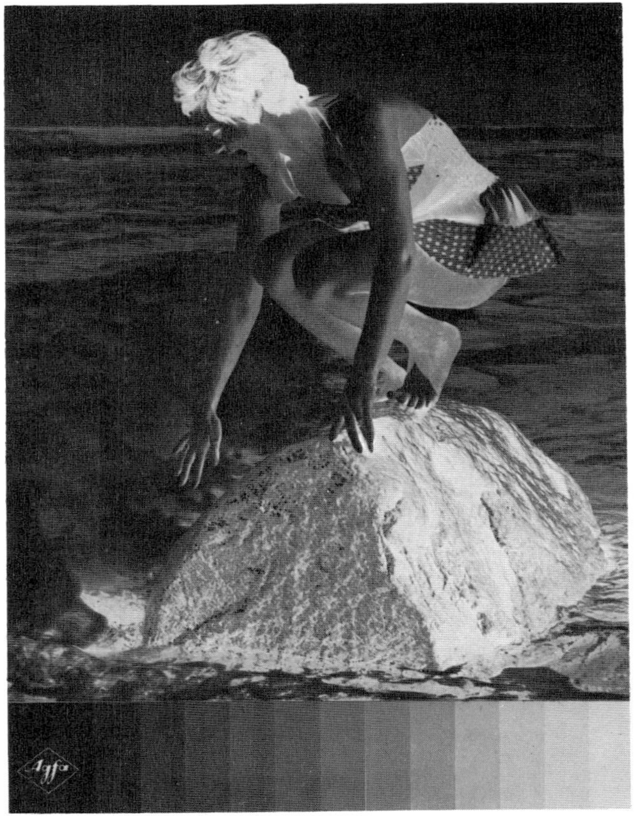

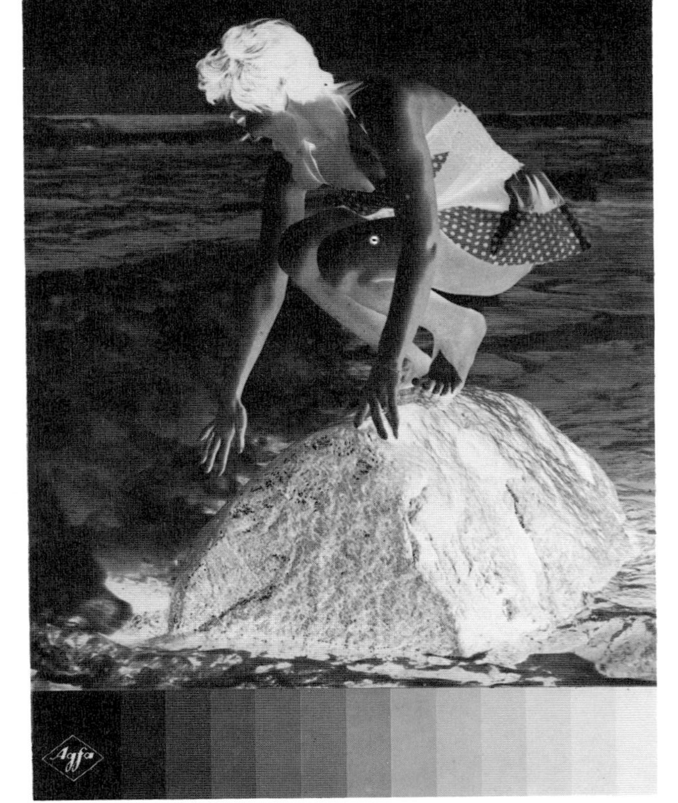


*Illustr. No. 67a* **Halftone Negative with Conventional Contact Screen**

*Illustr. No. 67b* **Halftone Negative with Agfa-Gevaert Negative Contact Screen**

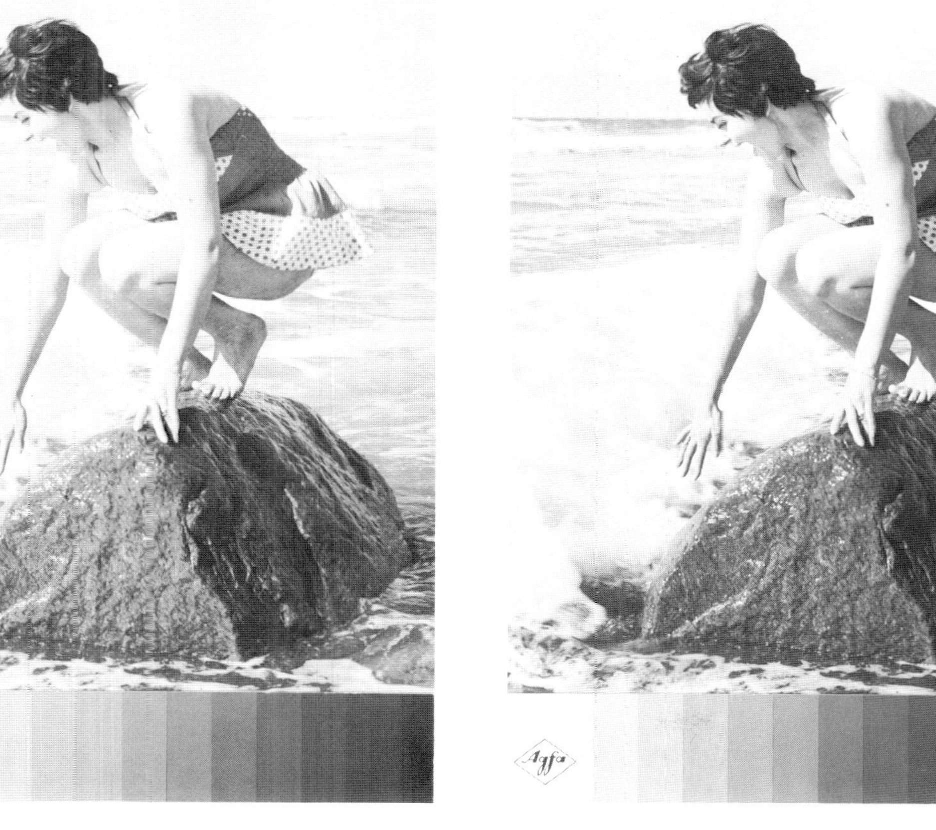


*Illustr. No. 67c* **Print from Conventional Contact Screen Negative**

*Illustr. No. 67d* **Print from Agfa-Gevaert Negative Contact Screen Negative**

## HOW IS IT POSSIBLE TO MAKE PERFECT CONTACT SCREENS

Extensive research and experience have shown that it is not possible to produce these screens on a productive basis by means of optical devices. Agfa-Gevaert went a completely new way by first of all designing and manufacturing a new double emulsion film which fulfills the basic requirements for such an accomplishment. With it completely new possibilities open up, as the dots can be influenced appreciably by exposure. There is no doubt that a film for this must meet exacting specifications, and the double emulsion must consist of extremely fine grain. After this task was mastered the final determination necessary was to select the most suitable dot structures. Illustration No. 67 shows the proper selections. It is easy to see how much they depart from conventional screens. The slight adjustment opposed to the theoretically correct screen dot structure compensates already for a minimum flare of 2% usually present when used in process cameras, and slight imperfection in following procedures.

It is simple to recognize that the Agfa-Gevaert Negative Contact Screen having a dome shape, is exactly contrary to the Agfa-Gevaert Positive Contact Screen. The bow shape determines the shape ob-

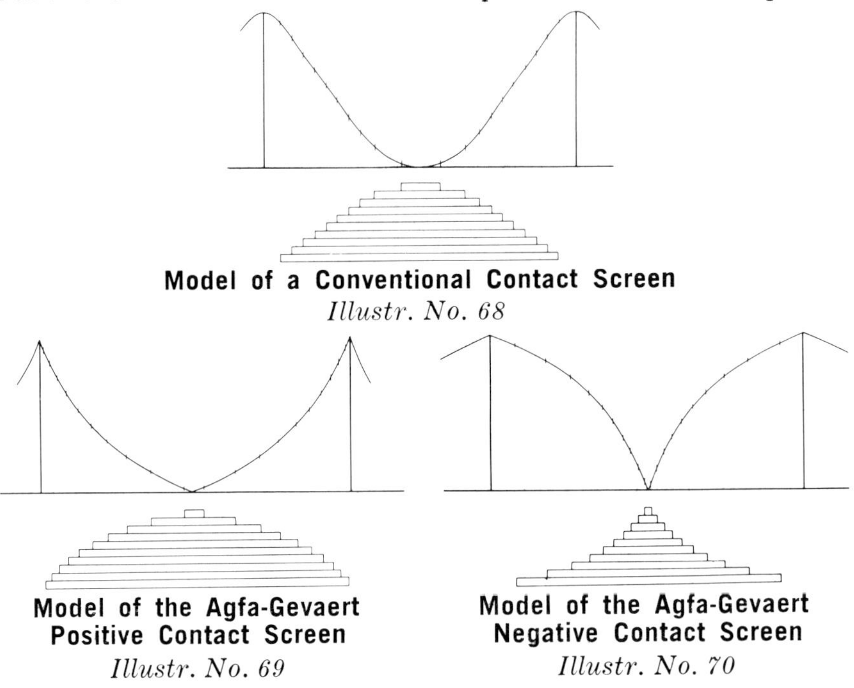

**Model of a Conventional Contact Screen**
*Illustr. No. 68*

**Model of the Agfa-Gevaert Positive Contact Screen**
*Illustr. No. 69*

**Model of the Agfa-Gevaert Negative Contact Screen**
*Illustr. No. 70*

tainable in the reproduction and must meet very tight tolerances. These illustrations No. 68-70 explain this relationship and confirm once more the necessity for two specifically different screens, one for negatives and one for positives.

Nevertheless exceptions confirm the rules and for special effects it is interesting to study the following applications.

## SPECIAL USE OF THE AGFA-GEVAERT NEGATIVE CONTACT SCREEN

As known, in four-color printing it is often good to make a skeleton black with distinct shadow details, empty middle tones and light highlight details. This can be accomplished very successfully by using the Agfa-Gevaert Negative Contact Screen to make halftone positives from the continuous tone color separation negatives. What the positive screen would exaggerate in the middle tones, the negative screen will belittle, and this is exactly what is required for making an outstanding black printer.

Another excellent area would be the making of improved halftone positives for offset printing where highlights are crisp, middle tones distinguished and shadows are very detailed. This is accomplished in the following way. From the original copy a continuous tone negative is made on Agfa-Gevaert CO23 highlight masking film, so that the mask has a range of about 30%. This can also be accomplished with a single emulsion film and a separate mask added. Then the Agfa-Gevaert Negative Screen is used to make a halftone positive. Thereby the mask in the negative guarantees genuine highlight details, the break in the middle tone gives nicely defined middle tones and the built-in bump in the negative screen guarantees very detailed shadows. In reality this would very closely meet "Person's" ideal curve.

This advantage can also be used when having difficulties with black and white halftone printing. Mainly in offset in connection with cheap paper and cheap ink, the middle tones intend to fill in and print too muddy and dirty. This can be prevented by making instead of a direct screen negative a continuous tone negative, which is then screened with the negative contact screen to a halftone positive.

Middle tones and the highlight bump effect can be governed up to a point with the kind of developing. Vigorous agitation makes the highlights jump up faster, resulting in more exaggerated middle tones. Still developing keeps the highlights down giving the middle tones a chance to develop up and therefore get lighter and flatter in the final print.

It is good to remember that the more a lith developer is used, the more bromide is accumulated. This results in a harder contrast and a shorter range, as the fine dots on the toe are not tickled out as well as with fresh developer. In any case, it is important that the film is always thoroughly developed, as the fine pinpoints only appear in the final stage and not if the developing time is rather short.

## DIRECT SCREEN SEPARATIONS FROM COLOR TRANSPARENCIES

This is by no means a new method. However, years ago it was not much used in practice for the main reason of not having been able to obtain good enough tone rendition and color saturation. In other words, the lack in color correction was so great that the alterations on the halftone separation necessary exceeded by far any practical score. Another reason was that the contrast range of many color transparencies was far too high to be covered by the screens available. Therefore, considerable flash exposure was necessary to obtain shadow dots, which by no means represented the actual details in the original.

Today the available one-stage masks in color as well as in black and white provide for easy premasking of the transparencies. These masks give excellent color corrections and, what is of great importance, reduce at the same time the range of color transparencies by about 40%.

The Agfa-Gevaert Negative Contact Screen should cover this remaining range, especially with the help of the Agfa-Gevaert Contrast Control Additive which is explained at the end of this chapter. In addition, the dot structure of this screen guarantees maximum tone rendition and color saturation.

The direct halftone color separations of course have to be made on panchromatic lith films with the recommended color separation filters. The speed of new lith films now available has greatly been improved and allows for comparatively short exposures with arc or other modern light sources like Pulsating Xenon lamps.

The silver content of a good panchromatic lith film such as Agfa-Gevaert P81p film is ample and allows any dot etching which might still be required.

Generally for all other procedures of the actual screening the methods as described in this book are applicable.

# Chapter Seven

## HOW TO USE CONTACT SCREENS

### THE NEGATIVE CONTACT SCREEN

It is designed to be used for making halftone negatives for offset as well as for letterpress when working from any positive original either reflection copy or transparency. The Agfa-Gevaert Negative Contact Screen is designed to give perfect tone-rendition from shadow areas through middletones into the extreme highlight areas with only one single exposure. As the screen is neutral gray it lends itself equally well for making black and white or direct halftone color separations.

### THE EVALUATION OF THE CONTACT SCREEN

To become familiar with the specific screen it is necessary to make a basic test to first of all determine the contrast range which the screen is able to cover under the particular conditions.

This range is largely depending on the type of lith film and developer used as well as on the kind of processing chosen.

The first step is to take a transparent gray scale and place it in the printing frame which must have a smooth backing. If this is not provided, a regular offset rubber blanket is used. It is absolutely smooth but yet tough and flexible to give perfect contact. The gray scale is placed emulsion side away from the pointlight source. The contact screen is put on in the same order. Then the lith film to be exposed is placed emulsion to emulsion with the contact screen. If the letters on the bottom of the Agfa-Gevaert Contact Screens read right, the emulsion side is facing up. Of course complete cleanliness is very important. Good vacuum assures immaculate contact. Two films are exposed with a pointlight source of about 40 Lux, or 4 ftcdl. for approx. 30 seconds. For the developing, a genuine lith developer is necessary. One film is developed with vigorous agitation for the time specified by the manufacturer at 20°C or 68°F. This is usually 2½-3 minutes. The other film is developed the same way, however with no agitation during the last two minutes. Still-development, however, might lead more toward a bromide drag (Eberhard or adjacency effect) and create some edge effect between extreme tone values.

The halftone negatives obtained differ noticeably when comparing the shadow and highlight areas. If the films are developed as recommened in the maximum sharpness tolerance of the film and developer combination, then practically no halo is apparent around the dots. The gray scale steps are now measured on a photoelectric densitometer with an aperture of at least 2 mm or 5/64 inch if the screens are not coarser than 24 lines per 1 cm or 60 lines per 1 inch. The integral densitometer readings are now plotted against the continuous tone grayscale in a coordinating system as explained.

The diagram obtained matches with about the same characteristics as shown in illustration No. 71 and proves the dependance as well as the flexibility on a certain type of developing characteristic in respect to the range which the screen is able to cover, as well as to the tone rendition obtainable.

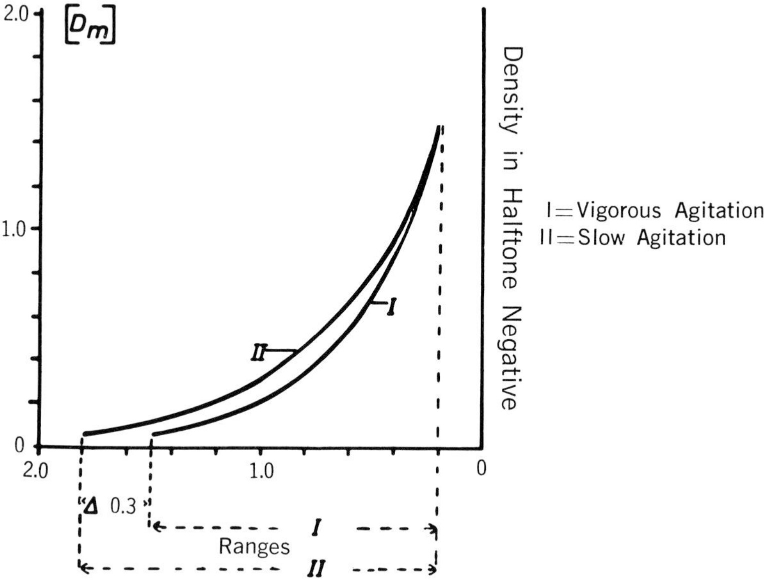


*Illustr. No. 71* **Agitation Against Still-development**

The density range the screen covers can be read on these gray scale steps which produced on one extreme a fine pinpoint and on the other end this percentage dot area which the printer can properly print under the conditions present. The integral readings on the film allow direct conclusion on the percentage of the dot area as shown in table No. 72.

| Integrated Halftone Density | Percent Dot Area | Integrated Halftone Density | Percent Dot Area |
|---|---|---|---|
| 0.00 | 0% | 0.34 | 54% |
| 0.01 | 2% | 0.36 | 56% |
| 0.02 | 5% | 0.38 | 58% |
| 0.03 | 7% | 0.40 | 60% |
| 0.04 | 9% | 0.42 | 62% |
| 0.05 | 11% | 0.44 | 64% |
| 0.06 | 13% | 0.46 | 65% |
| 0.07 | 15% | 0.48 | 67% |
| 0.08 | 17% | 0.50 | 68% |
| 0.09 | 19% | 0.55 | 72% |
| 0.10 | 21% | 0.60 | 75% |
| 0.11 | 22% | 0.65 | 78% |
| 0.12 | 24% | 0.70 | 80% |
| 0.13 | 26% | 0.75 | 82% |
| 0.14 | 28% | 0.80 | 84% |
| 0.15 | 29% | 0.85 | 86% |
| 0.16 | 31% | 0.90 | 87% |
| 0.17 | 32% | 0.95 | 89% |
| 0.18 | 34% | 1.00 | 90% |
| 0.19 | 35% | 1.10 | 92% |
| 0.20 | 36% | 1.20 | 94% |
| 0.22 | 40% | 1.30 | 95% |
| 0.24 | 42% | 1.40 | 96% |
| 0.26 | 45% | 1.50 | 97% |
| 0.28 | 48% | 1.70 | 98% |
| 0.30 | 50% | 2.00 | 99% |
| 0.32 | 52% | | |

**Comparison Between Dot Size and Percentage Dot Area**

*Ilustr. No. 72*

The minimum size of the densitometer aperture must meet the following conditions so that at least 15 dots are measured at the same time.

| Lines per: cm | or inch | Densitometer Aperture: mm | or 64/inch |
|---|---|---|---|
| 10 | 25 | 5,0 | 12 |
| 20 | 50 | 2,5 | 6 |
| 30 | 75 | 1,5 | 4 |
| 40 | 100 | 1,2 | 3 |
| 50 | 125 | 1,0 | 2.5 |
| 60 | 150 | 0,85 | 2 |
| 70 | 175 | 0,72 | 1.8 |
| 80 | 200 | 0,63 | 1.5 |
| 90 | 225 | 0,55 | 1.4 |
| 100 | 250 | 0,50 | 1.3 |
| 110 | 275 | 0,45 | 1.2 |
| 120 | 300 | 0,42 | 1.1 |
| 130 | 325 | 0,39 | 1 |
| 140 | 350 | 0,36 | .9 |
| 150 | 375 | 0,33 | .8 |

*Illustr. No. 73* **Densitometer Aperture Required**

To assure exact true reading it is suggested to zero the densitometer on an area where the ghost dots are just starting to show up but have not yet developed into an actual silverimage. At the same time this takes the base density of the film into consideration. The minimum density might average out to about D 0.1. The maximum density which is printable for black and white is approximately D 1.5, for color about D 1.2.

## SEMI-DARKFIELD DENSITOMETER

The new Sargent-Welch specular/diffuse semi-dark field densitometer is used with a linear Densichron photometer to provide accurate measurement of halftone dot areas on film. First generation halftone dots are usually not perfectly sharp but have some degree of edge gradient with a fringe density.

The Densichron Dot Area Densitometer represents a significant break-through for the graphic arts because it measures true effective size of the halftone image on film, regardless of dot softness. With a conventional densitometer, fringe densities which affect the transmission of light are incorrectly interpreted as representing part of the dot size and a dot size larger than actual is recorded. If the degree of fringe remained constant, then a conventional densitometer could be recalibrated for accurate measurement as described before.

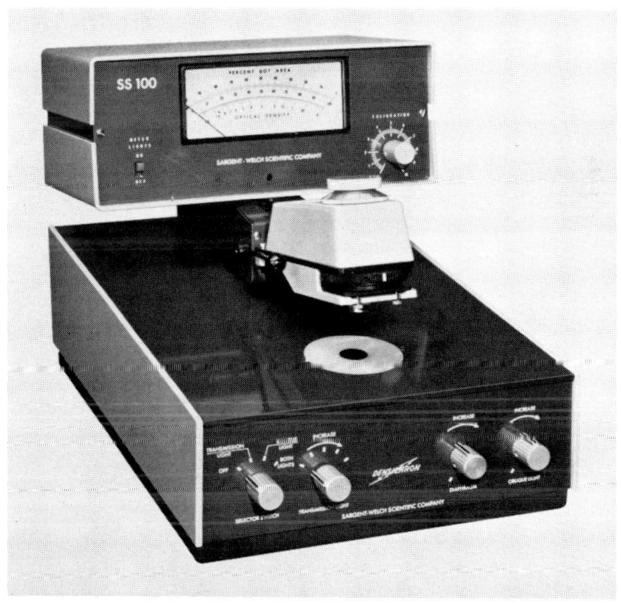


*Illustr. No. 73a* **Semi-Darkfield Densitometer**

Until the introduction of the specular/diffuse densitometer, dependable measurement of halftone images were difficult to obtain.

This new instrument employs a technique long used by the cameraman for visual evaluation of halftones — dark field illumination. Further, to achieve proper calibration, a second light source is used in the normal position. See next illustration.

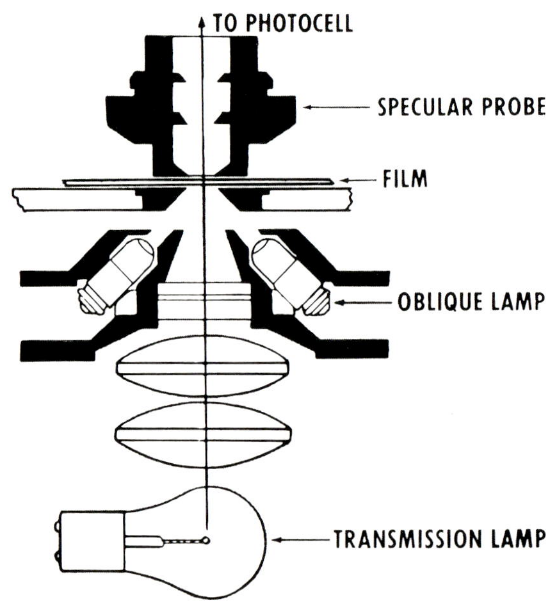


Obliquely positioned lamps provide proper illumination of fringe around each dot.

*Illustr. No. 73b* **Schematic of Semi-Darkfield Densitometer**

Adjusting the ratio of intensity between the two light sources calibrates the densitometer for use with any set of processing conditions. Accurate, consistent measurements of dot areas can be made regardless of the nature of the fringe once the instrument has been calibrated.

From these evaluations we can learn that there is quite a good possibility to standardize, doing away with sometimes very inaccurate guesswork. After the gray scale tests supplied the preliminary basis for practical applications, a regular picture is screened. By comparing the halftone reproductions differently developed, it becomes again evident how the tone values can be influenced between vigorous agitation and still-development as seen in illustration No. 71. The exposure given for curve II was twice as much as for curve 1 in order to compensate for the slower still-development and especially to be able to shoot more into the shadow end.

As the screening can be done in the contact frame, in the enlarger or in the camera, it is required to carry out these tests under the respective conditions. This is mainly because of the different influence of flare. Of course there is no flare when working with perfect contact. Most flare is present in the camera. When using a projector with a strong condenser the effective density range of the transparent continuous tone film original is usually increased. This is true only when using a silverimage, but not when transparent dyes are used. The more flare present, the more the reproducible density range seems to increase. In reality it is nothing else but the same as if a flash exposure were given. The supplementary exposure without a screen is not necessary, in fact it is absurd, as this special effect is built into advanced screens.

## COMPARISONS BETWEEN REPRODUCTION AND PRINT

As it was explained, there is an excellent opportunity to standardize by evaluating halftone reproductions with a densitometer by using the chart which compares the integrated halftone density reading with the actual percentage dot size.

This serves as a basis to make halftone reproductions from a gray scale which can then be plotted into a graph to see how far the reproduction made under the prevailing conditions meets with the expected ideal. As we have seen in previous chapters, a theoretically ideal halftone negative has a distinct bow shape, while contrary to this, a halftone positive has a straight line characteristic.

Integrated halftone density readings made from the test negatives enables one to judge what is really in the reproduction. It reveals whether negative meets with the actual printing requirement, or if it does not conform, it is easily recognized and can be corrected.

Naturally not the theoretical ideal, but the actual final printed result is what counts. As everyone realizes, considerable changes are created by the large varieties of paper and ink used. Further influences come up due to differences in the printing plates, mainly in the surface structure. In addition, not only the printing press but to a large extent the printer himself determines the final result. Variations sometimes occur in the same press run.

This is why the subject of standardization must be approached step by step. To be more specific, this means the preparatory steps such as the reproduction and platemaking should conform to a theoretical ideal. Naturally what is being done in the first test would have to be repeatable at any time to give it a real practical sense. The most critical area is the dependable processing of the film. By comparing halftone reproductions developed in different ways, it becomes readily evident how the tone values are influenced. The most reliable processing is obtained mechanically, provided the processing machine is kept in proper condition. To verify this, processing control strips must be developed at frequent intervals. A permanent record should be established by plotting the obtained results into a processing control chart. This is extensively explained in chapter eight.

Unfortunately, many cameramen don't have an automatic processing machine and are still confined to develop in a tray. This way, considerable fluctuations cannot be prevented. Not only the proper mixture and the exact temperature of the developer play a decisive part but also the agitation which is practically unrepeatable. About 10% fluctuations are inevitable. The graph in illustration No. 76 shows the great fluctuations caused just by a simple change in agitation.

Only after these preliminary steps have been established can the printing follow. In high quality printing, excellent results should be evident. This means the highlights are clearly defined, the middle tones should be properly saturated and the shadows should be well detailed. Naturally, this will not be true in many printed results and this is why the printing shortcomings must be studied in order to recognize the individual limitations.

For instance, if inexpensive paper and ink is used, due to the lack of brightness in the paper the highlights look very dull and compared to high quality coated stock a considerable tone value is inherent to the cheap paper itself. In addition, the ink on uncoated paper does not properly trap but rather spreads considerably. This enlarges the dots a great percentage more so in the middle tone and shadow end of the print. This dot gain has to be reliably established. For instance, if under adverse conditions an 80% tone value on the plate prints just about to a solid, then the most extreme shadows in the original should be limited and represented by only an 80% dot on the plate.

As these deficiencies can vary unpredictably under different conditions only practical tests can determine the necessary adjustments for the halftone reproductions to compensate in advance for the limitations to follow.

Not much to the surprise of an experienced craftsman, it can frequently happen that the theoretically "wrong" screen must preferably be used in order to compensate for the deficiencies in the printing. This is particularly true in the web-offset newspaper field. If the halftone negative conformed to the theoretically ideal Harrison Curve, then (due to the tremendous gain when printing onto the "off-white" newsprint with cheap ink) the whole picture would gain so much that it would be muddy and unattractive.

To compensate for this, it is wise to use a positive contact screen, or at least a conventional screen when making the halftone negative. This reproduces the middle tone in the negative much lighter so when the inevitable gain in the printing takes place the picture will appear as attractive as can be expected.

This shows that it is required to approach the final result in a standardized way but then go backwards and readjust the intermediate steps to suit the final result which is most important.

## CONTRAST VARIATIONS WITH SPACERS

Experience has shown that it is often necessary to fight too high a contrast. For this reason it is appropriate to compensate when making continuous tone intermediates. To gain contrast is no problem. If vigorous agitation is not sufficient, there would be a chance to put spacers of different thicknesses between the contact screen and the film to be exposed. The results are shown in illustration No. 74.

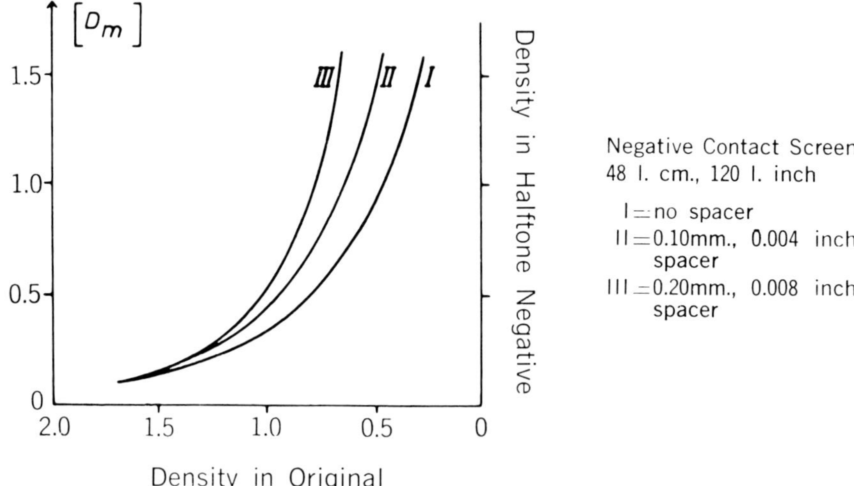


*Illustr. No. 74* **Contrast Variations with Spacers**

The diagram shows three curves. Curve I was obtained with the emulsion of the contact screen with 48 lines/cm or 120 lines per inch in direct contact with the film to be exposed, curve II with a 10/100 mm or .004 inch, curve III with a 20/100 mm or .008 inch clear spacer in between. Any values between Curve I and III can be obtained with adjusted development. It is important to notice that the change in contrast is not uniform when different size rulings are used. The coarser the screen the thicker a spacer required as can be seen in chart No. 75.

| Lines per cm or inch | Density range shortened by spacer thickness: No Spacer | 10/100 mm or .004 inch | 20/100 mm or .008 inch | 30/100 mm or .012 inch |
|---|---|---|---|---|
| 28 70 | full range | –.1 | –.2 | –.3 |
| 48 120 | full range | –.2 | –.4 | —— |
| 60 150 | full range | –.25 | –.5 | —— |

*Illustr. No. 75* **Effect of Different Spacers**

The values given are approximated results. One has to keep in mind that through the spacer some sharpness in the reproduction will be lost too. To prevent Newton Rings it is suggested to use certain cleared out Graphic Arts films which have clear anti-Newton layers.

## THE POSITIVE CONTACT SCREEN

It is designed to be used for making halftone positives for offset as well as for letterpress when working from continuous tone negatives. The Agfa-Gevaert Positive Contact Screen is designed to give perfect tone rendition from highlight areas through middletones into the extreme shadow areas with only one single exposure.

By evaluating the positive contact screen, basically the same is applicable as described for the negative contact screen. The characteristic curves obtained however match with about the same characteristics as shown in illustration No. 76.

This again explains the alterations possible with adjusted development. It also indicates the density ranges the screen can cover. This is of particular importance as, by working from an intermediate continuous tone negative, it is of great value to be able to choose the density range best suitable. The contrast range of the negative should be such that with only one single exposure and normal agitation the correct highlight and shadow dots are obtained. This leaves enough flexibility for some adjustments in lowering or increasing the contrast with different kinds of developments.

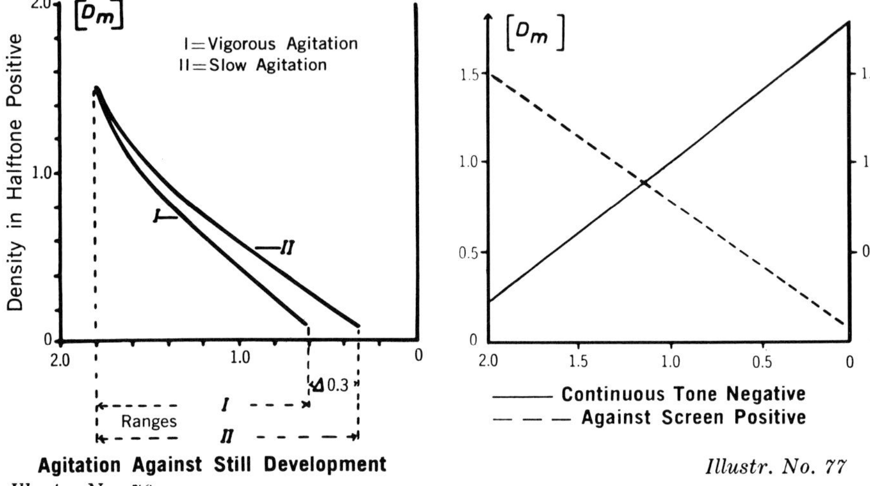


*Illustr. No. 76*

*Illustr. No. 77*

## THE PREPARATION OF THE CONTINUOUS TONE NEGATIVE

It is of utmost importance that these intermediate negatives have very closely the range which can be reproduced with the Positive Contact Screen in only one main exposure. Depending on the type of original available, it is necessary to choose a softer or harder film and developer combination to get the gamma required. The films used should produce a straight line negative curve.

In case the contrast of a continuous tone negative is too high, the highlight density can often be corrected with the help of the Agfa-Gevaert "Super Proportional Reducer" (PPa III). Due to its special characteristic it reduces the areas with heavy silver deposit considerably more than the ones with lesser density, thereby reducing the contrast range. For this reason it would not be useful for screen nor line reduction.

As the Agfa-Gevaert Positive Contact Screen is designed to give a tone value corrected halftone positive from a straight line continuous tone negative, there is no need to use a double emulsion film with a built-in highlight mask. This would even destroy the correct tone values by overemphasizing the middletones. In fact, real success is entirely depending on the quality of the continuous tone negative. The minimum density should not be less than 0.3, to assure to be out of the toe area. The highlight density is depending on the reproducible range the screen can cover.

Another drawback would be excess flare as it would injure the shadow details in the continuous tone negative. Unfortunately flare cannot be prevented completely, however, as 2% can be considered as an average flare factor, the Agfa-Gevaert Contact Screens are made to compensate for that.

As seen before, in black and white single color printing the highest density range obtainable is approximately 1.6. In color printing about 1.2. Therefore the Agfa-Gevaert Positive Contact Screen is designed to perform between these ranges, allowing for final adjustments through the developing procedure. Especially when screening to a positive, flash exposure is most harmful as the eyes catch the highlight details more than the shadows. If the continuous tone negative meets the correct specifications, one exposure is necessary only, eliminating any supplementary exposure without screen, as the "bump" effect is built into the screen which results in improvements of the shadow details.

For the processing and evaluation of the halftone positive basically the same is true as mentioned for the negative contact screen.

## IMPROVING QUALITY OF CONTINUOUS TONE NEGATIVES

If continuous tone separations are not in a balanced range and if this difference is not compensated with color compensating filter control which would be suitable for the magenta contact screen but rather with a flash — or bump exposure, then considerable color shift in the middle tones can occur.

As shown in Fig. A of the next illustration, if the range of the continuous tone negative is perfectly suitable and matches the range which the screen covers with one single main exposure, then the halftone positive will represent a straight line curve as would be expected under ideal circumstances.

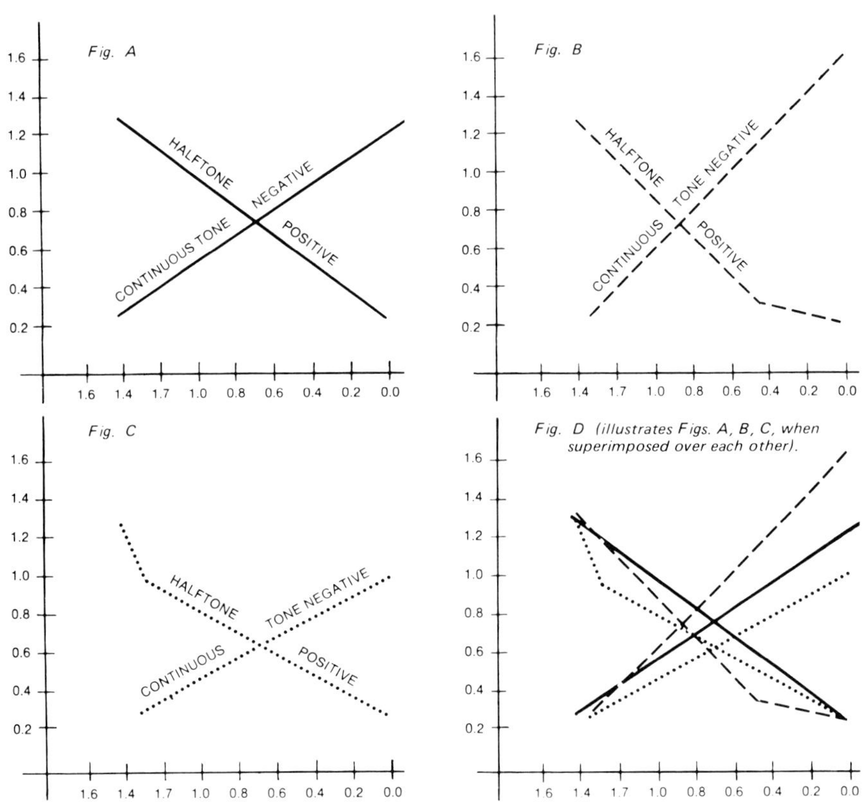


*Illustr. No. 76a* **Comparisons of Different Screening Techniques**

Fig. B illustrates a continuous tone negative which exceeds the range which the screen can cover with a single main exposure. In other words, the continuous tone range is too high and too contrasty and the highlights are too dense so that not enough light can penetrate to build up highlight dots in the halftone positive with a normal exposure. If a longer main exposure is given, of course, a highlight dot would finally be forced into the positive. Nevertheless, by that time the shadows would be hopelessly plugged up, which naturally would be intolerable. Therefore, the only alternative is to give a normal main exposure and substitute the otherwise dotless highlights with a flash exposure. As this is given from a no-picture white paper or with a flash gun, it cannot possibly be a substitute for capturing the actual highlight details. Again, when giving a flash exposure, when making a halftone positive, it is the most destructive thing one can do because it completely flattens the most important picture area — the highlights.

If one inspects a print and the highlights as well as the middle tones and shadows are in proper perspective, then one has the impression of a first class reproduction. If the shadows and middle tones are good but the highlights are flat, the picture gives a very poor impression.

Unfortunately, in too many cases, highlight flash exposures are given while it would be so easy to just shorten the processing time when making the continuous tone negative and thereby control the range.

Fig. C represents the opposite of that explained above. The range of the continuous tone negative is too low, for which reason the shadows in the halftone positive are too open and will print gray or the exposure must be lengthened to compensate for this, but as a result, the highlight dots will become far too large.

To prevent this, the main exposure must be normal and limited to the point where the highlight dots have the correct size. The lack of intensities in the shadow areas has to be compensated with a no screen bump exposure.

When comparing the three illustrations which are shown superimposed in Fig. D, it becomes obvious that, even so, the highlights and the shadows in the halftone positive exhibit the same dot size; the middle tones are considerably dislocated and vary quite a bit. Needless to say, a perfect tone and color balance is not obtained this way.

For the processing and evaluation of the halftone positive basically the same is true as mentioned for the negative contact screen.

## RECOMMENDATIONS

Dust is the worst enemy of the contact screen. When not in use, it is best to keep the screen in its original box. Before use, wipe with a soft antistatic cloth and clean with an antistatic camel hair brush. Spots might be removed with a good film cleaner or carbon tetrachloride.

As the contact screen is like a regular photographic film, it is sensitive for finger prints, scratches, water spots etc. To prolong its life it is very important to handle the screens with care.

## CONCLUSION

Special negative and positive contact screens are the latest developments in this field. In comparison to the glass screens these contact screens can be applied in a simpler way, and because of one single exposure required only, an easier, faster and more faultless operation is possible. The results obtained are in every respect of peak quality as the no screen exposure effect is already built into the screens.

*This kind of performance fulfills an old wishdream of the trade and means a genuine progress in the Graphic Arts Field.*

Contact screens with special characteristics are available also. Instead of being neutral gray, these screens have a magenta color which allows for increase or decrease of contrast with the application of blue or magenta, or yellow color compensating filters. Nevertheless, they are restricted for black and white work. Some screens have chain dots instead of square or round dots. It is claimed that this dot formation provides for smoother middle tones.

## PROS AND CONS OF SQUARE VS. ELLIPTICAL DOT SCREENS

Nevertheless, it is frequently debated whether the elliptical dot screen has an advantage over the conventional square or round dot screen. The advantages of elliptical dots (also known as chain dots) were originally recognized and appreciated by conventional letterpress operators. (See next illustration of dot structures.)

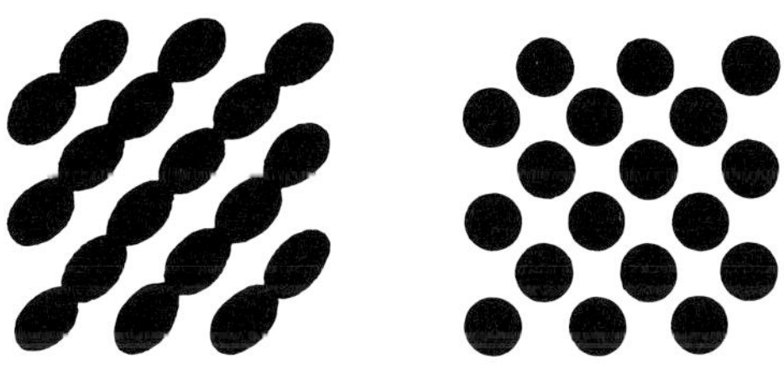

*Illustr. No. 76b* **Elliptical Versus Conventional Dots**

Many years ago, when conventional letterpress was predominant, it was quite common to make halftone negatives in which even the most extreme highlights were so open and flat that a 40 - 50% dot was obtained in these areas on the printing plate. A large percentage of the image which had to appear in the print with disconnected dots required considerable etching from a heavy connected dot.

If a smooth area of connected dots is being etched, it is obvious the checkerboard connection does not break smoothly and evenly on all four connections. Once a connection is broken, the etch attacks the dot structure considerably more, while the connected corners hold up disproportionately.

The result is an obvious unevenness that appears coarse and harsh. It is particularly disturbing in smooth detailed picture areas where it leads to hard breaks. Faces or flesh tones, in general, are quite characteristic of this phenomena.

When the screen was originally introduced it took especially the dot etchers quite a while to get accustomed to it. Their previous experience in visually judging dot percentages could not be applied. For offset it is easier, because an integrated densitometer reading can be made on the positive or negative which expresses an accurate dot percentage. Nevertheless, some printers were puzzled when they first experienced the oval dots which they associated with slur. The advantages being obvious, it did not take long to adopt the new screen.

Soon these advantages were also recognized in offset. When studying the particular use of the elliptical dot screen, it was surprising to find its use was much more pronounced in certain areas than in others. As an example, in Florida, where an abundance of outdoor and artistic pictures are produced in a majority of plants, they would not return to using a conventional screen.

One point must be understood: The shape of the dot has no direct influence on the tone reproduction. The latter is characterized by the density distribution of the contact screen dot whether it is square, round, or elliptical.

## CHARACTERISTICS OF GRAY VS. MAGENTA CONTACT SCREENS

It has been often claimed that a magenta contact screen against a gray contact screen, or a screen with elliptical dots against one with square or round dots automatically affords better tone reproduction with respect to highlights, middletones, and shadow saturation. Claims like this are very superficial and reveal that a full knowledge of the true function of the screen is lacking.

The color and shape of the dots in a contact screen have multiple functions. The tone reproduction of a contact screen is dictated by the density distribution in the contact screen dot itself. Whether the screen is neutral gray or has a magenta color is of no significance. The same holds true with respect to whether the dot is square or elliptical. Again, only the density distribution in the contact screen dot determines the tone reproduction.

It is possible to take advantage of this and design the screen to perform exactly as required.

As can be seen, the color of a contact screen has no significance with respect to the curve shape inherent in halftone reproduction. The only difference between the gray and magenta contact screen is that the former has a fixed contrast range, while with the latter filters can be used to change the contrast range.

The range a contact screen covers is governed by the density of the individual dots in the contact screen. A gray dot cannot be influenced. On the contrary, a magenta screen can be adapted to fit different range originals. This is done by selecting an appropriate filter, such as magenta or blue, to shorten the range while a yellow filter will extend the range. This is graphically explained in Illustration No. 76c, Figs. A, B and C.

*Fig. A Magenta screen dots used without a filter.*

*Fig. B Magenta screen dots used with a yellow filter.*

*Fig. C Magenta screen dots used with blue or magenta filters.*

*Illustr. No. 76c* **Dot Modifications with Magenta Screen**

It is obvious that the density of the magenta screen dots can be changed with appropriate filters. Fig. A shows the dots without a filter. A certain density which the screen manufacturer considers most ideal is built into the dots. This, together with the contrast of the film and developer used, determines the contrast range the screen can cover.

Generally speaking, a 1.3 range seems to be acceptable. It should be understood that this figure concerning the reproducible density range, can only be relative. Not only do the film and developer used have an influence on the basic range, but other factors, too, are involved, such as the development system; tray versus processor; and, if processor, the type used will in turn determine the developer turbulence, which also plays a role in ascertaining range.

The color of the exposing light source is yet another factor. Tungsten light, which is yellowish, increases the density range more than a Xenon or arc light would. There are also differences from screen to screen. Even if all these factors were standardized, it would still be of significance if the screen is used in a contact frame or in an optical system, such as an enlarger or in the camera. A longer range is usually obtained in a camera than in a contact frame because of the influence of stray light and flare, while in an enlarger the range would be shorter due to the Callier effect or Q factor.

The distinction between the density range a screen can cover also depends upon the purpose it is used for. In offset, where high contrast reproductions are usually made, the range can be judged from an extreme highlight to an extreme shadow. In letterpress, larger highlight dots are used which automatically shorten the range.

Fig. B shows the same magenta screen dots used behind a strong yellow filter. It was not accidental that a specific magenta color was chosen for the screens; it was scientifically selected. Behind the yellow filter the magenta color increases density considerably. This adds to the opacity of the dots. It is for this reason that the connected dots in the reproduction do not close up as fast, making it possible to give a longer exposure and capture more reflection from the dark areas of the original which will establish dots and details in an otherwise unregistered area.

Conversely, as evidenced by Fig. C, if a magenta screen is used behind a blue or magenta filter the dots in the screen become very transparent and transmit an excessive amount of light. The connected dots close up rapidly, and thereby limit the exposure to the point where small dots cannot be established in the reproduction from the darker areas in the original, resulting in a short screen range.

Any range between the maximum and minimum can be obtained by an appropriate selection of a certain percentage of yellow to blue filter, or with color compensating filters for the exposure.

It is needless to emphasize the importance of individually establishing the range a screen gives under specific conditions. These explanations are relevant for both negative and positive screens. To adapt a negative screen to an extremely high range of a first generation original, for instance a contrasty reflection copy, a flash exposure might be necessary, because the yellow filter exposure might not extend the range sufficiently. This should be as short as possible and longer than the minimum flash exposure only if absolutely required. (This refers to half of the flash exposure time which by itself would create a dot.)

Fortunately, a flash exposure, which is always a no-picture exposure (because it is given from a white paper or a flash lamp), can be tolerated more when making a negative. Again, in opposition, when screening to a halftone positive, a flash exposure cannot be tolerated as it would destroy the highlight details which are of utmost importance for a good quality picture.

It can be seen from the explanations, in addition to all the advantages which are equally built into a gray contact screen as well as into a magenta contact screen, the latter has a unique feature and possibility for contrast control with filters which guarantee the best picture quality. This makes the magenta screen a more versatile and more desirable screen. The only system a magenta screen cannot be used for is direct color separation screening.

## PREANGLED SCREENS

The Agfa-Gevaert magenta screens are supplied individually (screen angle: 45°) or - for color work - per set of 4 screens (screen angles 15°, 45°, 75° and 90°). Each screen has one or more notches. If the screen is held in such a manner that the notches are at the upper right hand corner, then the emulsion side faces you. The exact position of the screen angle is then determined by the long side at the left.

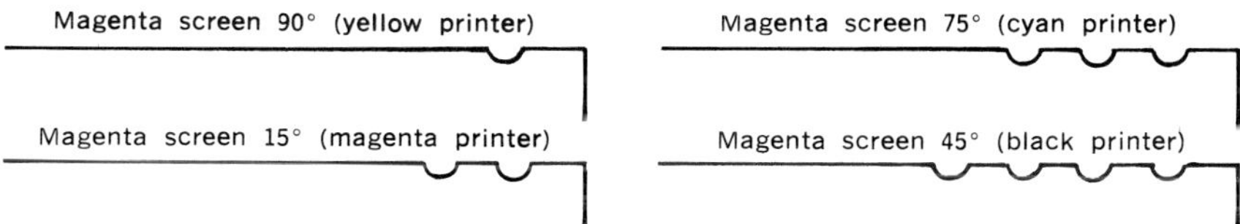


If one single screen is preferred and the separations are angled, the following sizes can be covered:

| SCREEN SIZE | SIZE OF SEPARATIONS | SCREEN SIZE | SIZE OF SEPARATIONS |
|---|---|---|---|
| 9½ x 12 inch | 5½ x 7 inch | 22 x 22 inch | 18 x 18 inch |
| 12 x 16 inch | 6½ x 9 inch | 26 x 26 inch | 16 x 20 inch |
| 16 x 20 inch | 10 x 12 inch | 30 x 30 inch | 18 x 23 inch |
| 20 x 24 inch | 12 x 15 inch | | |

To obtain cm. sizes, multiply by 2.5

There is also available Kodalith Autoscreen Film, a special material with a built-in 133 line screen.

## SPECIAL EFFECT SCREENS

These screens are available mostly as contact screens and are made in almost limitless patterns. Some are shown in the following illustrations.

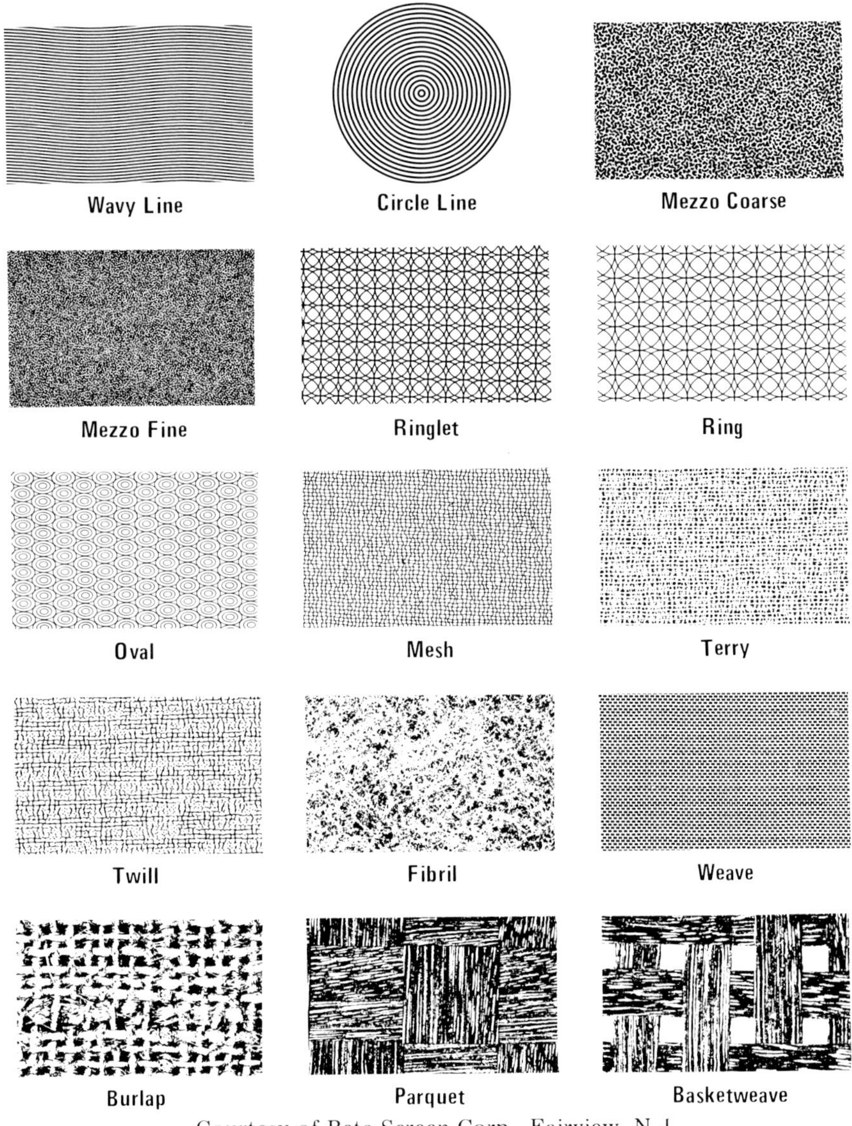


Courtesy of Beta Screen Corp., Fairview, N.J.

Very artistic results can be obtained with ease as long as the application is known and an appropriate pattern selected.

# CHAPTER EIGHT

## LITH-PROCESSING CONTROL

The results obtained on any light sensitive material largely depends on two main factors: Exposure and Processing.

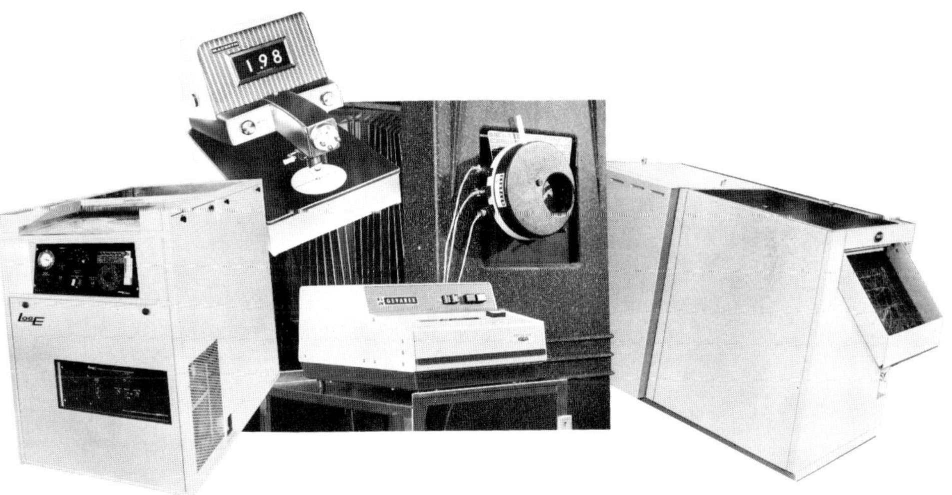


*Illustr. No. 78a* **Exposure and Processing Control**

Proper exposure really depends on too many intricate influences and it is not the intent of this chapter to clarify these involved matters. Needless to say, the correct exposure is most essential, however, it makes sense only if the proper exposure gets activated into a predictable image by reliable processing. This necessitates exacting control in all phases of the processing cycle but mainly during the developing which is best carried out in an automatic processing machine. Trays can be utilized also but to standardize these conditions, it is a must to be in a position to repeat all phases exactly the same way. This is easier said than done since even the slightest, and to some people "neglectable" differences, play a decisive role on whether a result is excellent or just acceptable. Once a developer has been used, it it not the same as when it was fresh. Whether it has been used immediately after mixing, or after it has been standing around for a "little while", makes quite a difference. On the other hand, if developer is mixed fresh every time, who can guarantee equal amounts of "A" and "B" solution to the drop and whether exactly the same proper parts of water are used again. Keeping the temperature the same is almost as impossible. This is true with temperature controlled sinks as well, because the room temperature and the cooling of the developer in the tray, due to surface evaporation, creates at least some deviations and we all realize that ½°F plus or minus creates changes like day or night. On top of this, the quantity and agitation of the developer solution in the tray gives quite some alterations. Further influences are created on whether the film is stationary in the tray or how it floats in the developer.

These adverse effects go on and on and there is only one very limited way to try and offset these and this is to manipulate with the processing time while inspecting the film in the last phase of the developing and interrupt processing only if the result is acceptable. This, however, means that a transparent tray with a red light underneath is necessary but it is quite difficult to evaluate a film in its rapidly changing final processing stage. All in all, it proves that 10% deviation must be content with in manual processing of lith film in an infectious "A" & "B" formaldehyde type chemistry.

Modern requirements and time commitments do not allow these deficiencies anymore which explains why progressive plants are spending considerable money to overcome the above mentioned problems, which in time, would be much more costly.

## AUTOMATIC MACHINE PROCESSING

There are not too many graphic arts processing machine manufacturers but they make several diversified processors, some with special features. It depends on each plant on what processor would best suit their individual requirement. It is highly suggested to first make a comprehensive study of all the available features before making the final decision for purchasing a processor which has to serve for a great many years to come.

Included in this must be an evaluation of available floor space and the best central location because the necessary installation with under-floor drainage, hot and cold water supply etc., would run considerably expensive if additional changes would be necessary. It is wise not to interrupt the present processing procedure until the new machine is in proper working condition. For the actual installation it is possible to get diversified and experienced help because the manufacturer of the equipment as well as the dealer will make sure that everything goes well as anticipated. It is also possible to get the help of the chemical and film manufacturer who is most interested to get his material successfully established in the machine.

When choosing the proper material, it is necessary to get the film and chemistry which is compatible assuring the highest possible contrast which is equivalent with the sharpest reproduction of dots and lines. The chemistry must have a reliable replenisher to provide for a long life and capacity of the solution.

## FILM INCOMPATIBILITIES

To keep a permanent check on the chemistry's behaviour, it is essential to use processing control strips. Even so different control strips are available, it is an absolute must to use the control strip which, in its developing characteristics matches with the film used for the actual work. This is necessary because different films get into different speed and especially sharpness maximum zones at different times. A film with slow developing characteristics might reach its best sharpness maximum only when a film with fast developing characteristic had already past through this stage and is loosing contrast by kicking out the toe resulting in a noticeable halation and dot unsharpness.

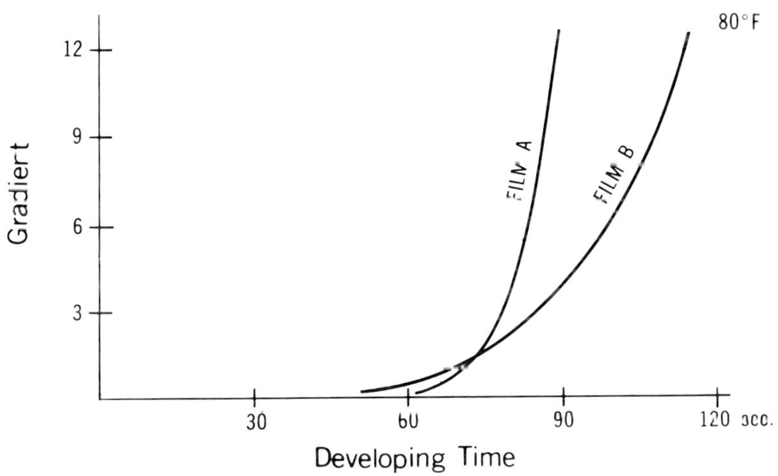


*Illustr. No. 78b* **Films With Different Processing Characteristics**

## FILLING OF THE PROCESSOR

After the processing machine is installed, it is most important to make sure that the inside of the tanks are immaculately clean and free of any grease. After a final check of all hose connections is completed, the fixer tank is largely filled up with water. The correct amount of fixer concentrate is added and after proper stirring the hardener is mixed in. Then, the transport rack is lowered into the tank. Finally, water is filled in, up to the right level. It is a good practice to always mix the fixer first and also use a splash guard in order to prevent the fixer from splashing into the developing tank.

Thereafter, the developing tank is half filled with water, than part "A" of the developer is put in and stirred up before part "B" is added. Finally after the developer rack has been put into the tank the water is filled up to the proper level and the recirculating pump, which is now switched on will homogeneously mix the solution. At the same time, the trapped air is bled which would otherwise create oxidation.

It is also possible to pre-mix the chemicals in two separate containers which, however, is rather complicated especially as different containers have to be used for developer and fixer. Needless to say, exact calculations for the proper chemical mixture have to be worked out. In addition to the tank volume, the displacement of the hoses, heat exchange and filter units have to be taken into consideration. It is better to mix first of all on the shy-side and then fill up to the proper level.

The temperature is chosen and obtained while the chemistry recirculates. A commonly used temperature is 80°F. This does not mean, however, that a higher or lower temperature could not be used as well. The main influence the temperature has is on the activity of the developer. With a higher temperature everything goes at a faster rate allowing for faster throughput time which is of advantage for high volume requirements. On the other hand, the latitude is not as wide as when using lower temperatures. This, however, is offset by the accuracy a high quality processing machine provides.

First of all, to see whether there is a perfect correlation between the thermometer reading in the machine and the actual temperature of the developer in the tank, a direct tank reading should be made with a reliable thermometer. The side panels and top covers should be kept in place as otherwise the temperature could be influenced. The actual transport speed of the film should also be clocked to assure perfect transport speed and developing time correlation.

## FINDING THE PROPER DEVELOPING TIME

Only by now are we about ready to start actual film testing. For example, if the temperature was set to 80°F., most films are expected to get into their proper sharpness maximum at about 90 seconds. Nevertheless, this can only be an approximation. A whole series of tests have to be run reaching from predicted under-processing to over-processing in rather short intervals. It would be appropriate to start at 75 seconds and go to 105 seconds with 5 seconds interval. Always make sure that the previous film is already in the hypo before the machine speed is altered. Whether the emulsion must be put in up or down depends on the construction of each individual machine. Generally, some roller processors ask for emulsion up and some for down, while machines with roller-belt combination transport require emulsion up in order not to have the belts obstructing the processing.

Another very important factor is that the control strip is always fed facing the same direction. In order to prevent excess influence by bromide drag, which amounts to a falsification due to adjacency effect, it is best to feed the part with the least exposure first.

## PROCESSING CONTROL STRIPS

Several different kinds of control strips are available. Some are comparatively short and require taping onto a leader. This, however, should never be a film which produces a developed image because bromide would again influence the result on the test strip. It is not advisable either to use an actual film with a gelatine coating over and over again as especially with fast processing times, the hypo trapped in the emulsion is not completely removed in the washing and thereby gets re-introduced into the developer. Some strips are actual step wedges, others contain a continuous tone image.

Agfa-Gavaert's advanced strip even utilizes next to a continuous tone image an actual halftone wedge which was exposed through a contact screen thereby truly representing the actual dot-sharpness which can be expected in a camera halftone.

This strip is also most practical to evaluate. The 0.3 and 3.0 density is simply located on the continuous tone wedge with a densitometer and this distance is transposed to a built-in gradient meter, immediately expressing the gradient obtained during the developing of this strip. The speed judgment is made on the 0.3 density. This claim could be argued because in lith-photography, only the density maximum plays an important role and, at least theoretically, a toe density is not even desirable. The very light density in the toe area is much more influenced by processing fluctuations than the extreme density maximum, for which reason the first serves as an excellent medium to detect minute indications of upcoming changes before they actually influence the practical work. The other way around one would rather produce a good looking test strip which would defeat its actual purpose.

*See Illustr. No. 78c on following page*

AGFA-GEVAERT

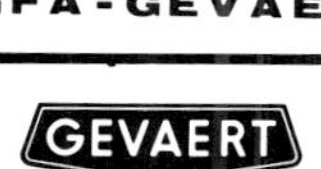


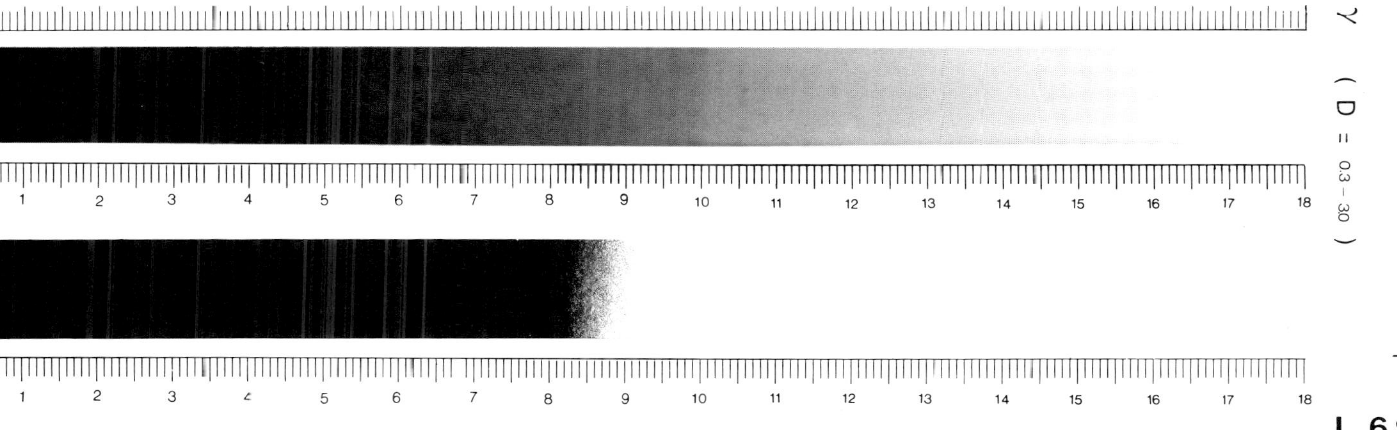


*Illustr. No. 78c* **Advanced Control Strip**

## PROPER USE OF CONTROL STRIPS

Processing control strips should never be fed directly after life work.

When film is being developed the developer becomes partly exhausted and loses activity. At the same time by-products are created and released out of the emulsion. To a large extent, they consist of bromide which is a restainer and slows down developing. The result is, that when actual work, especially large negative films are developed, the by-products accumulate and trail the film. A control strip fed directly behind it would not get fully activated and therefore greatly falsify the evaluation. This is true, both in respect to speed as well as contrast. Dependable evaluation would therefore not be possible.

This phenomena even occurs within the film itself and is known as bromide drag and recognized as adjacency effect. In half-tones, when dark and light areas are next to each other and the dark area is leading in front of the light one, then the small dots, due to the developer activity loss, are not activated properly and fall below the inertia of the emulsion resulting in a dotless area or fringe immediately adjacent to the dark area. Vice versa, when a dark area trails a light one, the developer retains its maximum strength and heavily activates the dark area which trail tones which developed lightly. Not only lithfilm but also continuous tone films are influenced by bromide drag. Because the image is so much softer it is not as obvious in the continuous tone stage.

It is even important to always feed the control strip in the same direction because if the part with the light exposure is developed first, the toespeed indicated on the control strip gets more activated resulting in a lower expression of gradient when evaluating a continuous tone image or the screen range seams longer. Quite contrary, if the part with the heavy exposure is developed first, the exhausted developer and by-products slow down development even more in the low density areas. This would again influence the evaluation and by comparison give the impression of a developer activity fall off. When erroneously compensating for this with more replenisher, the actual work would be overdeveloped.

## FINDING THE PROPER DOT SHARPNESS

The 7 test strips obtained as described before are evaluated this way and a time gradient curve can be established very easily, as shown in the following illustration.

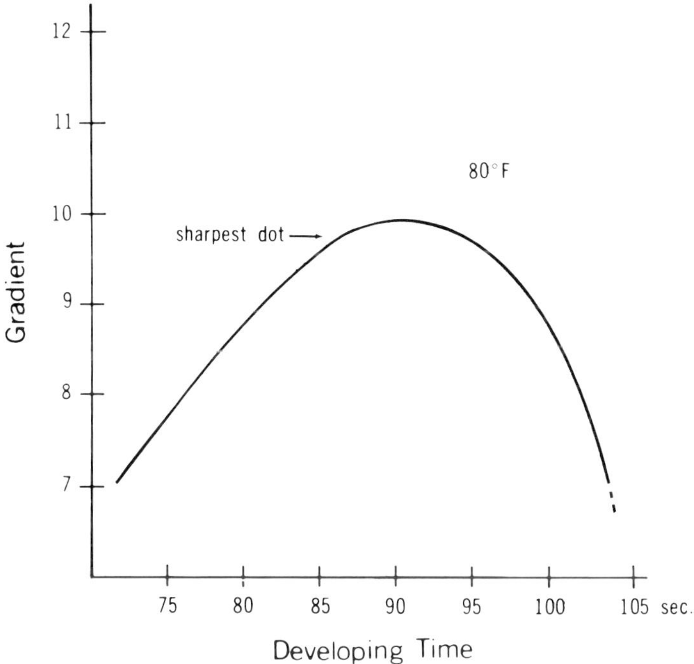


*Illustr. No. 78d* **Time-Gradient Curve**

It should by no means be neglected to carefully study the dot-sharpness with a strong magnifier. Theoretically, the highest gradient produces the sharpest dot. Although there is a definite relation, it is mostly found, that the cleanest dots are obtained just before the highest gradient is obtained. In any case, one should always settle for the developing time which has produced a gradient slightly before it has reached its peak gradient, thereby, still laying on the ascending part of the curve. On the descending part of the curve the dots produced show a distinct fuzziness which rapidly increases into very unsharp dots. This is easily explained because the toe of the curve kicks out which is responsible for the halation as can be seen in the next illustration.

Because different films can reach their optimum performance respectively maximum sharpness at different developing times, it is of necessity to use the control strip which has the same characteristics as the film being used, this is best guaranteed by using the control strip supplied by the film manufacturer who's film material is utilized for the practical work. However, it can occur that different films even when they are made by the same film manufacturer can have different processing characteristics to the point where the developing time has to be changed considerably in order to get optimum dot sharpness.

Nevertheless, the direct comparison between the control strip and the actual film is often debated, because some people claim that there is no need for a relationship from one to the other. The explanation is that in any case the characteristics of the actual film material should be evaluated by itself. Once this is finally established a control strip should be run at the same time and temperature and could then serve on a "relative" comparison basis. As long as the control strip would indicate the same result one could be reasonably sure that the function of the developer has not changed and this of course is the main reason why control strips are being used. Naturally this theory is definitely right, but I strongly believe that due to other variables which might not express themselves equally between the control strip and film emulsion, one should not just accept the statement that: if the control strip remains that bad it is still a proof that the developing conditions are stable. No doubt, in the long run, if at all possible, rather use an equivalent control strip which truly expresses what is going on.

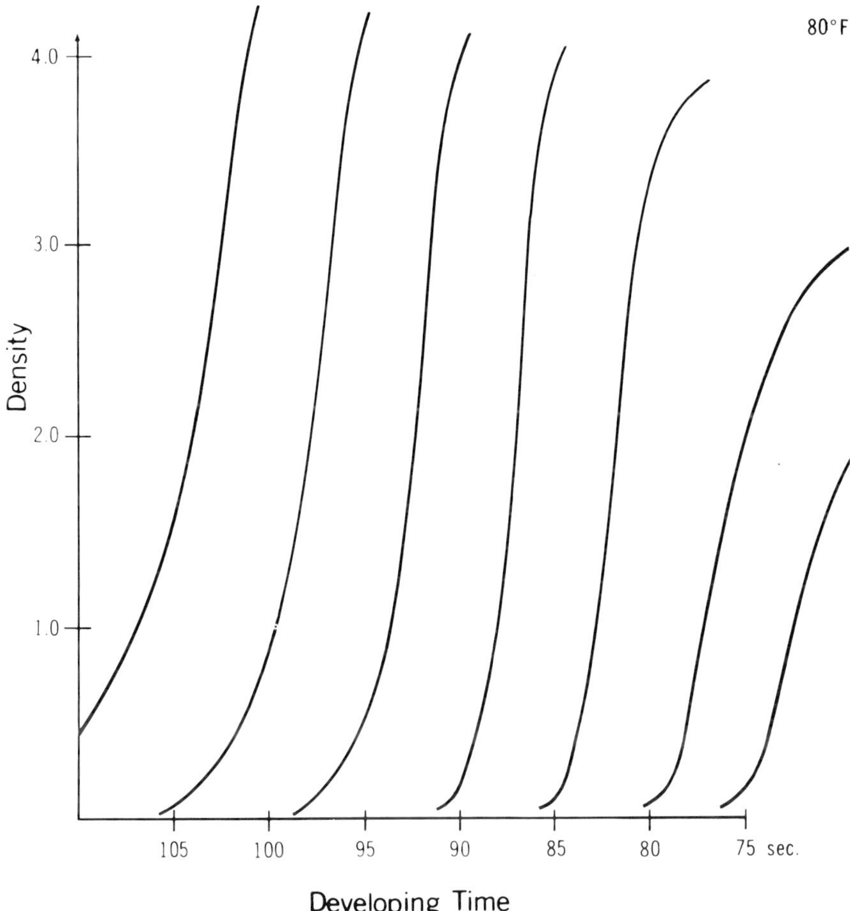


*Illustr. No. 78e* **Influence on Dot Sharpness by Gradient**

After the best suitable developing time has been chosen, this time must be fixed on the machine. Only after this has been established are actual exposure tests run to find out the proper exposure time. Reliable exposure computers are available to guarantee proper exposure. Once a standard has been established to compliment this, the proper function of the processor guarantees the circle of reliable and predictable control.

From there on it is most important to keep the processor in constant working condition which is accomplished by proper replenishment which must be started immediately after running the first seven test strips which have allowed the selection of the most desirable processing time. If this would be neglected to be done one would drain on the actual capacity of the developer. Unfortunately, quite a few people think replenishing is necessary only when a decline in activity is beginning to be noticed. This situation would mean that one is working on the extreme edge of tolerance, thereby having lost all latitude which could at one time or another amount to a complete falloff in developer activity, especially after long down times.

Processing control is monitored by using a "Processing Control Chart" in which all evident characteristics are noted. How wide the latitude is set depends on the quality requirements of the shop.

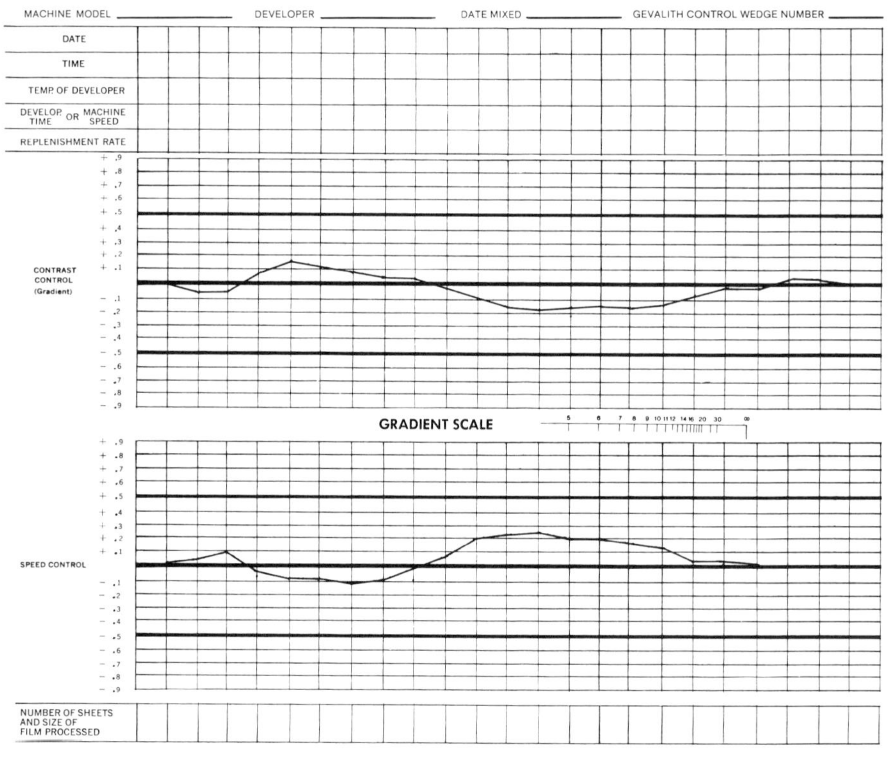


*Illustr. No. 78f* **Processing Control Chart**

## REPLENISHING

When replenishing is started, the recommendations from the chemical manufacturer should be followed. Those are based on the size of the film and also on the percentage of the developed area. These suggestions however, are merely a guide and by no means blindly reliable. This is why it is necessary to run control strips in short intervals 'til a certain pattern indicates no more necessary modification of the established replenishing rates. This should be done slowly, but surely, in order to prevent any erratic function of the developer. Replenishing can be accomplished automatically or monitored manually. It is also necessary to find out what replenishing rate is necessary for overnight and weekend fall off. In this case it has been proven that much more stable results are obtained if the replenisher is added in the evening instead of the morning. Not only might it amount to lower replenishing rates, but most important, the developer is ready to be used immediately in the morning as no mixing and reaction time has to elapse.

Not only the developer but also the fixer must be replenished. It is a rule of thumb to replenish fixer at the rate of 1 to 1 for negatives and 2 to 1 when making positives compared to the developer replenisher used the previous day. It is drained out of the bottom of the fixer tank and thereby carries away possible slush too. Then it is topped off with fresh hypo. Automatic fixer replenishing is also available.

New improved processors provide advanced concepts for replenishment. Automatic scanning of the film with photocells evaluates not only the width and length but especially the density of the processed film. It thereby compensates automatically for the total amount of developed silver with the predetermined quantity of replenisher according to the memory bank setting. For oxidation during time elapse a "stand by" circle is available. Thereby the machine is never shut off completely, only the mechanics such as the roller transport, but at certain time intervals replenisher is added and the short in-flow circulation keeps the solutions at perfect temperature. This way the processor is ready for use at all times with no waiting not even after long weekends.

Proper hypo concentration it not only essential for sufficient fixing, but just as well for the appropriate amount of hardening of the emulsion. The hardening creates a compression of the otherwise too much swollen gelatine, which can make the emulsion tacky and not dry properly. As a matter of fact, 90% of all problems encountered in the dryer are created from improperly replenishing the hypo. This includes proper recirculation of the solution in the fixer tank as well. Fixer is heavy—developer is lighter—for which reason the developer which is carried over can accumulate on top of the fixer and create a pocket. Developer carryover can be minimized by assuring that the last roller pair in the developer tank has a proper squeezing action. The developer level should thereby remain just lightly below the center of the last roller pair to prevent back run streaks.

To enhance best fixer circulation, the filter must be frequently changed. Dichroic fog is a sure sign of fixer contamination.

It is often asked how long a developer should be used in a machine.

As a matter of fact the developer originally put into the machine does not remain there very long because it is constantly replaced with replenisher. As it takes about two weeks to learn about the exact function of a new machine filling, it would be quite wrong to strive for a frequent developer change. The longer it runs, the better the control. The same is true for high volume machines as there is very little influence by air oxydation which is created by plenty of down time. In very low volume machines this can create fluctuations if not carefully watched.

Last, but not least, it must be stressed that good housekeeping is one of the secrets of satisfactory automatic processing. In case a machine cleaner is used, it is most essential to neutralize and carefully flush out all residues from the tank, hoses, etc. and a new filter should frequently be used.

If these simple rules are followed, it is a great pleasure to have a processing machine to assist you in making your work more pleasant and rewarding. It is an accepted fact that machine processing can increase productivity almost 100% over tray processing. An extra bonus is obtained by saving large quantities of chemicals which would otherwise be dumped into the sink constantly. A silver recovery unit represents an additional small "silvermine".

## BROMIDE DRAG—ADJACENCY EFFECT

Bromide drag is a general terminology for adjacency effect, the latter which is caused by the former.

Although it is mostly noticed in high contrast material, especially with lith film, it is also evident in continuous tone photography. It occurs in tray processing as well as in machine processing. In machines, however, it becomes more pronounced due to the one directional motion of the film.

When photographic material is being developed, in addition of loosing developing agents and a drop in ph, by-products are created in proportion to the amount of the developed area. These by-products, to a large extent, contain bromide which flows into adjacent areas. Bromide, being a restrainer, retards developing in these neighboring areas to the point where image areas, which have only been exposed lightly, become so much retarded that they drop below the inertia of the emulsion giving insufficient density, or in case of halftone dots, do not produce a printable dot anymore. The higher the contrast of a film and developer combination, the more pronounced this effect becomes.

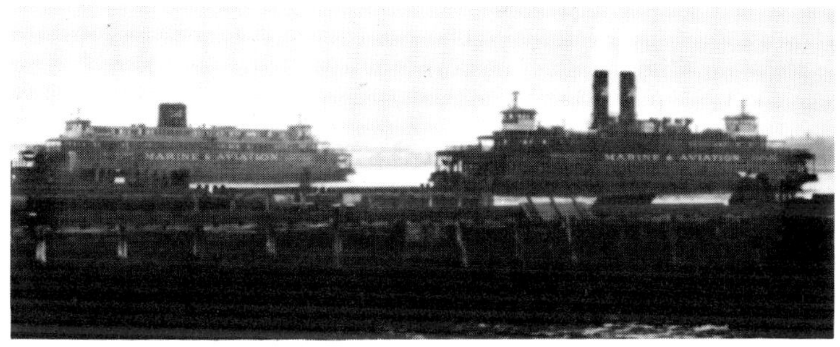

*Illustr. No. 78g* **Effect of Bromide Drag**

Bromide drag can be minimized by creating an adequate turbulence in the developer solution while developing. In a tray this is done by vigorous agitation or better, by using a brush developing technique. Thereby a 3″ - 4″ wide camelhair brush is moved over the film in a slow smooth motion in all directions. The weight of the brush is entirely sufficient and no additional pressure is to be applied. Even though this is quite an awkward way to develop a film, the results are so good that it is at least worth to make you aware of it.

For machine processing it is quite important to have as much developer circulation as possible. Some processors have built in "Cross flow circulation" or "spray bars" or a slotted "uniflow" design which helps wash away the bromide, thereby adjacency effect is kept down to a minimum.

As unrealistic as it might sound, adjacency effect is largely dependent upon the kind of screen used. Due to the special dome-shaped dot structure in a negative contact screen it exposes and activates the area where pin points are formed much more than conventional screens. This strengthens the dots to the point where they are not subject to bromide drag anymore.

*Illustr. No. 78h* **Negative Contact Screen Dots**

Due to the special dot structure the highlight is "funnelled" in much more precisely to a particular spot so that the dots form freely without being subject to deterioration which is the case with dots which have obtained minimum exposure only.

With positive or conventional type contact screens, one is more prone to get adjacency effect.

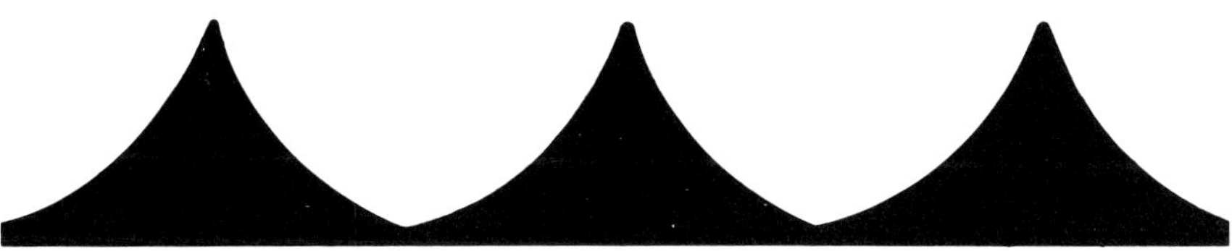

*Illustr. No. 78i*

**Positive Contact Screen Dots**

As can be observed, the areas between the dots of the positive contact screen are wide open. Besides very exacting exposure a very high contrast film and developer combination is necessary to get a fine dense dot which would easily fall below the threshold of the emulsion if it were influenced by bromide drag.

# Chapter Nine

## HALFTONE DUPLICATING WITH CONTACT FILM

### HIGHEST GAMMA-BEST QUALITY?

The desire to improve halftone and line films has always led to an increase in the contrast of the film; in other words, in the steepness of the curve. From this point of view, the most suitable materials are the lith films. Their steep gradation is unsurpassed, and they are in every respect the latest step in technical development.

However, there are many areas in reproduction work in which steep gradation for halftone and line work is not necessary, and sometimes not even desirable.

The following table shows various groups of reproduction applications and their most suitable gradation requirements.

| GEVALITH FILM | | GEVALINE CONTACT FILM | |
|---|---|---|---|
| Steepest gradation required | Steepest gradation desired | Steepest gradation not required | Steepest gradation not desired |
| Contact screening | Screen and line Reproduction in the camera, Projection | Contact duplicating | Contours, Hachures, Contrast masks |

*Table No. 79* **Proper Selection of Film Material**

This table describes when to use a lith and when to use a contact film. The properties of the films determine which of the two types should be used for specific purposes.

Agfa-Gevaert has provided for a special material, called Gevaline Contact Film. It lends itself in an outstanding way especially for making contact duplicates of even fine halftones as well as for making screen tints.

### PROCESSING

Compared to lith films, the processing of Gevaline Contact Film is much simpler: The developing latitude is wider and the Metol-hydroquinone developer has a longer life and is more consistent than any formaldehyde type developer. There is practically no change in the final result when the developing reached its peak in about 2½-5 minutes as shown in illustration No. 80. No temperature control is needed, nor is a stop bath necessary; only the regular fixing bath is required.

In lith processing a definite gradation maximum occurs. This can best be determined toward the end of the processing cycle with a magnifier under a fairly bright darkroom safelight. If one develops too long, this maximum contrast is lost and the gradation becomes softer again, noticeable by a halo and as a larger dot. In the development of Gevaline Contact Films in M.Q. developer, the gradation hardly changes after the recommended developing time of 3 minutes as shown in illustration No. 80.

2 1/2 min. developed

5 min. developed

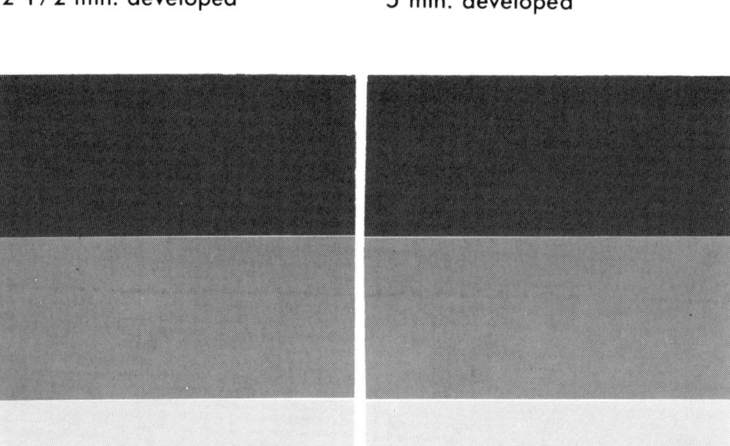

*Illustr. No. 80* **Developing Latitude**

If a lith developer is used for Gevaline Contact Film, a steeper gradation is obtained, although this contrast does not quite reach that of the lith films. Conversely, if an average lith film is developed in a Metol-hydroquinone developer, gradation is less than that of the Gevaline Contact Film in Metol-hydroquinone developer. Such an exchange of developers defeats the purpose and is usually not recommended.

Lately, a trend towards a combination lith-contact film could be noticed. A considerable step forward in this direction is the Gevalith Film.

# Chapter Ten

## FLARE AND ITS INFLUENCE[11]

Flare is the greatest secret enemy in respect to damaging the shadow details in tone reproduction. Flare is diffracted or stray light which is not directly reflected from the original. It puts a fog over the whole film and is very destructive in this respect. Therefore shadow areas on the film obtain more light than anticipated and influence the actual gamma value of the film, resulting in a softer negative as shown in illustration No. 81.

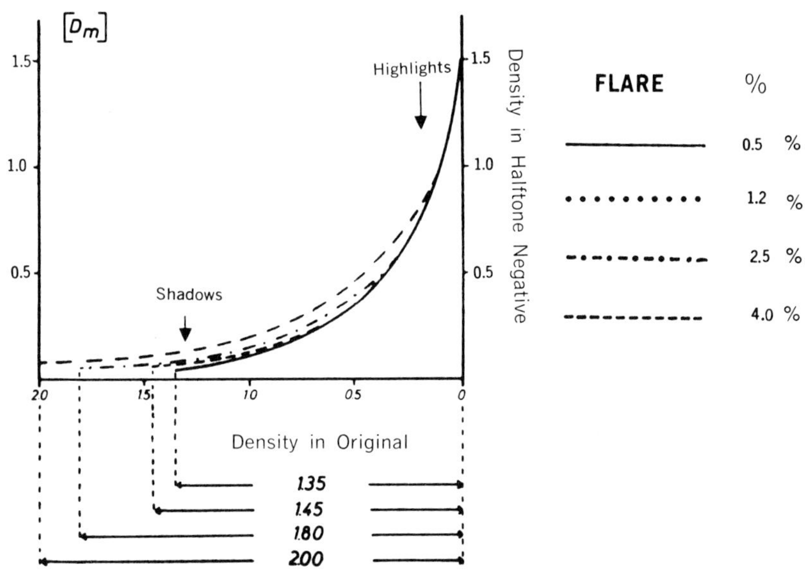


*Illustr. No. 81* **Destructive Effect of Flare**

Fortunately, the lighter the tone values the lesser the influence there is.

## THE CAUSE OF FLARE

Excessive white areas around the lens cause flare. This means not only the immediate surroundings of the original, but also bright walls being too close reflect immense light. The light source of the camera can reflect itself in the glass of the copyboard and throw a tremendous amount of stray light into the lens. It is also very disadvantageous if a camera is standing close to a window or any other light source. Flare can also be created from dirty lenses or scratched filters, just as well as from excessive dust on the inside of the bellow in the camera.

*It is possible to minimize flare.* First of all a big lens hood is very important. Under all circumstances must the copyboard and its surroundings be dull black to stop reflections. Windows or other light sources should not be close to the camera and the intermediate walls should be painted in a matte dark gray. The copyboard glass, the lens system, filters as well as the inside of the camera must be dust free. To prevent flare inside the lens system, the surfaces of all lenses have an anti-reflex coating. All apertures or filter holders used in the lens must also be black. Last but not least all light reflective borders around originals should be covered up with black paper.

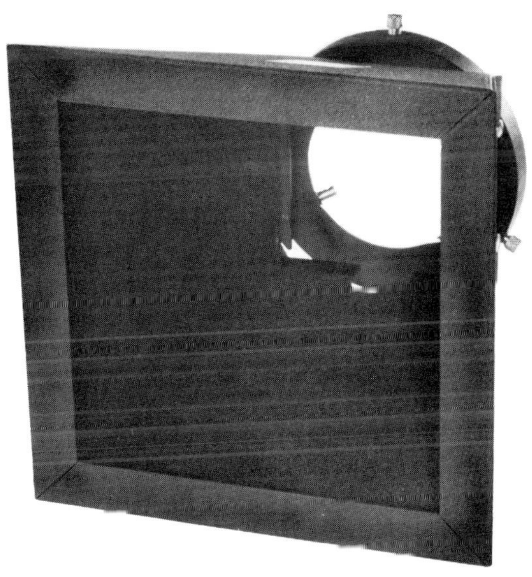

*Illustr. No. 81a* **K & M Lens Shade with Filter Holder**

Flare not only destroys shadow details in continuous tone reproductions but just as much in halftones. If the flare were absolutely equally distributed over the complete film area, and its effect would be below the intensity of a minimum flash exposure, then in many cases it would not cause harm. Nevertheless, the flare might be unevenly distributed and therefore create even more harm. By taking all these precautions into consideration, it is possible to control flare. However, flare cannot be completely prevented. An acceptable minimum is about 2% flare. The dotted line of the previous illustration No. 81 represents 2% flare in a reasonably good camera set-up.

## HOW TO DEFINE FLARE

To be able to determine flare it is customary to express it in percentages. The brightest spot on the original or on an equivalent gray scale step is the basis. Because it reflects all the light possible it is equal to 100%. As we know, minimum flare of 2% is acceptable, and for up to 5% flare it is possible to compensate. More than 5% flare can be prevented. Now it is necessary to learn how flare can be detected.

For easy visual illustration it is best to show the effect of flare with a stepwedge. If no flare is present, a stepwedge with equal steps is obtained as shown in illustration No. 82.

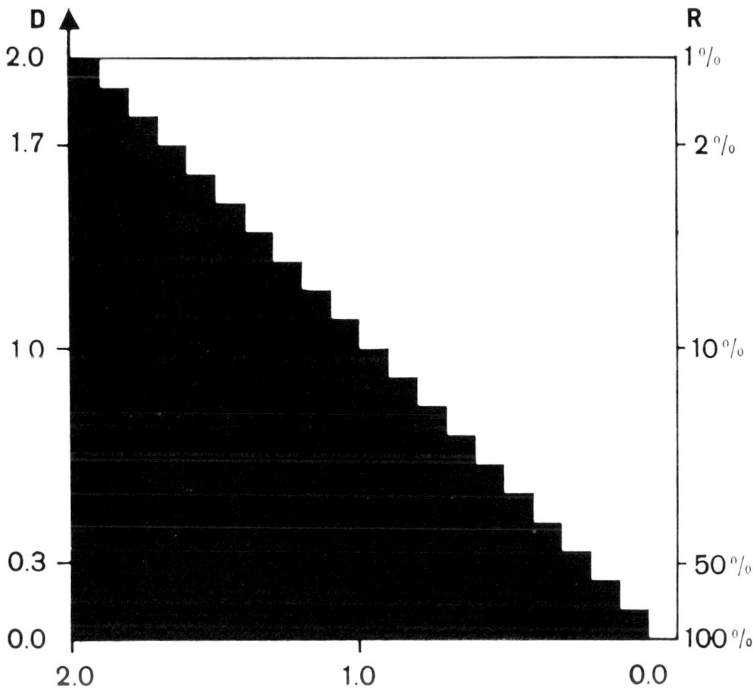


*Illustr. No. 82* **Illustration of Flare**

Flare influences the reproduction in this way that it lowers the contrast range and adds density to the shadow areas of a negative, or highlight areas of a positive. If 2% flare is present, then in addition to its own reflection of the dark areas another 2% of exposure calculated from 100% reflection is given in excess. To be able to calculate with these values it is best to transfer the densities in the gray scale steps into percent or reflection (R) as seen in table No. 83.

| Density in Original | Reflection % | Density in Original | Reflection % |
|---|---|---|---|
| 0,0 | 100 | 1,1 | 7,94 |
| 0,1 | 79,4 | 1,2 | 6,31 |
| 0,2 | 63,1 | 1,3 | 5,01 |
| 0,3 | 50,1 | 1,4 | 3,98 |
| 0,4 | 39,8 | 1,5 | 3,16 |
| 0,5 | 31,6 | 1,6 | 2,51 |
| 0,6 | 25,1 | 1,7 | 2,00 |
| 0,7 | 20,0 | 1,8 | 1,59 |
| 0,8 | 15,9 | 1,9 | 1,26 |
| 0,9 | 12,6 | 2,0 | 1,00 |
| 1,0 | 10,0 | 3,0 | 0,10 |

*Illustr. No. 83* **Density Versus Reflection**

As can be seen, "white" paper with a theoretical density of 0.0 reflects 100% light. A density of 1.0 reflects only 10% and a density of 1.7 only 2% light. To these reflections, expressed in percentages, the percentage of flare has to be added as shown in illustration No. 84.

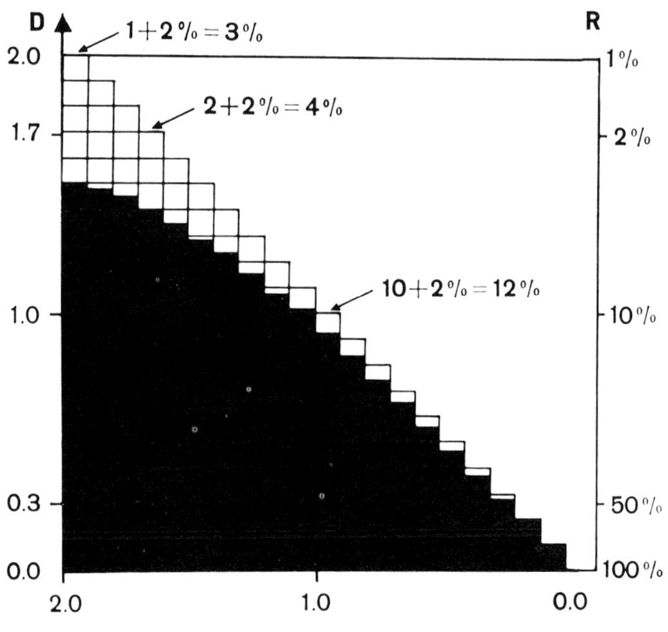


*Illustr. No. 84* **Effect of Flare**

It is surprising that the reflection created by flare can be much higher than the own reflection of the dark areas in the original. However the lighter the original the lower the effect of flare as seen in illustration No. 85.

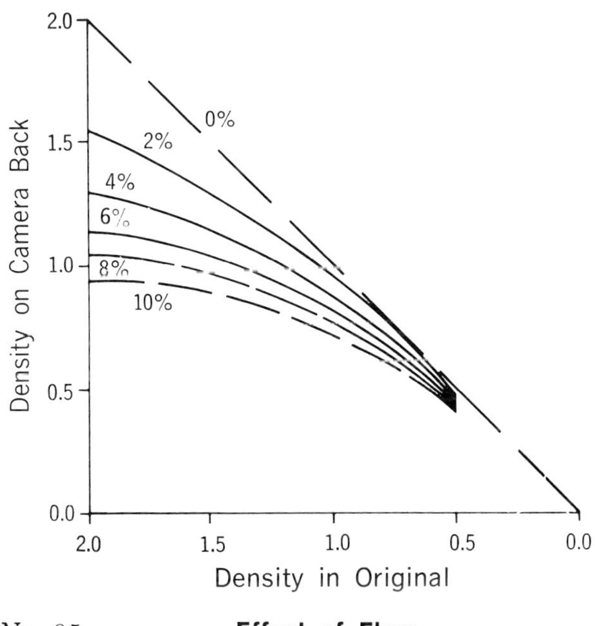


*Illustr. No. 85* **Effect of Flare**

*Quite frankly, it is not sufficiently recognized how severely flare destroys shadow details.* Exact measure has to be taken to prevent excess flare of more than 5%. Below that some compensation and corrections can be made by adjusting to a higher gamma when making continuous tone reproductions.

## VARIATION OF FLARE UNDER DIFFERENT WORKING CONDITIONS

In the following, various sources of flare are described. These evaluations were made on a vertical camera equipped with a lens F:36 cm or F:14.5 inch and four arclamps of 45 amps. each. The average flare on the camera was 2%. These conditions are characteristic for a normal camera setup and are supposed to give close informations to safe endless practical tests.

## EXPOSURE VERSUS FLARE

The length of exposure has no influence on the percentage of flare, as can be seen in illustration No. 86.

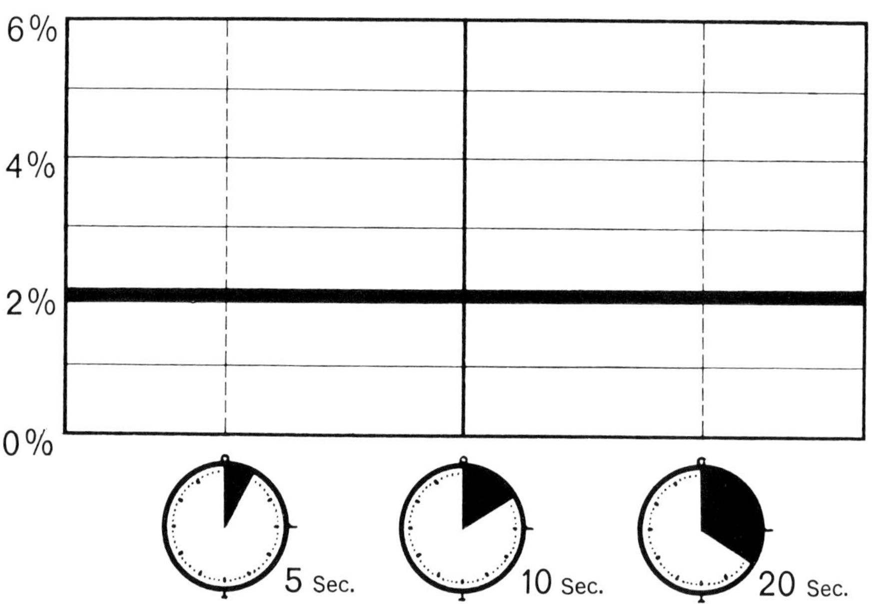


*Illustr. No. 86* **Exposure Versus Flare**

## APERTURE VERSUS FLARE

Small apertures, for instance F:64 compared to F:32, noticeably increase flare at equal size ratios. This is mainly because of the diffraction of light on the edge of the diaphragm, which on a small stop is much more compared with the actual opening of the aperture as shown in illustration No. 87.

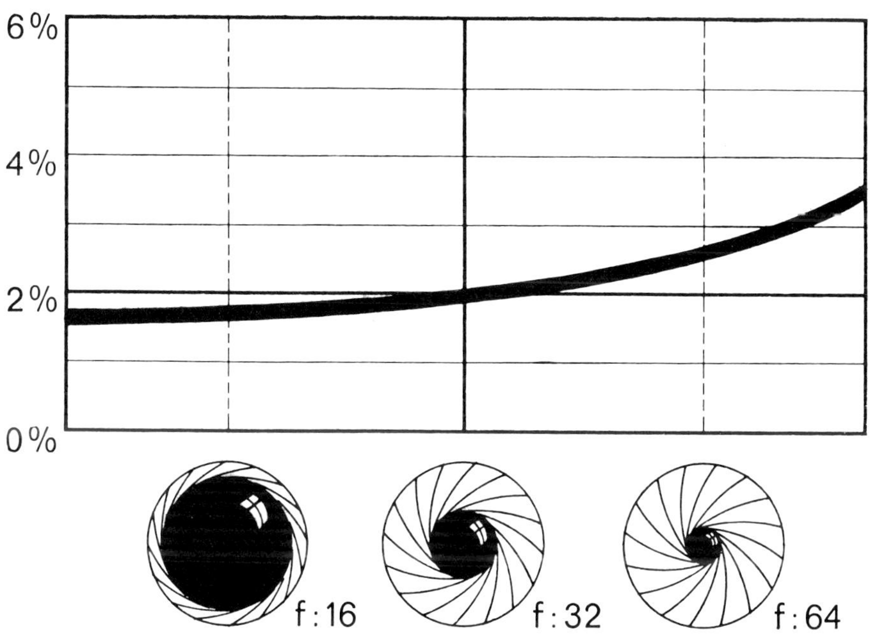


*Illustr. No. 87* **Aperture Versus Flare**

## SIZE RATIO VERSUS FLARE

Enlargements compared to reductions increase flare. Mainly responsible is hereby the reproducible size of the original, as shown in illustration No. 88. However, if an equivalent lens ratio is taken, hardly any changes are noticeable as enlargements will be made with larger apertures than reductions.

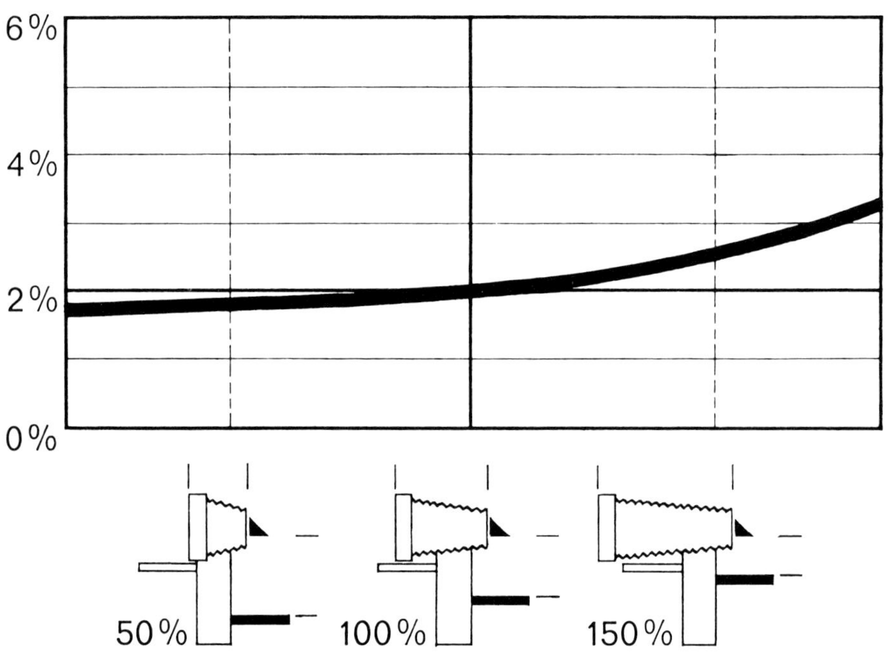


*Illustr. No. 88* **Size Ratio Versus Flare**

## SIZE OF ORIGINAL VERSUS FLARE

The larger the original the more flare is created. In order to equalize flare, a dark gray copyboard, rather than a total black one serves a good purpose.

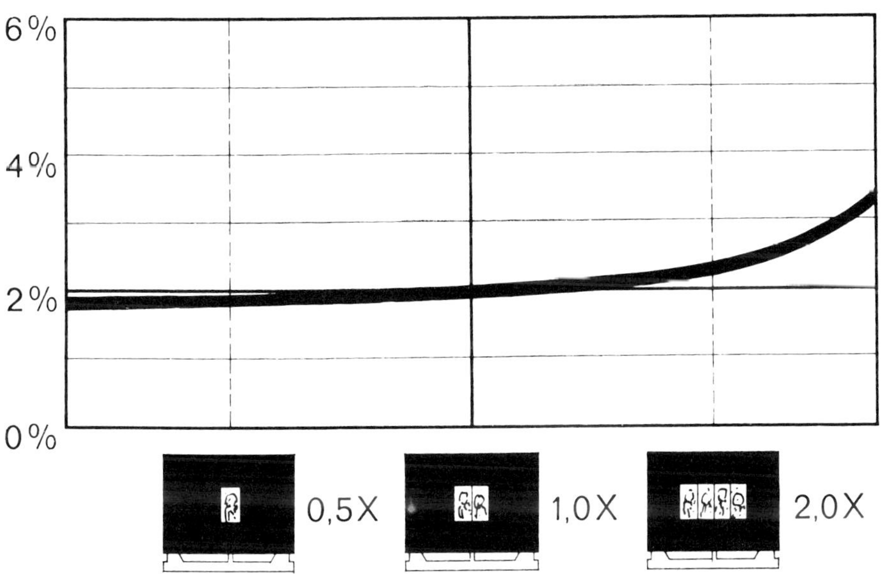


*Illustr. No. 89* **Size of Original Versus Flare**

## DIFFERENT ORIGINALS VERSUS FLARE

The previous evaluations were made with an average original. If all other conditions remain the same then bright originals create more flare than rather dark ones as illustration No. 90 shows.

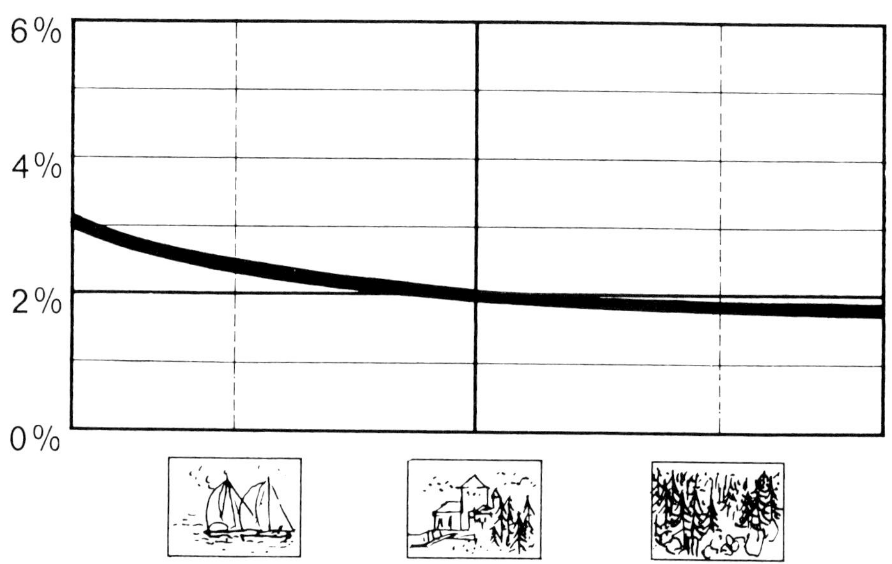


*Illustr. No. 90* **Different Originals Versus Flare**

## SURROUNDING OF ORIGINAL VERSUS FLARE

Much more flare is created when white backgrounds are used on copy holders. This is very obvious in illustration No. 91.

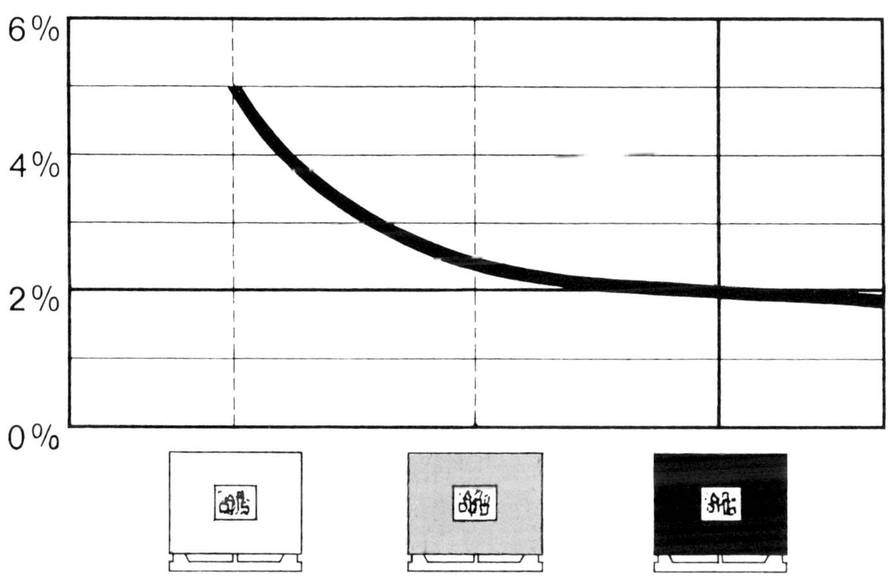


*Illustr. No. 91* **Surroundings of Originals Versus Flare**

## USE OF FILTERS VERSUS FLARE

Basically, color filters as well as genuine neutral density filters do not increase flare as long as they are immaculate. If however, scratches, fingerprints or dust are present, then not only flare is increased rapidly, but also color saturation is degraded as evident in illustration No. 92.

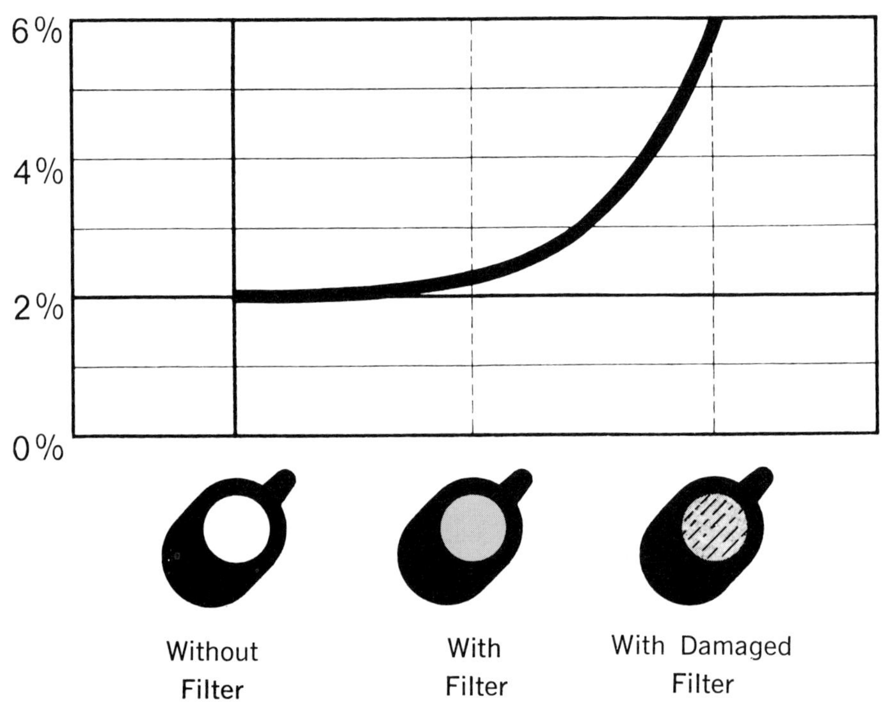


*Illustr. No. 92* **Use of Filters Versus Flare**

## HOW TO IDENTIFY FLARE

For convenient testing Agfa-Gevaert developed a special flare tablet together with a flare calculating disc as shown in illustrations No. 93 and 94.

*Illustr. No. 93* **Flare Tablet**

## FLARE CALCULATING DISC

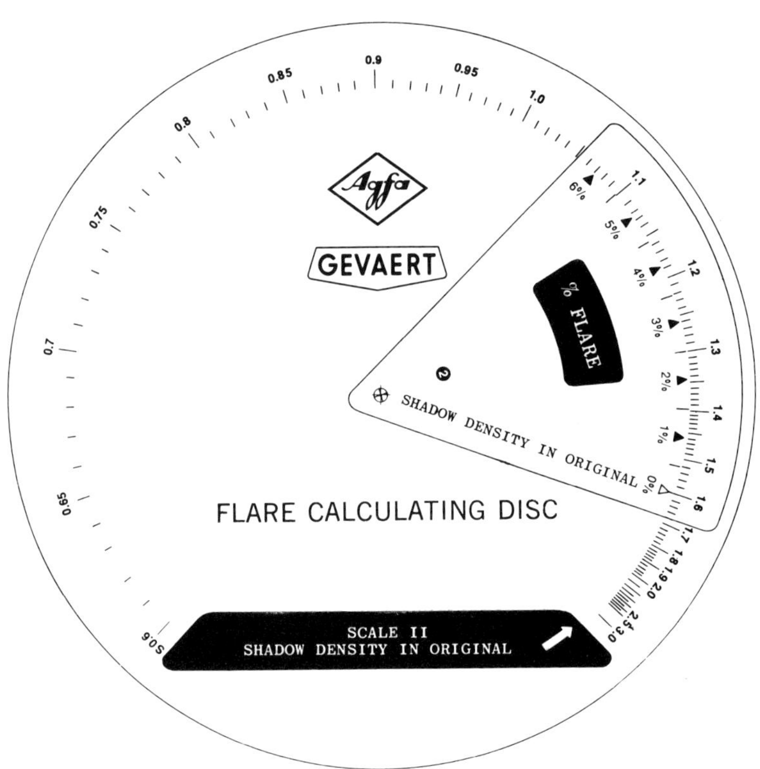


*Illustr. No. 94* **Flare Calculating Disc**

## FLARE CALCULATING DISC

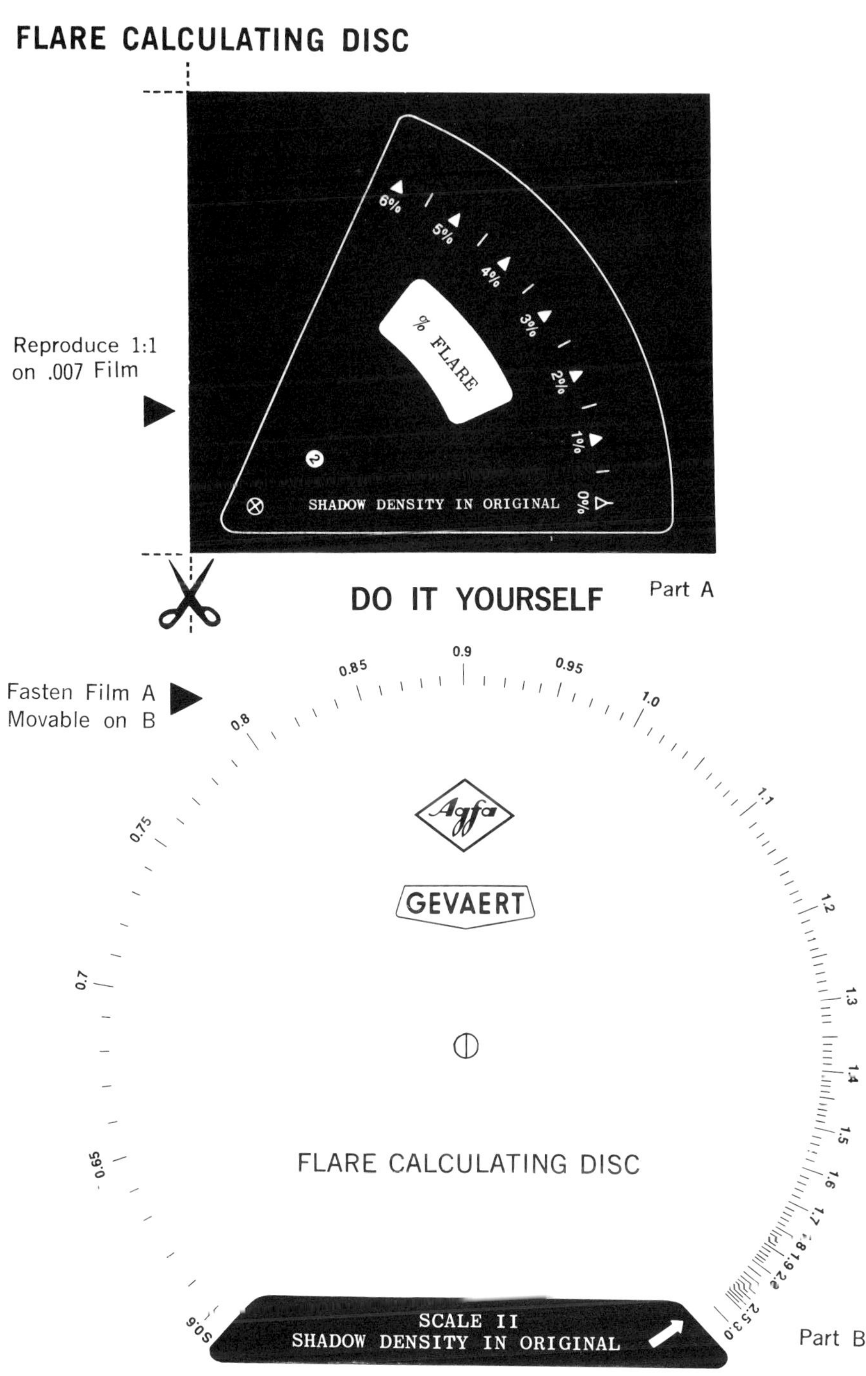


*Illustrs. No. 94a A and B* **Flare Calculating Disc**

## PREPARATION OF THE CAMERA

The flare tablet is put on the copyboard next to an average original. The latter can be simulated with equal size black and white strips of glossy photographic paper, approximately 5 cm. or 2 inches wide and reflection densities of .05-2.10. The area to be covered should be at least twice the square size of the focal length of the lens used. The camera is then focused and the flare tablet located in such a position that the white area A meets with a transparent stepwedge when it is attached over a blue sensitive commercial film (N31) for the exposure on the cameraback. A big clear transparent film helps to keep it in place. See illustration No. 95.

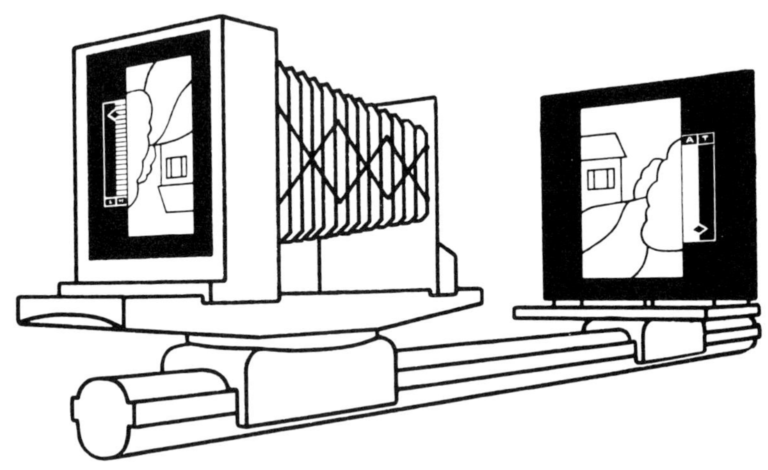

*Illustr. No. 95* **Preparation of the Camera**

## EVALUATION OF THE NEGATIVE

The exposure should be such that the black area T with its density of 2.10 produces a density of at least 0.5 on the film. The actual density is read on a transmission densitometer. Then an equivalent density has to be found on the exposed gray scale created by the exposure through the transparent stepwedge in area A, as explained in illustration No. 96.

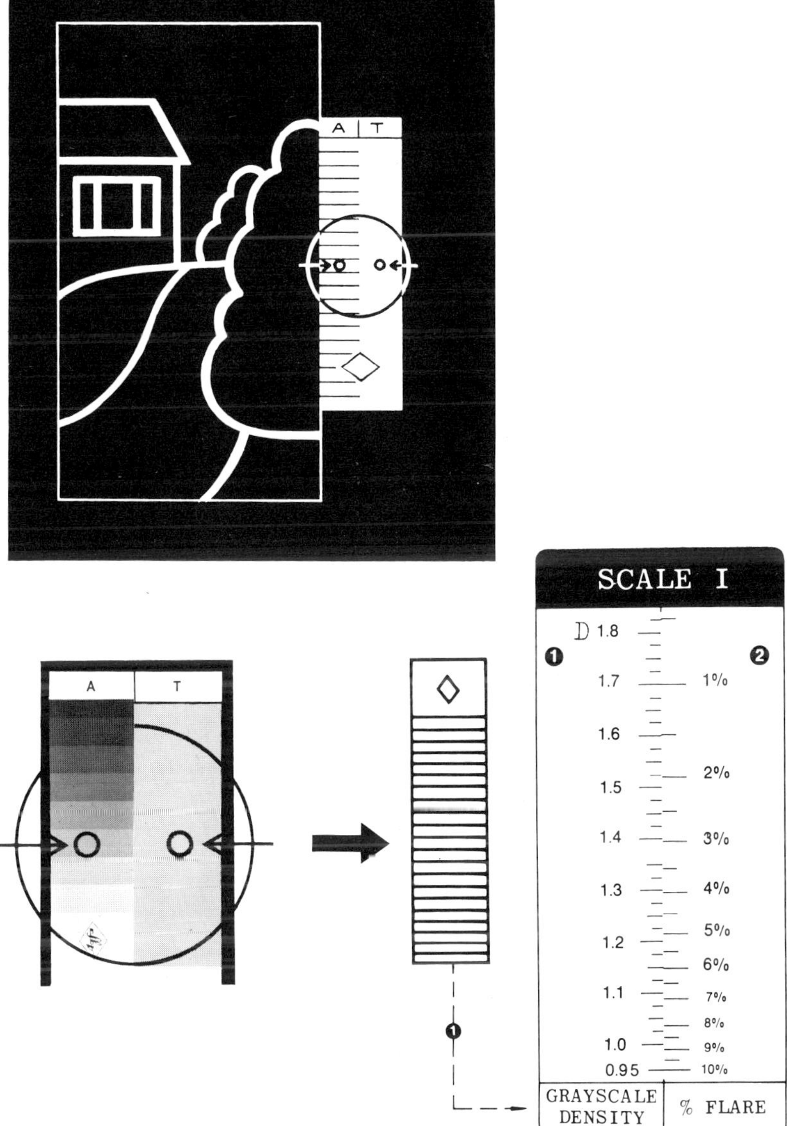


*Illustr. No. 96* **Evaluation of the Negative**

The same step has to be located on the original transparent gray scale stepwedge, and its density read through the clear transparent film which was used to hold the stepwedge in position while on the camera. This density is located on the left hand side ❶ of scale I, then, opposite on the right hand side ❷ the percentage of flare can be simply read off. See illustration No. 96. This result expresses the flare present in this camera. The flare can be read of scale I only, if an original photographic flare tablet is used which has a reflection density of .05 in field A and a reflection density of 2.10 in field T. In case an original flare tablet is not available, it is rather easy to make one with photographic paper.

## DO IT YOURSELF

To be able to make an own flare calculating disc, illustration 94a part A and B is provided. Both parts are reproduced at same size. From part B a copy on photopaper is made. The film reproduction from part A is already final. Part A is put in register with part B and the combination is ready for use.

## USE OF THE FLARE CALCULATING DISC

It serves to find out the effective range of the original.

## PRACTICAL APPLICATION

First of all the reflection densities are read on the darkest and lightest areas of the original in order to figure out the density range. The shadow density, for example 1.6, is located on part B, scale II, of the disc and matched with the indication 0% flare on the movable flare indicator part A or ❷ as seen in illustration No. 94.

The percentage flare obtained with the camera test (and as indicated on scale I) was for example 2%. This is now located on the movable part A or ❷ and the effective density of the original under these particular conditions is then found opposite on part B or scale II and indicates D 1.34.

It is fortunate that light areas are not much influenced by flare, for which reason the calculation for the highlights can be neglected.

## EXAMPLE I

The test exposure on camera A was made at same size and F:32. The original was a black and white print on photopaper.

Evaluation of the original:

| | |
|---|---|
| Density in the shadow | = 1.60 |
| Density in the highlight | = 0.05 |
| Density range | = 1.55 |

Evaluation of the test negative:

| | |
|---|---|
| Density in area "T" | — 0.55 |
| Identical density in step 12 in area "A" | = 0.55 |

Evaluation of the original stepwedge:

| | |
|---|---|
| Density in step 12 | = 1.52 |

Evaluation of Scale I:

D 1.52 is located on the left side ❶ on scale I
2% flare is indicated opposite on side ❷

Calculation for the reproduction:

| | |
|---|---|
| Shadow density with 2% flare | = 1.34 |
| Highlight density with 2% flare | = 0.05 |
| Effective range | = 1.29 |

In case 8% flare were present, the movable part A would have to be forwarded twice 4% + 4% = 8%.

## EXAMPLE II

The test exposure on camera B was made at 90% size and F:45. The original was in watercolor.

Evaluation of the original:

| | |
|---|---|
| Density in the shadow | = 1.45 |
| Density in the highlight | = 0.15 |
| Density range | = 1.30 |

Evaluation of the test negative:

| | |
|---|---|
| Density in area "T" | = 0.48 |
| Density in step 10 | = 0.44 |
| Density in step 9 | = 0.52 |
| Average | = 0.48 |

Evaluation of the original step wedge:

| | |
|---|---|
| Density in step 10 | = 1.33 |
| Density in step 9 | = 1.21 |
| Average | = 1.27 |

Evaluation of scale I:

D 1.27 is located on the left side ❶ on scale I.
5% flare is indicated opposite on side ❷

Calculation for the reproduction:

| | |
|---|---|
| Shadow density with 5% flare | = 1.06 |
| Highlight density with 5% flare | = 0.15 |
| Effective range | = 0.91 |

These indications also give information whether a screen reproduction can be made with one single exposure, or whether and how much flash exposure is necessary to overcome an excess density range which a particular screen might not be able to cover. For continuous tone reproductions it would indicate to what gamma one has to develop.

As proven with these results, flare is much more harmful than generally realized. These unconsidered facts very often seem to be the course of undetectable variations in otherwise well standardized operations. Nevertheless, being able to calculate and compensate for the destructive flare puts us into a position where the techniques of exposure and developing can be adjusted to diminish this destruction for black and white as well as for color reproductions.

There are several different flare tests available now. One, published by Eastman Kodak Co., is a visual flare test which should prove very revealing. DuPont also provides information about their flare test.

## BEWARE OF UNSAFE "SAFELIGHTS"

Similar to flare, unsafe darkroom illumination is equally harmful.

Safelights and the recommended filters are designed to be used with 25 watt bulbs maximum. Stronger ones give too intense light and heat as well. Actinic light will expose the film and lead to more or less fog. The filter is usually imbedded between two glass plates but the too intense heat will not only bleach the filter but also create hairline cracks which will further expand to the point where white light will strike the film and fog it. A safelight filter is best inspected with a complementary filter to reveal these otherwise hard to detect deficiencies.

## SAFELIGHT TESTS

To make meaningful safelight tests it is not sufficient to expose the film to the safelight only. Even so, this might not give a visible fog by itself, it would certainly add to the actual exposure and this way give built-in destruction.

For this reason a regular halftone exposure is given to the film. To take an 18 x 24 cm. or 8 x 10 inch stepwedge would be ideal. It is carefully protected from the safelight first but after the halftone exposure has been made 3 cm. or 1¼ inches are covered completely and safelight exposures added in 3 cm. or 1¼ inch strips for ½, 1, 2, 4 and 8 minutes. After the film is developed only a smooth grayscale should be visible. If however darker stripes are visible this reveals that from this time on the safelights have a destructive effect which cannot be tolerated. They should then be checked to find out whether the filter is still perfect, whether the bulb is within the 25 watt limit and that the safelight is a least 1 meter or 3 feet away from the working area. If everything would check out alright, it would indicate that the safelight filter is too transparent and a darker one would have to be used.

This is particularly important if lith film is developed in a one solution metol or phenidon developer because in it the speed increases about 3-4 times over a lith developer.

## ULTRAVIOLET LIGHT INFLUENCE

Similar to flare, other disturbing difficulties can arise due to the influence of U.V. radiation. Again like with flare and stray light, U.V. rays cannot be seen with the naked eye. Xenon and arc light contains a large portion of ultraviolet which, depending on the characteristic of the original copy and the artists paint used, could reflect or absorb the U.V. rays.

In addition, it could also make the paper and the paint fluoresce. The latter can be revealed by illuminating the original with a U.V. lamp. Naturally, because U.V. light is invisible it cannot be detected whether the U.V. rays are reflected or absorbed.

Due to the spectral sensitivity of photographic film, the effect is not necessarily in line with what one might expect. For instance, areas which fluoresce gives less density on the film than areas which just reflect U.V. the latter which gives the highest density. This is because the photographic emulsions are generally very sensitive to U.V. For this reason the lowest density is obtained from areas which absorbs U.V.

To overcome these often unpredictable difficulties it is best to eliminate U.V. rays before they hit the copy. A special clear mylar film is put in front of the light source and absorbs the U.V. radiation before it can create any problems which is much more effective as if a U.V. filter would be used in the lens. Even so the U.V. sheet is transparent, the exposure has to be doubled.

## RE-SCREENING

It is often necessary to make halftone reproductions from already screened prints. To simply photograph these as a fine-line reproduction is usually not possible because the print does not have the quality necessary. In addition, the dot sizes might be so extreme small or large that a true reproduction is not possible.

Many different attempts have been practiced to overcome the original screen pattern while re-photographing it. To go the indirect way does not help much, to make the image unsharp, rock the camera or wiggle a clear film in front of the lens while exposing, is a very unpredictable way and leads to detail deficiencies. The main trouble is that while making a halftone from an already screened image, a moiré pattern appears. Some mechanical devices are available to overcome these problems and simplify the procedure and get optimum quality.

A comparatively simple way is to use an optical device consisting of a set of re-screening lenses known as the Caprock Re-Screener. It is used for direct re-screening of halftones without moiré, for producing continuous tones from halftones and for eliminating graininess from enlargements.

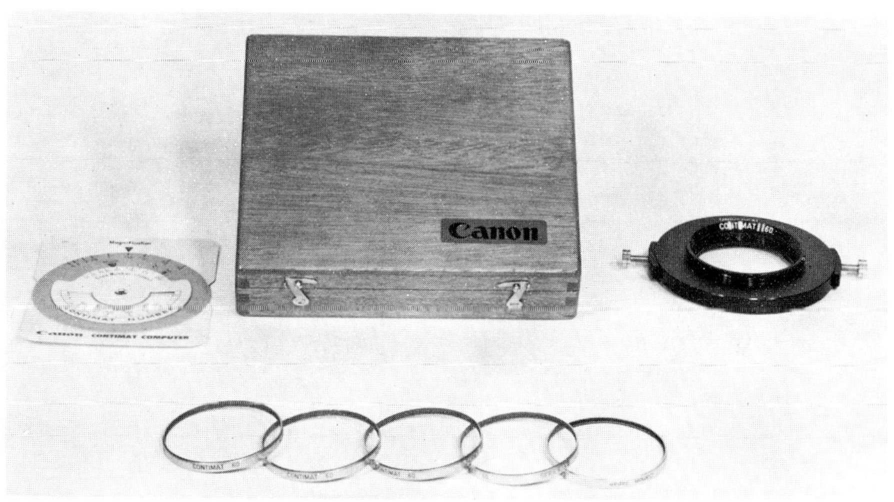

*Illustr. No. 96a* **Caprock Re-Screener**

It permits the screening of black and white and colored halftone copy without moiré using any desired enlargement, reduction, or halftone screen, all in one step, without re-makes. It prevents moiré when screening continuous tones containing textile patterns, and allows one to inspect the result before the exposure is made. Consisting of a set of five filters, clear glass, holder, computer and instruction booklet.

A highly sophisticated re-screening device is available from Klimsch known as the "Variomat". It is also used in connection with the camera lens to reproduce halftone copies free of moiré with the highest degree of detail. The Variomat works on the principle of the difracting effect of a plane-parallel glass plate in front of the lens. The glass is rotated by a motordrive and is oscillated with an appropriate cam during exposure. The cams can be exchanged to meet the exact requirements for different screen rulings. The principle hereby is that the halftone dot image in the copy is displaced with such an exactness that a continuous tone original is simulated.

## HOW DOES STILL DEVELOPMENT FUNCTION

Still development is of advantage mainly when originals of extreme contrast have to be unified. For instance, when the original has extremely fine detail in both shadow as well as highlight areas, it is quite difficult to hold both ends. Unfortunately by the time the shadow details are developed, the highlights are closed up. Conversely, if development is stopped just in time when the small highlight details are perfect, then, the fine shadow details are not sufficiently established. This is the case with halftone as well as with line originals.

With halftones this is generally overcome by giving a flash exposure, which when over done can again jeopardize the quality. Even so a short minimum flash exposure is helpful for line work if it is not commonly used. There, still development is a real asset.

Naturally this is in respect to developing with super high contrast Lith A & B developer. The contrast is so great that it supresses the extreme details if its function is not fully understood and properly controlled.

Actually, it is quite easy to understand how still development functions.

When the developer is agitated as usual, the chemistry being used-up by processing the exposed areas is washed away and constantly replaced by fresh developing agents. This way, the highlights are quickly developed to completion while the shadows lack behind. If processing is continued the shadows are obtained while the highlights are lost.

In still development one takes advantage of the developer getting exhausted. To start with, processing takes place as usual, in other words vigorous agitation for about 1 minute until the image starts to appear. Then the tray is left alone. The tray must be absolutely flat without any ribs. Also it must be horizontally placed and sufficient developer must cover the film with a uniform layer. Air bubbles can be eliminated by slightly blowing onto them.

Since the developer gets used-up and partly exhausted on the areas which develop first, it slows down in proportion. Conversely, in the shadow areas where no developing takes place for quite some time, the developer actively works out the small details. Exposure as well as developing time is to be extended by about 25% It is also important to have a good safelight in order to inspect the film while it must remain in the tray. The film can not be taken out of the tray and inspected by holding it in front of a safelight, otherwise the effect of still development is jeopardized when it is re-inserted into the tray.

# Chapter Eleven

## STANDARDIZATION IN HALFTONE REPRODUCTION[12]

*It is of utmost importance to take full advantage of all knowledge gained at all times.*

Undoubtedly there are many very efficient automatic exposure devices available. Naturally like with most computer equipment, the outcome is only as good as what has been pre-programmed into it. Therefore the following evaluations will be at least very helpful by themselves in order to understand these important functions much better and get more use out of them.

To be able to get the full benefit, a strict pattern must be followed. As will be explained, not even too many tests are necessary, however they have to be very thoroughly evaluated. Unfortunately, in too many cases people depart more or less from set procedures, and as they get lost, they cannot keep track of what is happening. As a result, due to lack of confidence, they go back and stick to their old method, leaving no chance for improvements.

## THE EVALUATION OF THE ORIGINAL

Standardization already starts with the evaluation of the original. For this reason the highlight and shadow densities must be read. After the highlight density is subtracted from the shadow density, the contrast range is obtained. These facts as well as the size ratio should be marked on the back of the original.

The exposure adjustment for the size changes is compensated for by applying an equivalent lens ratio.

Depending on the contrast of the original two or three exposures are necessary with a glass screen. These are:

Main Exposure
No Screen Exposure
Flash Exposure

With an Agfa-Gevaert Contact Screen, only one or two exposures are necessary as the no screen exposure is built into the screen. The tests for each of these three individual exposures should be made from a wide 18x24 cm, or 8x10 inch step tablet* $\sqrt[3]{2}$ containing 20 steps between D 0.1-2.0. Besides this gray scale, graph paper is required to be able to prepare the necessary graphs as will be described. Plain universal standard graphs for main, flash and no screen exposures are provided in the four illustrations No. 98, 101, 104, 106. These can be reproduced to larger sizes and will serve as a basis in which all findings can be marked as shown in the illustrations No. 99, 102, 105, 107. Especially the combined graph No. 103 is very simple to use, as it gathers all three exposures on one sheet.

To assure exacting exposures the camera must have a built-in shutter. If the camera is not provided with it originally, it can be installed later on.

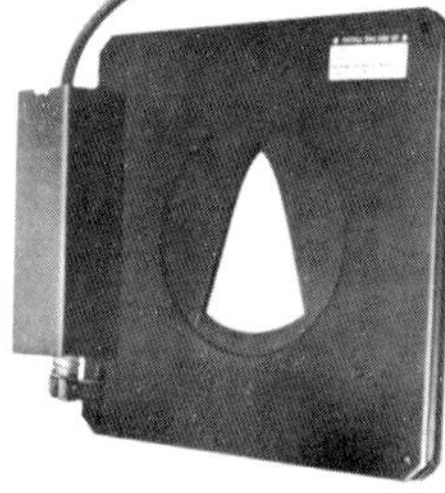

*Illustr. No. 96c* **EMPCO Auto-Electromagnetic Shutter**

## THE PRACTICAL TESTS

The following tests were made under these conditions: Camera No. 1, Light source: Pulsating Xenon, Footcandles: 150, Lux: 1500, °Kelvin: 5500, Lens ratio: F:22, Flare: 2%.

Exposure: With light integrator, one unit basically equal with one second.

Film used: Gevalith Ortho, O81

Developing: In Agfa-Gevaert Lith Developer at 20°C or 68°F with constant agitation.

Screen used: Glass screen No. 80217, 54 lines per cm or 133 lines per inch.

Correct screen distance setting: 1 mm or 2½/64.

For etching method: Offset.



*Available through Perfect Graphic Arts Supply Company, P.O. Box 62, Demarest, N. J. 07627

## THE MAIN EXPOSURE

The first test was exposed with e.g. 100%. It was just one single main exposure in order to learn about the basic contrast range the screen is able to cover. Besides that it is possible to determine the correct main exposure time. It should be as such that the integral density reading on step D 0.1 in the original, reads on the halftone negative.

D 0.3 for conventional letterpress etching

D 0.5 for powderless etching

D 0.6 for offset.

This leaves enough space to be able to add the necessary amount of no screen exposure in order to get a final higlight density reading of D 1.4-D 1.5 for powderless etching or offset. Nevertheless if the Agfa-Gevaert Contact Screen is used it does not require a supplementary exposure without screen and the main exposure alone must be longer to produce the density of 1.4-1.5 right away.

The first exposure with the glass screen produced a density in step D 0.1 of D 0.7. However, as this step should have a density of only D 0.6 for offset, the exposure had to be shortened to only 80% of the first test exposure, and came to 30 seconds.

This exposure adjustment can very easily be read of a slide rule. For example, the exposure time of 100% or the exact amount of units exposed is lined up on the "C" scale on top of the "L" logarithmic scale, matching the density 0.7 obtained in the first negative. The cursor is then lined up on the "L" scale with the density required in this example 0.6. On the "C" scale the correct exposure such as 80% or the amount of units can be read of, as shown in Illustr. No. 96d.

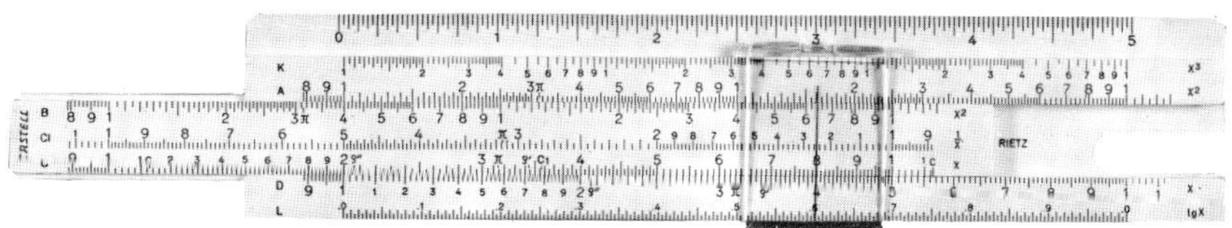


*Ilustr. No. 96d* **Exposure Time Calculation with the Slide Rule**

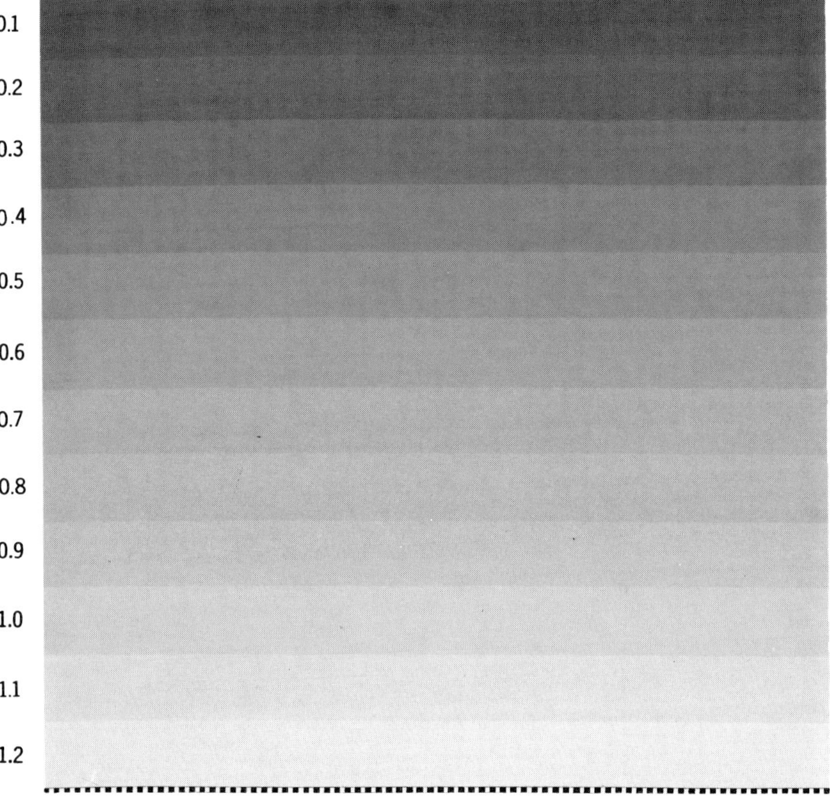


*Illustr. No. 97* **Result of the Main Exposure**

The second main exposure test was therefore exposed accordingly and produced the correct density of 0.6 in step 0.1, however variations of + 0.1 or —0.05 are allowed. On the other end a printable pinpoint was obtained in step 1.2. The useable range the screen can cover is therefore 1.1 as can be seen in illustration No. 97.

The values obtained in this main exposure negative are now characteristic and serve as a basis for all further work. To be able to apply it easily to originals with highlight densities different than 0.1, a graph is set up in the following way, as shown in illustrations No. 98 and No. 99.

## THE ESTABLISHMENT OF THE EXPOSURE GRAPHS

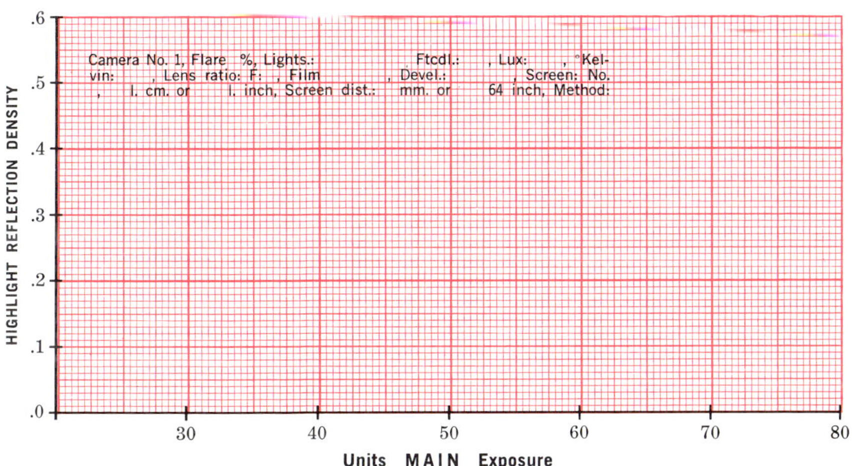


*Illustr. No. 98* **Plain Graph for the Main Exposure**

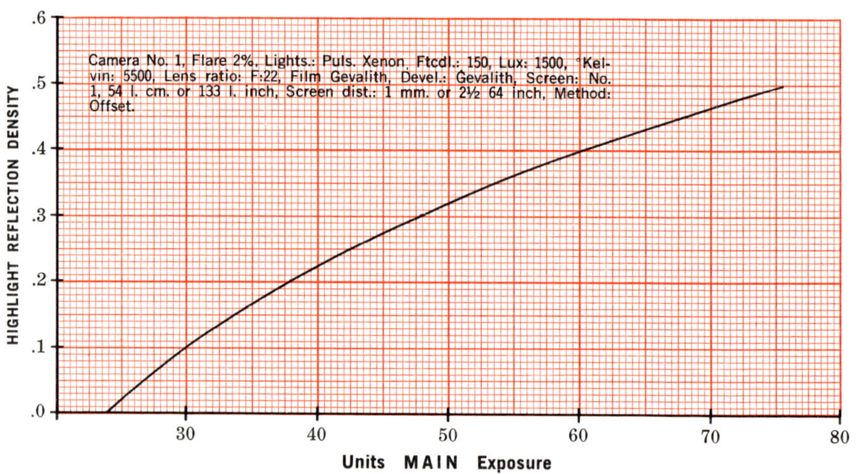


*Illustr. No. 99* **Final Graph with Main Exposure Results**

An increase in density by 0.1 needs an increase of 1.26 in exposure. With this in mind the graph is established on millimeter paper. The exposure is marked in units or seconds on the axis of abscissas, and the highlight densities of the original are marked from 0.1-0.6 on the ordinate axis. The curve then results from the following values:

Exposure with highlight density 0.1 = 30.0 sec.
Exposure with highlight density 0.2 = 30.0 sec. x 1.26 = 37.8 sec.
Exposure with highlight density 0.3 = 37.8 sec. x 1.26 = 47.6 sec.
Exposure with highlight density 0.4 = 47.6 sec. x 1.26 = 60.0 sec.
Exposure with highlight density 0.5 = 60.0 sec. x 1.26 = 75.6 sec.

These values are marked in the appropriate position of the coordinating system and connected with a French curve or more exact with a logarithmic spiral to get intermediate values.

Example: If an original has a highlight density of 0.27, then this value is located on the vertical axis. It is transferred to the right till it meets with the characteristic curve of the main exposure. That point is followed straight down and the horizontal axis shows the indication of a necessary exposure of 44.5 seconds.

Of course, it would also be possible to read these values directly from the "L" respectively "C" scales on the slide rule.

## THE FLASH EXPOSURE

It is necessary to make a flash exposure test to find out what exposure is required to overcome a certain excess density range in the original.

A step tablet is exposed with the same suitable main exposure as previously determined. After this, different additional flash exposures of 2, 4, 6, 8, 10 seconds are stepped onto the film. It is important to use the same stop as used for the main exposure. This is absolutely necessary when using a glass screen to keep the perfect screen distance. The basic exposure time can be regulated by means of a neutral density filter to avoid too short exposures when working with this large aperture. However, it would even be easier to select a bulb weak enough when working with a flash exposure lamp. If no flash lamp is available, then it is advisable to give the flash exposure with a gray paper rather than with a white one.

After the film is processed under the same condition as the main exposure test, the effect of the different flash exposures can be seen easily. This density step which has produced the required printable pindot is underlined as explained in illustration No. 100.

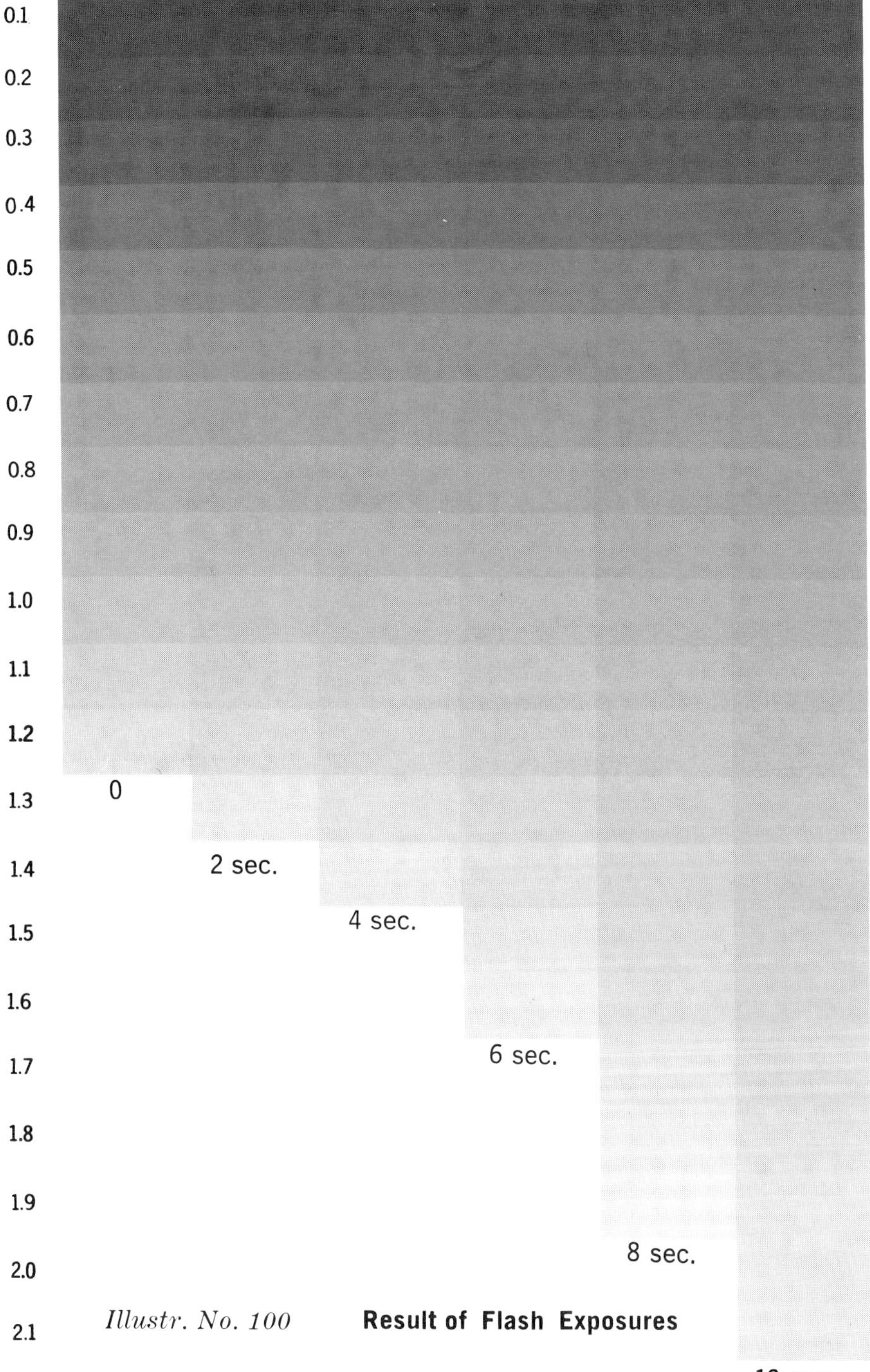


*Illustr. No. 100* **Result of Flash Exposures**

In evaluating the densities in the original step tablet, it is now possible to find out the contrast range which the screen can cover with the different flash exposures. For exact and easy practical application it is best to set up a graph for the flash exposure as shown in illustrations No. 101 and 102.

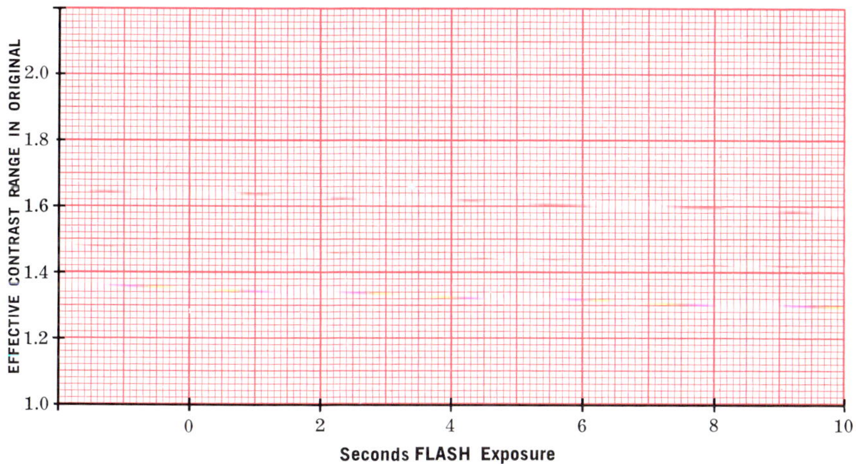


*Illustr. No. 101* **Plain Graph for the Flash Exposure**

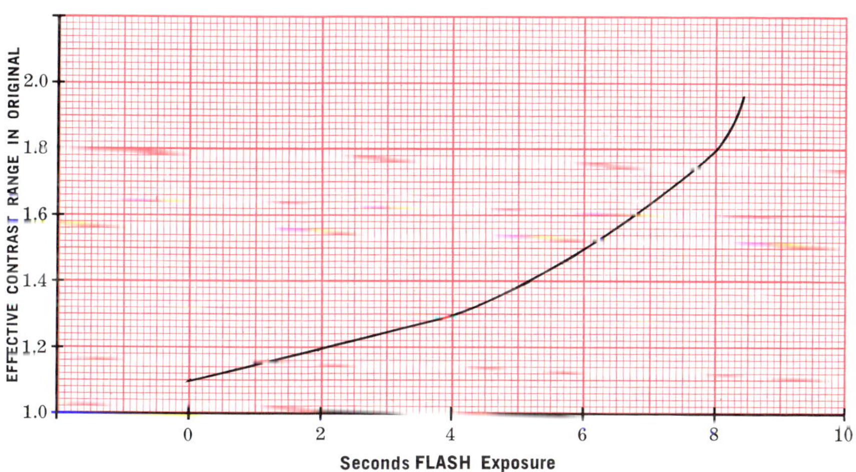


*Illustr. No. 102* **Final Graph with Flash Exposure Results**

On the ordinate axis, possible excess densities are marked. On the axis of abscissa, the different flash exposure times are marked. The excess ranges possible to cover are marked in the height of the particular densities above the exposure given.

| Flash Exposure Given: | Density Range Covered: |
|---|---|
| none | 1.1 |
| 2 seconds | 1.2 |
| 4 seconds | 1.3 |
| 6 seconds | 1.5 |
| 8 seconds | 1.8 |
| 10 seconds | 2.1 |

All necessary flash exposures to suit different originals can now be read from the graph.

| Effective Contrast Range in the Original: | Excess Densities in the Original: | Flash Exposure Required: |
|---|---|---|
| 1.25 | 0.15 | 3.0 seconds |
| 1.40 | 0.30 | 5.1 seconds |
| 1.57 | 0.47 | 6.6 seconds |
| 1.70 | 0.60 | 7.5 seconds |
| 1.95 | 0.85 | 8.4 seconds |

## THE HIGHLIGHT EXPOSURE

This exposure must be made without a screen to assure best results as explained in detail in chapter four. The test is made in the following way. A film has to be exposed through the screen from the gray scale with an average medium main exposure and an average flash exposure learned from the last two tests. After this the screen is removed and actual line exposures of 5, 6, 7, 8, 9% based on the main exposure time, are stepped onto the film. For more exact exposure control a neutral density filter can be applied. It is important to compensate for the glass thickness of the screen to assure perfect registration.

Developing is again carried out under identical conditions as before. The exposure which produced the correct highlight dots, in this case amounts to 7%, or 2.1 seconds, serves as a basis for further calculations.

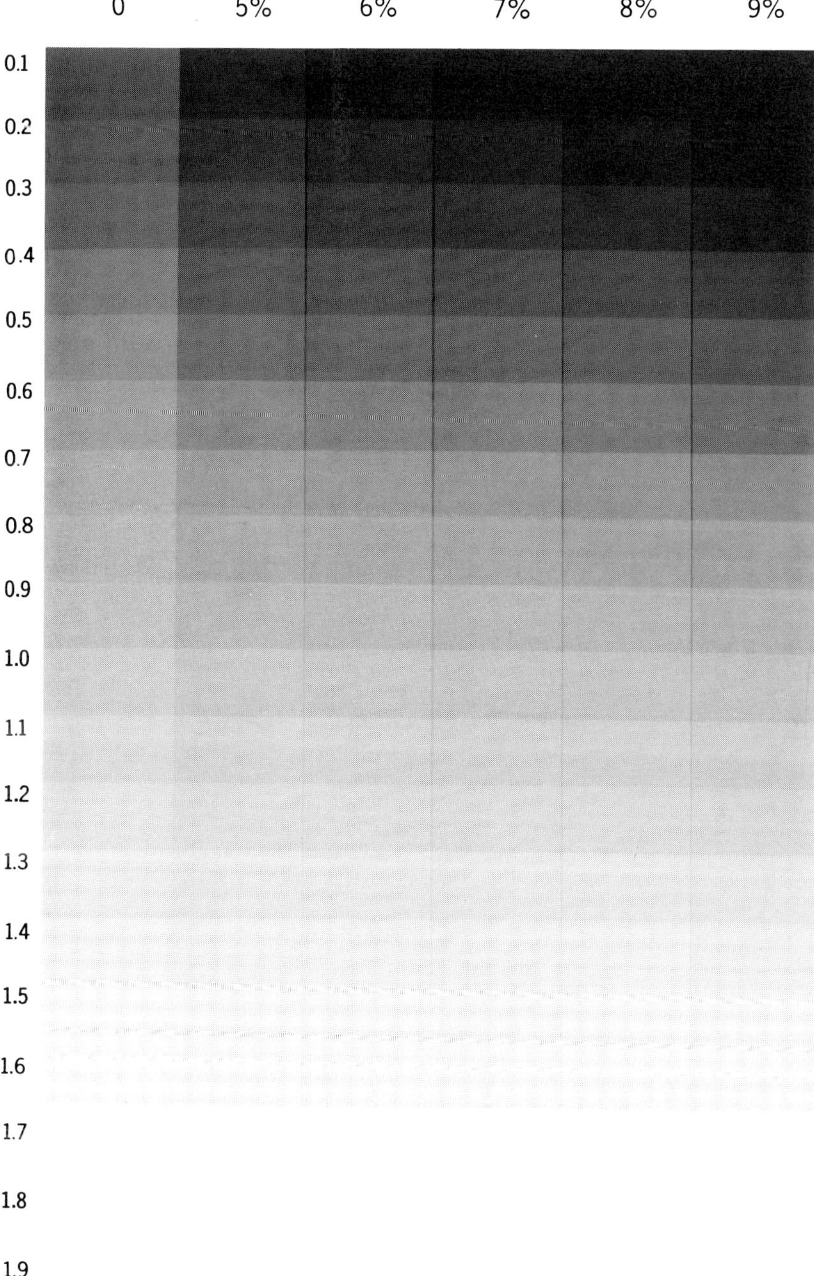


*Illustr. No. 103* **Results of No Screen Exposure**

The exposure increase for originals of different highlight reflection can now be calculated in the same way as it is explained for the main exposure where a factor of 1.26 of exposure adjustment compensates for a 0.1 difference in reflection density. With these informations the final graph for the highlight exposure can be established as shown in illustrations No. 104 and 105.

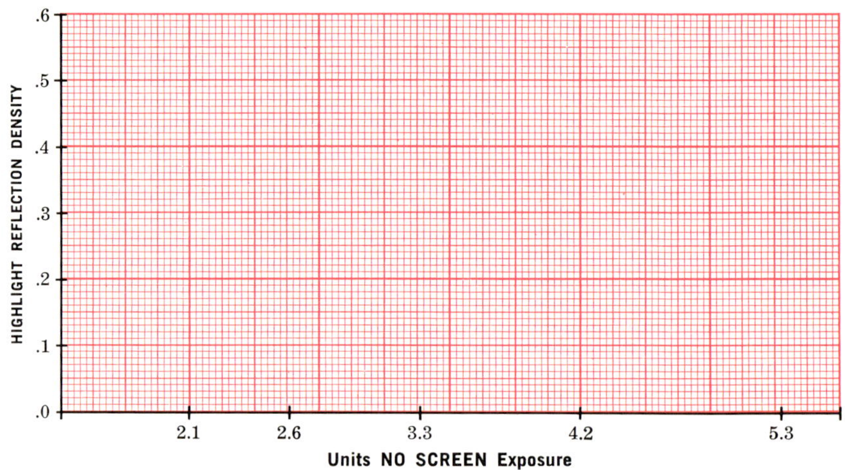


*Illustr. No. 104* **Plain Graph for No Screen Exposure Results**

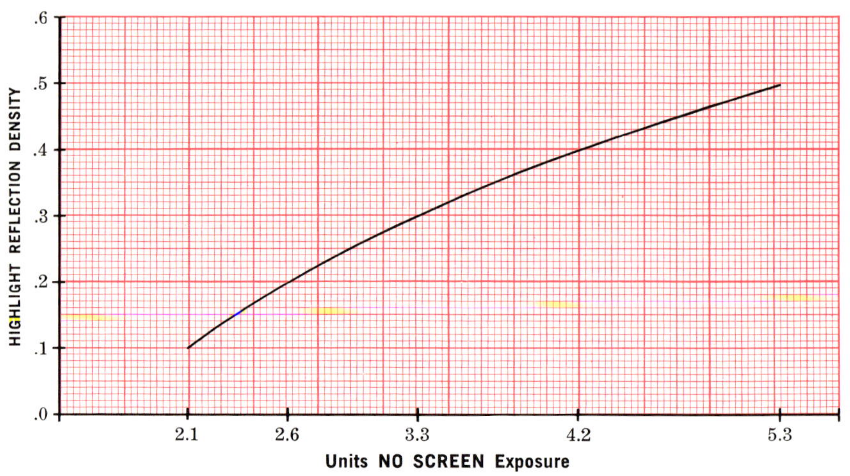


*Illustr. No. 105* **Final Graph with No Screen Exposure Results**

EXAMPLE:

| Highlight density in the original | No screen exposure |
|---|---|
| 0.1 | 2.1 seconds |
| 0.2 | 2.6 seconds |
| 0.3 | 3.3 seconds |
| 0.4 | 4.2 seconds |
| 0.5 | 5.3 seconds |

For more exact exposure control a suitable N.D. Filter can be applied.

## PRACTICAL USE OF THE EXPOSURE GRAPHS

The following explanations show again how the graphs can serve for practical use. The screen used for these tests, reproduced a basic contrast range of 1.1 with the single main exposure.

| Test Original: | Shadow density | 1.80 |
|---|---|---|
| | Hightlight density | —0.20 |
| | Density range | 1.60 |
| | Influence of flare 2% | —0.25 |
| | Effective density range | 1.35 |

As the main exposure can only cover a 1.1 range, a flash exposure must be given to overcome the excess density from 1.1-1.35 = 0.25. The 1.35 is located on the ordinate axis of the flash exposure graph and followed horizontally till it meets with the characteristic curve. From there a vertical line is drawn to the axis of abscissa where a necessary:

Flash exposure = 4.6 seconds

is indicated.

As the highlight density in the original is 0.2, this density is located on the ordinate axis of the main exposure graph and followed horizontally till it meets with the characteristic curve. From there a vertical line is drawn to the axis of abscissa where the necessary:

Main exposure = 37.6 seconds

is indicated.

The no screen exposure is also based on the highlight reflection density of 0.2. This is again located on the ordinate axis of the no screen exposure graph and followed horizontally till it meets with the characteristic curve. From there a vertical line is drawn to the axis of abscissa where a necessary:

No screen exposure = 2.6 sec.

is indicated. Needless to say that if the original is within the range the screen can cover, no flash exposure is required.

## UNIVERSAL STANDARD EXPOSURE GRAPH

These three separate curves can be combined into one single universal standard graph sheet as seen in illustration No. 106.*

For simplification the graph is set up in such a way that all values can be obtained at a glance. The basic exposure ranges provided in the graph are balanced for average conditions and allow a good exposure latitude. In case they canot be met, the lights or aperture can be adjusted, neutral density filters can be applied or the basic values in the graph could be changed. Besides the basic provisions to set up the individual characteristic curves, notations are made to state all equipment, respectively processing characteristics, etc. which are quite often overlooked. See illustration No. 107.

If the Agfa-Gevaert Negative or Positive Contact Screens are used to make halftone negatives or positives, the same kind of graph is applicable except that the no screen exposure and eventually the flash exposure can be eliminated.

The main difference might be the adjustment of the exposure time. Exactly the same applies, when the screening is done in the contact frame rather than in the camera.

Basically the combined graph is established on the same principles as the three separate graphs, but it is much more convenient for daily use. This is of utmost importance as only a handy easily to use aid is carried to full use. Complete standardization with hardly any efforts can be achieved by first measuring and marking all exposure details right on the original. The last and final step would be the processing in an automatic developing machine which eliminates processing fluctuations. The exposure step, which evidently had to be considered the most critical one, boils now down to a simple, easy to control step, when applying the exposure graphs as described.

*These procedures fulfill a long wish-dream and comply with the necessities for combined quality and quanity requirements of our modern times.*



*These plain multicolored standard graphs 30 x 40 cm or 12 x 15 inch can be obtained from Perfect Graphic Arts Supply Company, P.O. Box 62, Demarest, N. J. 07627.

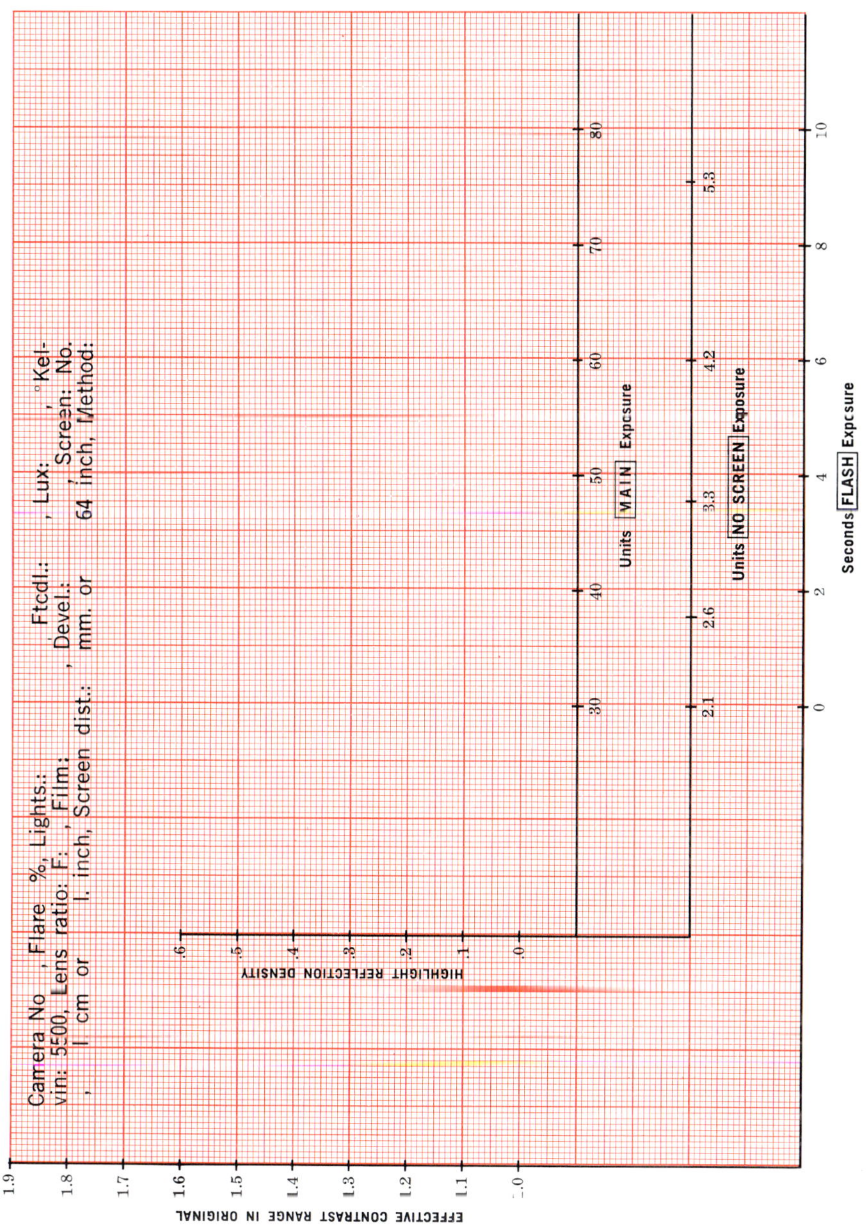


*Illustr. No. 106* **Plain Universal Standard Exposure Graph**

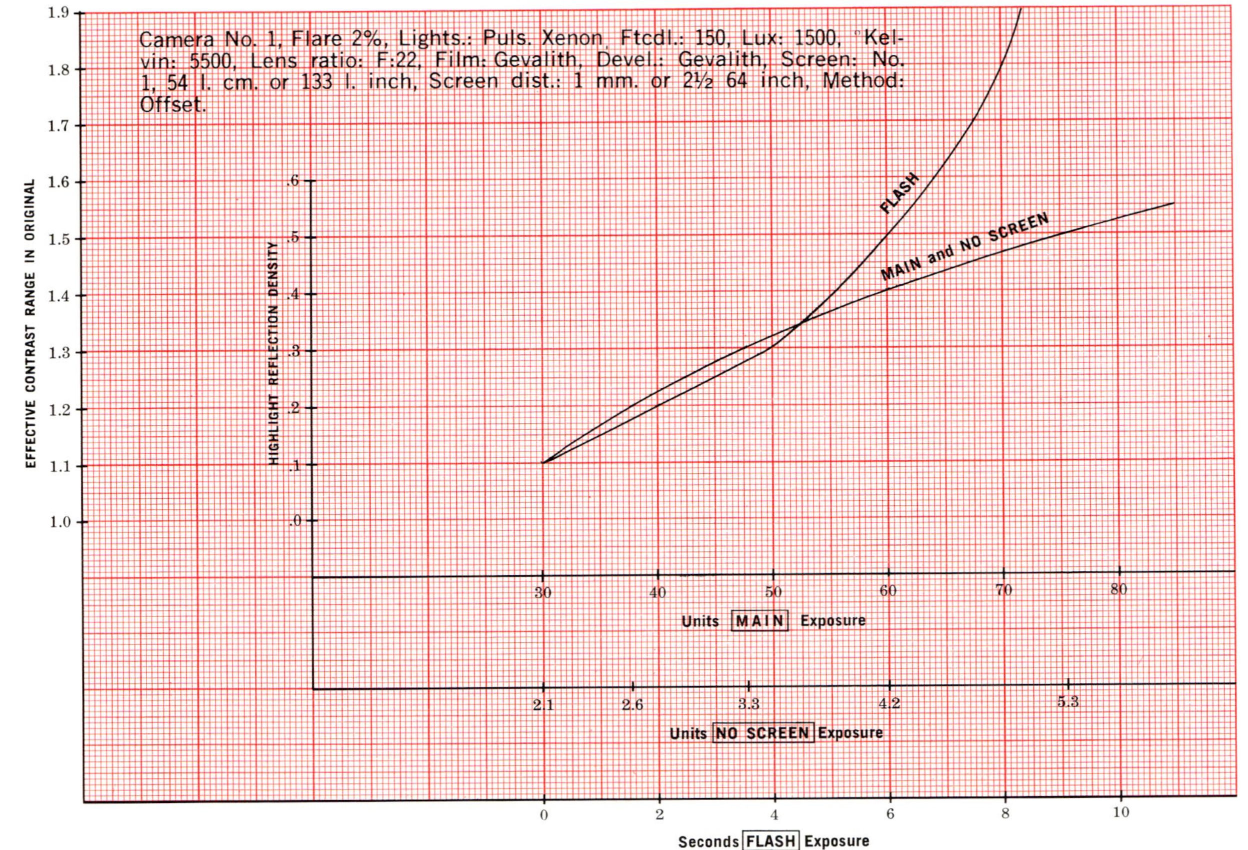


*Illustr. No. 107* **Final Universal Standard Exposure Graph**

## R.I.T.'s "STORC SYSTEM"

Rochester Institute of Technology, Graphic Arts Research Center announced a new product. This is now offered as a new non-graphical method for achieving optimum black and white halftone reproduction called STORC, Screening Test for Optimum Reproduction Conditions.

The procedure includes a special test object which is photographed and then printed. This introduces the characteristics of the camera, plate, and press conditions. An evaluation of the printed test shows what main, bump, and flash exposure values should be used. There is also a Copy Classifier to determine if the illustration is contrasty, normal, low contrast, or very low contrast. Copy can be classified prior to the exposure.

The STORC test is not difficult, but it must be done carefully. And for volume procedure it is an efficient approach for making optimum black and white halftones. It also provides a systematic method for handling poor copy and can be set up as a routine test and compensation for changes in film speed.

The STORC kit contains instructions, test objects, a Copy Classifier, and data forms. For more information, contact the Graphic Arts Research Center, Rochester Institute of Technology, One Lomb Memorial Drive, Rochester, N.Y. 14623. U.S.A.

## Chapter Twelve

# DOT ETCHING ON HALFTONE FILMS

The film's silver content plays a large role in etchability of screen dots, as do dot densities. Here are formulas for etchants and reducers, plus instruments for efficient application.

Even if dependable photo-mechanical masking and reproduction methods are used, some manual tone corrections and color corrections still remain necessary.

Some halftone films lend themselves more to dot reduction than others. They are distinguishable as films which can be etched. The degree of "etchability" is expressed in percentage. In other words, if a film is expected to stand 30% etching, it is required to be able to reduce a 30% dot to a pinpoint. Most important, however, is that the remaining dots retain sufficient density in order to withstand the subsequent exposure in platemaking.

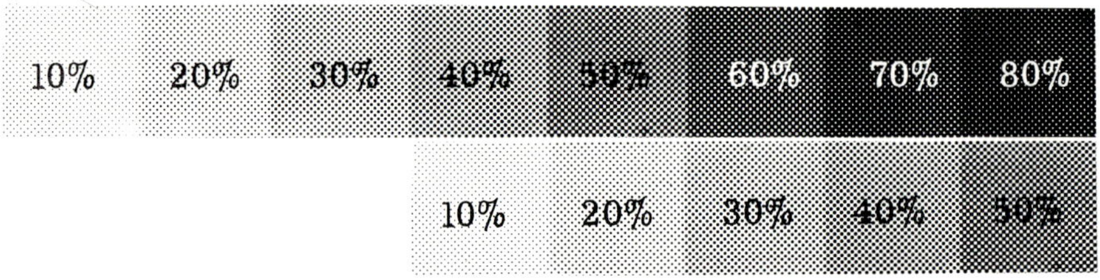

10% 20% 30% 40% 50% 60% 70% 80%

10% 20% 30% 40% 50%

*Illustr. No. 108* **30% Dot Reduction**

Illustration No. 108 shows how the dot sizes in a gray scale reduce after a 30% etching has taken place. Fifty percent dots, also known as checkerboard dots, should withstand a reduction to 20%. It must be expected, however, that extremely heavy areas, which contain 95% dots, reduce somewhat less. This is because disconnected dots are attacked faster and more easily from the sides by the reducer.

It is possible to read an equivalent density of the dot with a densitometer, provided a completely solid area was exposed onto the same film. Nevertheless this holds true only if the entire film was uniformly etched in a tray. If the etching is only carried out partially, for instance with a brush, then a densitometer reading cannot be secured. In this case, it is necessary to check the dot density by inspecting the film against a dark background. Gray or halated dots will then disappear and look as they would finally be obtained on the plate. An experienced eye is necessary to make a predictable judgment. It is therefore suggested that a dependable dark field illuminator (see Illustration No. 73a) be used. A device of this type will reveal the actual printing dot value without any difficulties.

It is generally known that the inspection of dots with bright light does not easily disclose halation, which is why the sophisticated dark field illuminator is used. A light box with an open area for inspection has a movable diffusing glass mounted between the light source and the inspection area. For bright field illumination, the film is inspected with the diffusor in place. For dark field illumination, the diffusing glass is removed and the dots appear as shown in Illustration 41a, clearly revealing the amount of halation.

## THE SILVER CONTENT OF FILMS

The etchability of a halftone dot depends mainly on the silver content of the film used. It is also greatly influenced by the structure of the halftone dot and the dot densities. This is easily understood after studying illustrations No. 109a and No. 109b.

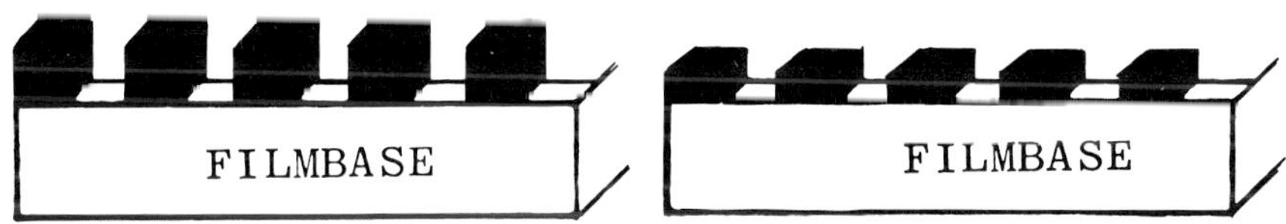


*Illustr. No. 109a* *Illustr. No. 109b*

**Films with Different Silver Content**

Film A and Film B have basically the same dot size, in this example, 50%. Although the dot size is the same in both films, there is a distinguishable difference in the density between the dots in the two films. This is due to the higher silver content in Film A.

When a film is etched, naturally the dots are attacked from the top first. If the etching solution penetrates deeper into the emulsion, then the sides of the dots are attacked, and more and more reduced. Film A withstands much more dot reduction because of the higher silver content. The dots in Film B will lose density rapidly so that the dot size reduction is very limited. In Film A, however, one can afford to lose density while the dots are reduced in size, because enough density will remain to withstand the plate exposure.

## DOT STRUCTURE AND ETCHABILITY

The dot structure is of great influence too. Illustration No. 110a shows dots which are created when exposing through a glass or contact screen. The dots shown in Illustration No. 110b are obtained when hard dot, straight contacts are made.

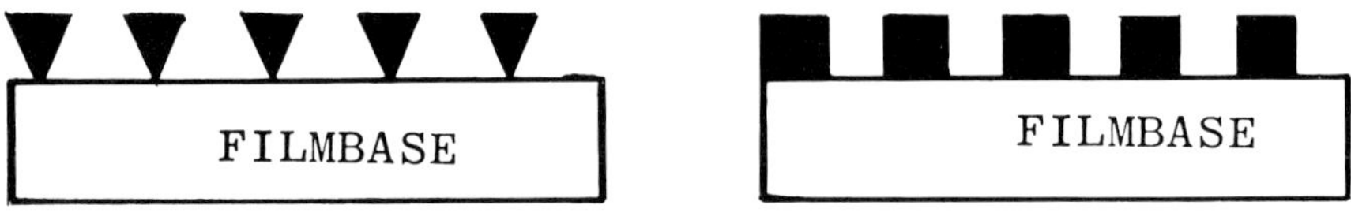


*Illustr. No. 110a* *Illustr. No. 110b*

**Films with Different Dot Structures**

When the dots in Illustration 110a are etched and density is removed from the top, then at the same time the dot size is reduced as well, and can therefore be etched much further as can be seen in Illustration No. 111.

10% 20% 30% 40% 50% 60% 70% 80%

10% 20% 30%

*Illustr. No. 111* **50% Dot Reduction**

The etchability of dots as seen in Illustration No. 110b depends largely on the exposure time and intensity. If not enough exposure is given, the dots have a minimal surface density only and get gray as soon as the etching solution acts (see Illustration No. 112).

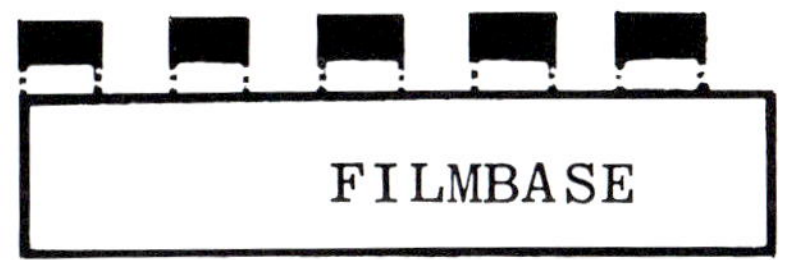


*Illustr. No. 112* **Underexposed Halftone Film**

## CHEMICAL REDUCERS

The most widely used reducer is Farmer's. However, there are ready made reducers available too. It is important to mix the reducer properly if one intends to make his own. Here is a formula for Farmer's reducer:

Solution A:
- 150 grams or 5 oz. sodium thiosulphate
- 12 grams or 0.4 oz. thiourea (in powder form, and very harmful for photographic emulsions. Therefore for optional use only!)
- 1000 cc. or 1 quart water (end volume)

Solution B:
- 50 grams or 1¾ oz. potassium ferricyanide
- 1000 cc. or 1 quart water (end volume)

*Usage:* Mix one part of A with one part of B, plus water, to get the desired etching control.

It is good practice to add a few drops of wetting agent into the solution as it helps to achieve smoother etching.

It is also important to mix only a small amount of A & B just before etching, as the combined solution deteriorates very fast. In bright light, it goes even faster! The same will happen if too much of Solution A is used. This can easily be noticed by the discoloration of the reducer. During the etching procedure, the following chemical reactions take place. The potassium ferricyanide oxidizes the metallic silver into a soluble silver complex, which is dissolved by the sodium thiosulphate. The thiourea prevents the formation of a yellow ghost image on the areas which were etched. Chemically expressed, it results in the following reaction:

$$4K_3Fe\ (CN)_6 + 4AG = 3K_4\ Fe\ (CN)_6 + AG_4\ FE\ (CN)_6$$

It is therefore essential not to use too much potassium ferricyanide as it would bleach out the dots rather than etch them. The etchability of the film in this case would be diminished, because the gray dots would not withstand the exposure during the platemaking. If too much sodium thiosulphate is used, the etching solution decomposes very rapidly. If no thiourea is used, some films show a rather distinct yellow after-image which falsifies the dot reproduction. It must be mentioned, however, that thiourea is a very strong fogging agent when it gets into contact with any unprocessed photosensitive materials. It has to be handled, therefore, with great caution.

More or less dilution of the reducer determines the rate of speed at which the reducer works. It is better to etch slowly rather than risk ruining the film by hurry.

At this point, mention should be made of a relatively new reducer formula which has the same etching characteristics as Farmer's. The advantage is a longer life of the etching bath after A and B have been mixed.

Solution A:
150 grams or 5 oz. potassium ferricyanide
1½ gram or 0.05 oz. potassium metabisulphite
Water to make 1000 cc. or 1 quart end volume

Solution B:
350 grams or 12 oz. ammonium thiocyanate
50 grams or 1¾ oz. potassium bromide
Water to make 1000 cc. or 1 quart end volume

*Usage:* mix 1 part A and 2 parts B, + two parts water.

It is important not to use metal trays as this reducer attacks iron and can even effect stainless steel. One must keep in mind that etching should only be a resource for special correction requirements.

*The goal must always be to take full advantage of most modern photomechanical processes and systems in order to comply with ever increasing demands to stay competitive.*

# ACKNOWLEDGMENT

1. Dr. Werner Rebner: Der Rasterschlüssel, Agfa Leverkusen, Repro-Mitteilung No. 8/1956.

2. Dr. Werner Rebner: Der Richtige Rasterabstand, Agfa Leverkusen, Repro-Mitteilung No. 13/1960.

3. Dr. Werner Rebner: Die Tonwertwiedergabe mit Gravur-und Kontaktraster, Agfa-Leverkusen, Repro-Mitteilungen No. 18/1964.

4. F. J. Tritton and E. T. Wilson; Tone Rendering by Transparent Screen Negatives and Positives, The Photographic Journal, London 1939, p. 396-406.

5. V. G. W. Harrison, G. A. Mitchner and L. E. J. Lawson, The Photographic Science, London, 1955, p. 97-106.

6. Dr. Werner Rebner: Die Anwendung des Kreuzlinienrasters, Agfa Leverkusen, Repro-Mitteilung No. 10/1957.

7. J. H. Bow: Gradation with Cross-Line Screens and Lithographic Emulsions, Journal of Photographic Science, London, 1955, p. 121-123.

8. Dr. Werner Rebner: Rasterpunktschärfe und Lithgradation, Agfa Leverkusen, Repro-Mitteilung No. 15/1962, No. 19/1964.

9. Dr. Werner Rebner: Anwendung des Kreuzlinienrasters, Agfa Leverkusen, Repro-Mitteilung No. 10/1957 III.

10. Dr. Werner Rebner: Positiv-und Negativ Kontaktraster, Fachhefte 2/1964, S. 94-100.

11. Agfa Leverkusen, Doku Sonderinformation 11/1963, Der Streulicht Einfluss in der Repro-Photographie.

12. Agfa Leverkusen, Repro Sonderinformation 12/1960, Das Rasternegativ nach Mass.